TRANSYLVANIA
AND BEYOND

T0204499

Other books by the author

FULL TILT

TIBETAN FOOTHOLD

THE WAITING LAND

IN ETHIOPIA WITH A MULE

ON A SHOESTRING TO COORG

WHERE THE INDUS IS YOUNG

RACE TO THE FINISH?

A PLACE APART

EIGHT FEET IN THE ANDES

WHEELS WITHIN WHEELS

MUDDLING THROUGH IN MADAGASCAR

TALES FROM TWO CITIES

CAMEROON WITH EGBERT

TRANSYLVANIA
AND BEYOND

a travel memoir by

DERVLA
MURPHY

THE OVERLOOK PRESS
WOODSTOCK • NEW YORK

First paperback published in 1995 by
The Overlook Press
Lewis Hollow Road
Woodstock, New York 12498

Copyright © 1992 Dervla Murphy

All Rights Reserved. No part of this publication may be reproduced or transmitted
in any form or by any means, electronic or mechanical, including photocopy,
recording, or any information storage and retrieval system now known or to be
invented without permission in writing from the publisher, except by a reviewer
who wishes to quote brief passages in connection with a review written for
inclusion in a magazine, newspaper, or broadcast.

Library of Congress Cataloging-in-Publication Data

Murphy, Dervla, 1931-
Transylvania and beyond : a travel memoir / Dervla Murphy.
p. cm.
1. Transylvania (Romania) - Description and travel.
2. Murphy, Dervla,-Journeys-Romania-Transylvania.
I. Title.
DR279.64.M87 1993
914.98'4-dc20   93-26235   CIP
First published in the United Kingdom by John Murray
ISBN: 0-87951-603-8
135798642

*To my many good friends in Transylvania and beyond
— Rumanians, Magyars, Szekelys, Jews, Gypsies,
Saxons, Swabians and Serbs*

Contents

Acknowledgements

Many Rumanians gave me valuable advice during the writing of this book, especially certain Cluj academics and those friends who came to stay with me in Ireland while work was in progress. (For obvious reasons, all personal names have been changed.)

In Budapest Rudi Fischer read the first draft and made many essential corrections and constructive suggestions.

In Cimpulung Moldovenesc my doctor and his wife and daughter, and the staff of the local hospital, made a nasty experience much less so and did their best, against grotesque odds, to succour the maimed foreigner.

From Skopje my daughter Rachel uncomplainingly undertook three wearisome journeys to assist her accident-prone mother.

In Hampstead the long-suffering (twenty-eight years long) Diana and Jock Murray attended what proved to be a rather difficult birth with their usual patience and skill.

To all, my thanks.

Historical Note

Modern Rumania consists mainly of three territories previously separate though sharing a common religion, Greek Orthodoxy, and the Rumanian language. These territories are known to English-speakers as Moldavia, Wallachia and Transylvania. In 1859 Moldavia and Wallachia were united to form the state of Rumania, to which Transylvania was ceded by the Treaty of Trianon in 1920.

During the Paris Peace Conference, in 1919, most of the British delegation found Balkan politics intolerably confusing and Lloyd George was heard to ask irritably, 'Where the hell is that place [Transylvania] Rumania is so anxious to get?' Probably only Harold Nicolson, Britain's Balkan expert, could have told him that – for the Conference's purposes – Transylvania was the land between the bend of the Carpathians and the Apuseni Mountains, plus Crisana, Maramures and part of the Banat – some 40,685 square miles.

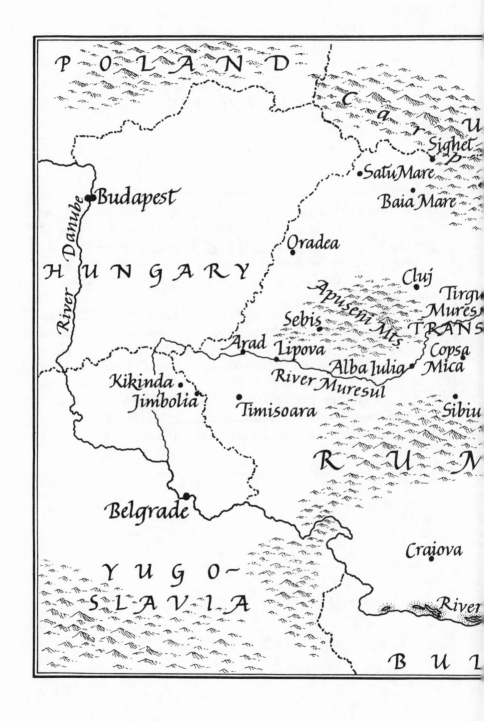

POLAND

Carpa...

Sighet

SatuMare

Baia Mare

Budapest

Oradea

River Danube

HUNGARY

Cluj

Tirgu
Mures

Apuseni Mts

TRANS

Sebis

Arad Lipova

Copsa
Mica

Alba Iulia

River Muresul

Kikinda

Jimbolia

Timisoara

Sibiu

R U M

Belgrade

Crajova

YUGO-
SLAVIA

River

BU

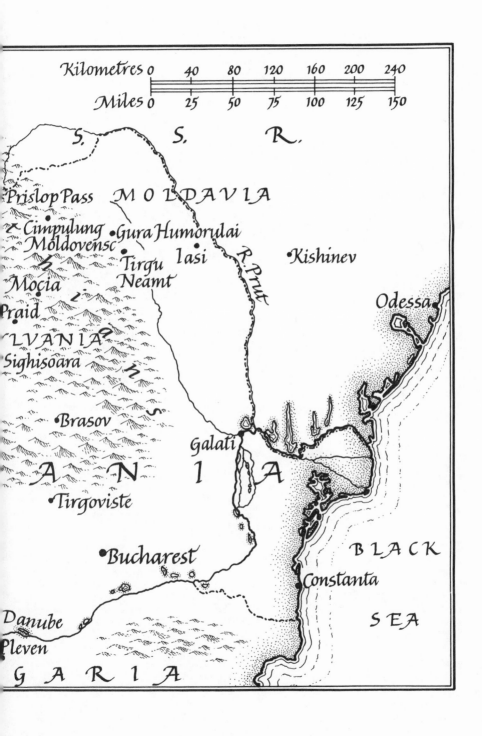

Kilometres 0   40   80   120   160   200   240
Miles   0   25   50   75   100   125   150

S.   S.   R.

Prislop Pass   M O L D A V I A

Cimpulung   •Gura Humorulai
Moldovensc
                •   •Iasi   •Kishinev
           •Tirgu
Moçia   Neamt
                                    Odessa
Praid
LVANIA
Sighisoara

•Brasov

          •Galati
A   N   I   A

•Tirgoviste

                                    B L A C K
     •Bucharest

                    •Constanta
                                    S E A
Danube
Pleven

G A R I A

Foreword

On New Year's Day 1990 we were all euphoric. Within months the Communist Bloc had become Europa Felix, countries suddenly made happy by freedom. And I was revelling in my own freedom to explore regions hitherto inaccessible.

A long time ago Fate had ordained that my first Europa Felix journey should be through Transylvania. The year must have been 1940; I can dimly recall my parents discussing the Vienna Diktat, when Hitler forced Rumania to surrender the northern half of Transylvania to Hungary. I was aged eight and had been temporarily weaned off Just William, Biggles and the Coot Club by Walter Starkie's *Raggle-Taggle* – grown-ups' books did not usually have such tempting titles. At least half of it was way beyond me, yet by the last page I had decided that one day I, too, would wander with the Gypsies through Transylvania: the very name seemed a one-word poem. But the region's contemporary fate didn't interest me; for the next several years the Transylvania eventually to be explored and the Transylvania on my father's flag-pocked map remained two quite separate places.

Then Churchill did his infamous swap with Stalin – 'You can have Rumania and thereabouts if we can keep Greece within our sphere of influence'. By 1950, when I set off on my first European cycling tour, Rumania had been a Communist state for three years. Transylvania, like Tibet and Central Asia, had sadly been written off as a Never-Never Land.

Towards the end of the 1970s Nicolae Ceausescu became – it is now generally agreed – mentally ill in a peculiarly unpleasant way. And his wife Elena became more and more ruthless, avaricious and domineering. Throughout the 1980s increasingly grim reports trickled out from the Ceausescus' 'State of Terror'. A harsh censorship had mentally isolated the population. Too much food was being exported to repay Western loans and many were starving. To stymie any samizdat movement, every typewriter had to be registered with the police. Five children were demanded of each couple, abortion was outlawed and Elena founded the 'Baby Police' to screen women monthly. When the President revived an old plan to raze more than 7,000 villages, churches and all, and to force the peasant (mainly elderly) into cramped blocs, the Western media gave widespread coverage to this brutal campaign. In April 1989 the EEC belatedly suspended trading relations with Rumania because of its deteriorating human rights record. But for far too long the West had fawned on the Ceausescus, choosing only to see Rumania as a lucrative trading-partner and cherished anti-Soviet ally within the Warsaw Pact.

Early on the morning of 22 December 1989 the World Service broadcast a report from one of the threatened villages. Gently the interviewer asked how this perverse exercise in social engineering would affect the peasants. 'In a bloc we can have no pig, no hens, no cows' – the voice of that elderly woman trembled with despair, yet also held a note of incredulity. How to imagine life without pigs, hens, cows? An elderly man sobbed while beseeching the interviewer to try to save the village's 400-year-old church; its frescos, he said, were famous throughout Europe and what about all the foreigners who used to come to study them? Could these important people not now rescue the church from the bulldozer? The interviewer's own voice trembled as he described this ancient Transylvanian village (unnamed: the Securitate were still in power) with its still vigorous tradition of folk art – wood carving and weaving, song and dance. Waves of grief and angry frustration surged through me; at breakfast-time my daughter found her tough mother almost in tears.

'Cheer up!' she said. 'Those villagers will be OK. Haven't you heard the latest news? In Bucharest the army is turning against the Ceausescus!'

On Christmas Day I resolved to go to Transylvania as soon as possible; I felt impatient to share in Rumania's happiness. Of course I must also expect to find much hardship, tension, dissension, suspicion: once the challenge of learning how to use freedom had been confronted, the prevailing euphoria could not long survive. As a political zombie, it would ill become me even to try to understand the consequent machinations – which would anyway be an urban phenomenon. I was only eager to travel among the ordinary countryfolk of 'the other half' of my own continent during the dawn of their New Age.

Just as 'everyone' leaves London in August, 'everyone' was converging on Timisoara and Bucharest during January 1990. Apparently I too was being attracted by Rumania's new aura of tragic glamour, and friends refused to believe that I was going simply to enjoy a Transylvanian trek – not to gather material for a book. In their eyes, travelling and writing were – for me – part of the same process. They said, 'A *holiday*? It's not possible!' And events proved them right.

On the bus to Munich I tardily recognised that I was taking quite a risk. The pursuit of fifty-year-old dreams is a dangerous sport. Was it reasonable to expect more than a faint resemblance between Walter Starkie's Transylvania and post-Ceausescu Transylvania? Yet already I knew, in that cellar of the mind where we store our illogical certainties, that my journey was not a mistake.

1

Dispossessed on the Frontier

I paused, startled, in the doorway of Budapest's empty West Station restaurant. Had I strayed into the 1890s section of some Central European Victoria and Albert Museum? Gilded chandeliers shed a mellow light on immaculate damask table-linen. The tables stood far apart on a floor of inky blue and carmine marble. The mahogany dining-chairs, rather pompously carved, were upholstered in dark green velvet. Slowly I moved to the centre of the room, passing fluted porphyry pillars. Burgundy and silver tapestry wall-hangings shimmered beneath golden rosettes sprouting from the cornice. Silver candelabras gleamed on square marble corner pillars and on either side of intricately bevelled window embrasures. One expected several archdukes to appear at any moment.

Instead, the door was pushed open by a tall, thin, slightly stooped young man with longish mousey hair and pale blue bloodshot eyes. He too seemed momentarily bemused by this imperial left-over. Then, taking courage from me and my rucksack, he asked, 'OK just to sit?'

I nodded. 'There's no staff around to object.'

Noticing my London–Arad luggage label, Klaus suggested, 'Reporter?'

'No,' I said, 'just a tourist.'

'A *tourist*? Why? There is no tourist comfort in Rumania, no food or heat in the hotels – nothing!'

'But I have a tent – and lots of dehydrated food.'

'A *tent*!' snorted Klaus. 'Don't you know there's snow? And the Securitate won't let you camp, they hate foreigners. You go home!'

'Mine is a Himalayan tent,' I soothed. 'And aren't the Securitate gone – disbanded, defeated?'

'Only foreigners believe that,' said Klaus. 'They still have the

1

best weapons and could be more dangerous now. The other Ceausescus could be organising a counter-revolution. Last week my cousin ran from Timisoara, he doesn't like to live in a country without a government. He wants the army to take over until the election. Now all the criminals – Securitate, Party activists, policemen – can do what they want.'

Klaus, a Swabian from a village near Timisoara, had been working in Germany since illegally crossing the border near Kikinda in 1988. That escape route, across the flat Banat, was not too difficult by night yet required courage. If caught, Klaus could have been sentenced to three years' imprisonment. His only sibling, a fourteen-year-old brother, had been badly wounded during the uprising on 17 December and though his farmer parents were against his returning, he felt they needed him. His arrival would be a surprise – 'I wish they won't get angry. Now they have passports and I want to take them to Munich. There my brother can have good medical treatment to help him walk again. We are two hundred years in that village but since Communism came – and especially since Ceausescu came – most of our neighbours have gone back to Germany. I wanted my parents to escape with me but they were frightened. Not frightened to make the journey but frightened to live outside, in Germany.'

A waiter appeared in the distance, briefly considered us, then tactfully vanished.

Klaus frowned at my notebook; old habits die hard and I was keeping a daily journal for – as I then thought – my daughter Rachel's benefit. 'You *are* a reporter!' he insisted. 'Why do you not trust me? I am your friend. I tell you, if you write like this in Rumania, where people see you, it is dangerous. I am nearly two years in the Occident, I know how you think. For you repression is not real, you believe you can always act free. But in Rumania you will find trouble, saying you are a tourist but making reports!'

The door opened slowly, and a frail fur-hatted young woman dragged two bulging suitcases over the threshold – then retreated to fetch four cardboard cartons, roped together. When Klaus hurried to help her they spoke Rumanian.

Maria was a Szekely, now living in Vienna with her Szekely husband. They were trying to get visas for Canada, but losing hope ... She had not been home for three years; pre-revolution, she feared being forbidden to leave Rumania again. Even post-revolution, she seemed frightened; her hands shook as she chain-smoked. 'I must now bring luxuries to my family, but I cannot stay long – it is too horrible there!' She paused, looked intently at me, then asked, 'Do you know who are the Szekely people?' I assured her that I did. 'So you know we are persecuted?' Her voice rose shrilly. 'The Rumanians want to kill us if we won't give up our culture. You know Transylvania belongs to us for one thousand years? To the Szekely and the Magyars – until in 1920 we are tricked and cheated and Rumania takes it!'

I glanced at Klaus, who was staring at a chandelier. This was not his problem.

Maria leant forward and tapped my wrist with long shocking-pink nails. 'Do you understand all I say?' Her tone was desperate, her fear palpable. She needed to be reassured, on the eve of venturing back into a threatening – as she perceived it – environment, that the outside world sympathised with her situation.

Vaguely I remarked, 'We have a slightly similar difficulty in Northern Ireland. There, many people . . .'

Suddenly Klaus looked at his watch and shouted, 'Come! The train will be leaving!' Flinging his knapsack over his shoulder, he seized both Maria's suitcases and made for the door.

I left last; my giant rucksack was so abnormally heavy that loading up took time. On the uncrowded platform I was at once approached by four Rumanian Gypsy youths who politely pleaded, 'Change dollars?' Maria and Klaus, already boarding the train, observed this encounter and Klaus beckoned vigorously. 'Come!' he yelled. 'Leave those Gypsies, they are bad people! Come!'

The swarthy youths stood staring hopefully at me. They were offering only sixty lei to the dollar though the unofficial rate was then, Klaus had told me, eighty or ninety. Their anoraks and frayed jeans were filthy, their eyes red-rimmed with exhaustion, their dull uncombed hair betrayed serious vitamin deficiency. At that time most Western Europeans were riding on a wave of horrified sympathy for all Rumanians and I felt no temptation to haggle. We sat on a bench while I excavated twenty dollars from my money-belt. Counting the repulsively soiled and almost illegible hundred lei notes, I found one too many. On my returning it the youths were overcome with astounded gratitude; one of them took a small wrinkled apple from his pocket and pressed it into my hand. Then I hurriedly boarded the last coach moments before the train pulled out, punctually at 8.15 p.m.

Seeking my friends, I walked up the corridor; the last two coaches were empty. This service is described as 'the Orient Express' but the gravy-brown leatherette seats were hard, the corridor windows mud-caked, the floors strewn with sunflower seed shells, the loos noisome. And at the end of the penultimate coach a locked door prevented my joining Maria and Klaus.

Settling in a corner seat, I tied the rucksack's long waist-strap to my right wrist and read the *Rough Guide to Eastern Europe*, dozing at intervals. Never before had I carried such a weight. It would however be much reduced in Arad, when I had donned several layers of garments and distributed the heavy goodies: medicines, soap, chocolate, coffee beans. The light goodies – Kent cigarettes, tights, condoms, tampons, warm socks and sachets of shampoo – were for use *en route* as gifts or bribes.

The border control stop – an ill-lit rural station – seemed deserted at 1.15 a.m. Rumanian time (two hours ahead of GMT). But soon a couple of uniformed figures, with hard unsmiling faces, appeared at my carriage door. Oddly, they ignored my offered passport, stood staring silently at me for a moment, then vanished. Seconds later they reappeared nearby on the platform, talking to two other uniformed figures. On their return the customs officer said in English, 'Visa check! Quickly get off – quickly! Five minutes this train go!' I protested; normally passengers' visas are checked *in situ*. 'Quickly!' repeated the customs officer, advancing into the carriage as I – slightly alarmed by his harshness – untied the rucksack from my wrist. The police officer then pushed past him, seized me roughly by the forearm and half-dragged me into the corridor. Instinctively I leant sideways and grabbed the Hatchards plastic bag that held my notebooks and pens.

My captors hustled me far up the platform to join two heavily laden Magyar peasants, the only people here leaving the train. Given my need to re-board quickly, they would surely not have objected to my passport being stamped first. Yet I had to wait seven or eight minutes, while their documents were being carefully scrutinised and argued about. Then, without delay, my visa was stamped and an entry form provided.

Back on the train, I assumed myself to be in the wrong carriage – until I saw my discarded London matchbox. Otherwise the carriage was empty. Yet it was impossible immediately to accept the fact that my rucksack had been stolen. The magnitude of the disaster made it seem, literally, incredible. As though disbelief could somehow reverse the situation, I stood pushing this reality away. Then suddenly I accepted it and panicked. Leaping to the platform, I raced towards the distant officers, standing in the shadows near a half-open door.

'Everything's stolen!' I yelled. 'My baggage, it's all gone, *everything*! Someone has stolen my rucksack!' As I approached they shrugged and gestured dismissively, then sharply turned into the lighted room and slammed the door.

I looked up and down the dark empty platform, wondering about the other two uniformed figures ... My fellow-passengers were dormant; no one stood at the corridor windows and the silence was broken only by the panting hiss of the train's central heating pipes. Now I was trembling with shock. It seemed pointless to continue; the sensible thing would be to wait here for the next homeward-bound train. I hesitated, then realised I couldn't, at this stage, turn away from Transylvania. And the idea of trying to survive with nothing but the inadequate garments I wore had a certain macabre attraction; it appealed to what some people unkindly describe as my masochism. Of course the nature of this journey would be changed; the *Rough Guide* (also stolen) had just reminded me that in Rumania 'life is literally at risk during winter unless you come ... equipped as if for a short walk in the Himalayas' – which is exactly how I had come equipped. Therefore I couldn't trek deep into the mountains and would be totally dependent on Rumanian hospitality.

The train was jerking forward when I scrambled into a half-full coach with clean curtained windows and soft seats upholstered in old-gold velveteen. Briefly I considered looking for my friends, whose commiseration would have helped; but that would be feebly parasitic – they had enough problems of their own. In an empty carriage I took stock of my worldly goods: a compass, torch, comb and Swiss knife in my pockets. And in the Hatchards bag – apart from notebooks and pens – a map and a bottle of whiskey for which, mercifully, there had been no room in the rucksack. After a few swigs I stopped trembling and counted my money: £165 and $310. Irrelevant affluence; it was then impossible to buy even a toothbrush, never mind a flea-bag or tent, and Rumanians, however poor, won't accept payment for hospitality.

Arad's railway station restaurant – large, dirty, dreary, cold – stays open all night. On one damp-streaked beige wall an unfaded rectangle marked the spot recently vacated by Ceausescu. Under a solitary low-watt bulb a dozen shabby unshaven men sat around conversing in hoarse mutters – if at all – while sipping glasses of ground-acorn coffee-substitute. They surveyed me with swivelling eyes, not turning their heads. When I greeted a man sitting alone near the door his lips twitched in a nervous parody of a smile and he moved to another table. Turning to the bar, I reflected that men who spend all night in railway restaurants are not Average Citizens.

The long shelves behind the bar supported two dusty bottles of a pseudo-fruit juice that would seem drinkable – I later discovered – only if one were lost in the Sahara. The nourishment on offer consisted of a few grey slimy sausages, dreadfully resembling dog turds, and three pale pastry rolls from which oozed something yallerish-green. Recoiling from this display, I became aware that the barmaid was surveying me with concern; evidently I still showed signs of shock. She was a haggard young woman with rotting teeth and a nasty boil on her neck. 'Irlanda' puzzled her but she reached across the counter to shake my hand vigorously while welcoming me to Rumania. When I tried to pay for a large glass of luke-warm 'coffee' she laughingly returned my lei, tapped the glass, wrinkled her nose and said 'Nu bun!' (No good.)

Sitting at a small circular red plastic table, cigarette-burnt around the edges, I considered my next move. Should I report the theft to Arad police headquarters? In theory, yes. The guilty uniformed quartet – there were no alternative culprits – plainly formed a border mafia that threatened other unwary foreigners. Yet I lacked the courage to confront their Arad colleagues (a humiliating realisation) since these were likely to be of the same ilk and might well deport me on some trumped-up technicality. I recalled Klaus's cousin's comment about living in a country without a government. That national deficiency would not have worried me pre-theft, but now it did. There was nowhere for the buck to stop. If some Arad policeman decided to deport me, to whom could I appeal?

At that point the barmaid brought me a steaming hot glass of 'coffee' and apologised for the last having been cold. Her blunt-featured, coarse-skinned face became quite beautiful when she smiled. She was the first of many Rumanians whose spontaneous caring took the sting out of major misfortunes.

At 3 a.m., warmed by hot liquid and kindness, I left the restaurant – feeling an overwhelming compulsion to walk and walk and walk, on and on and on, until bodily exhaustion exorcised emotional pain. Striding east out of Arad, through unlit canyons between gaunt rows of high-risery, it suddenly seemed that all this could not be *true*, that I was about to wake up. In real life people don't set off in the middle of the night through freezing fog – hatless, ungloved and possessing only a bottle of whiskey – to explore an unknown and recently traumatised country. Until dawn, this strong sense of outrageous improbability persisted; without my gear, I felt as disorientated and vulnerable as an unshelled crustacean.

Near Arad's edge the faint light of a half-moon, filtering through the fog, revealed a stack of milk crates outside an *alimentara* (food shop). I took a litre bottle, leaving fifty lei in its place – forty-five and a half lei too many, I later learned. Then for four hours I followed a straight level icy main road, keeping to the rough verge, so treacherous was the tarmac.

One-storey dwellings lined the road on both sides for several miles and collective farm buildings provided powerful odours of pig-shit and silage: delicious aromas after four days amidst Budapest's nauseating air pollution. No motor traffic broke the cold windless silence but at about 4 a.m. long farm wagons, drawn by pairs of briskly-trotting horses, began to move towards Arad. The clip-clopping, gradually approaching and receding, was comforting; as was the cock-crowing, now weaving a strident sound-pattern all over the wide plain.

By then my numbed sense of unreality had been replaced by a sharp grief: the sort you can feel, like something physical, in your heart. I recalled another slightly similar crisis on the Galapagos Islands, way back in February 1979 when Rachel and I were returning from Peru. Addled by the equatorial heat, I left *all* our cash and travellers' cheques, and our return tickets to Guayaquil, and our return tickets from Quito to London, momentarily unguarded on the counter of the village store. Everything was stolen and on one level that was an even more dramatic crisis. There were then no postal or telephonic communications with the outside world and we might have had to sit indefinitely on the equator, 600 miles out in the Pacific, but for the trusting generosity of a young Norwegian couple who lent us our fares to Quito – where, pending the arrival of replacement funds, a British Embassy official magnanimously sustained the feckless Irish. Yet that loss had not been so emotionally shattering. It was my own fault; people who leave wallets on shop counters in deprived areas deserve the consequences. Also, it merely involved money. In contrast, the theft of my rucksack and its contents represented a bereavement. Several of the stolen items had formed part of my trekking gear on four continents for twenty-seven years and could not be thought of as replaceable, extraneous objects. They had become – or so I felt, immediately after their loss – an integral part of *me*, so unique were their associations. On the eve of a journey I am often accused of parsimony, advances in design and technology having long since made much of my gear obsolete; few seem to understand that the sentimental value of a traveller's equipment may far exceed its monetary value. To replace my stolen rucksack and contents would cost more than £1500, including the £400-worth of medicines, yet for weeks I was unable to focus on the economics of the calamity. First I had to recover from my bereavement – and from the disappointment of having to postpone, into the indefinite future, a trek for which I had already waited fifty years.

By six o'clock many groups of peasants were walking silently to their collective or state farms – never suspecting, in the pitch darkness, that a foreigner (for decades past a rarity in this area) was among them. It felt almost uncanny to be at last with the Rumanians yet unable to see them.

An hour later it was just light enough for me to read 'Ghioroc' on a signpost. I turned north off the highway onto a rough, narrow road. In that monochrome dawn – greyness gradually replacing blackness – it was hard to believe that somewhere on my right the sun had risen. All around flat brown ploughland stretched to the horizon; there was not a dwelling, a person, an animal, a fence, a tree – even a bush or a bird – to be seen. But soon a line of low humpy mountains became faintly visible not far ahead, through banks of dissolving cloud. Stopping for the first time, I sat on the frost-bound verge to drink my litre of milk – which proved, unsurprisingly, to be at least 50 per cent water. While walking fast my meagre garments had been adequate but now, within moments, I was shivering. After a swig of whiskey, to counteract the chilling milk, I hurried on.

Ghioroc is a mining settlement on the litter-strewn shore of a lake – in winter a large oval of solid bottle-green ice. At 8.15 scores of workers of both sexes were thronging the old village street, looking half-starved and either apprehensive or defiant. No one returned my greetings. The place had a taut, sullen feeling and I walked with downcast eyes lest some Securitate informer might suspect me of spying on Rumania's metallurgical activities. While 'breakfasting' I had planned my route: a dirt track through the mountains, from Ghioroc to the village of Siria, where someone would surely provide a night's shelter. However, my turning onto the track displeased a plump young man who moments before had been haranguing the workers. He shouted angrily at me, pointing down the tarred road. Unlike everyone else, he was well dressed in a smart suit and bum-length leather jacket. But for his tone, I would have assumed him to be a helpful character, trying to prevent my going astray. As it was, I meekly obeyed him, making no attempt to explain my situation; the shadow of deportation still hung over me.

Beyond Ghiroc the monotonous state farm landscape was replaced by hilly, partially wooded countryside that might have been in Ireland. On either side of the winding road stretched a succession of small villages, rows of red-tiled carefully maintained dwellings set in neat gardens. The few visible peasants were old or middle-aged. I made several attempts to communicate, unfolding my map and pretending to seek directions, but no one would speak to me; only a few weeks previously, it had been illegal to talk to foreigners.

9

Two hours later the sun began at last to disperse the high fog and, coincidentally, an ancient ruddy-cheeked man in a tattered smock smiled shyly at me from the arched gateway of his unusually large farmhouse. My greetings were returned in German; his family had been among a group of Saxons who generations ago settled here, far from the Saxon heartland in southern Transylvania. Now only he and his half-crippled wife were left in the homestead; he pointed to her as she hobbled across the spacious square courtyard beyond the archway. One son was teaching in Brasov, the other three and a daughter had migrated to Germany. It seemed that hospitality was about to be offered when the old lady noticed me, and there was fear in her voice as she summoned her husband. Hurriedly he shook my hand and retreated, closing the high wooden double door behind him.

Approaching the town of Lipova, another hour later, I again noticed that all the roadside houses – some new, or recently extended – were smartly painted and embellished and curtained. Looking at them, no one would guess that for years Rumania had been enduring a major economic crisis. But of course it was impossible for a stranger to buy food and by then I was ravenous, having walked twenty-one miles and eaten nothing since leaving Budapest. On the outskirts, I despairingly tried one last shop – much smaller than the standard *alimentara* – where an amiable woman behind the L-shaped counter took pity on me. Fumbling under the counter, she produced half a rock-hard loaf for which she would accept no payment. To make it chewable I bought a bottle ambiguously labelled 'Aperitif' and containing a mildly alcoholic red-brown liquid derived from who knows what. In retrospect, that ranks among my least palatable meals. Yet I was hungry enough to finish the loaf and empty the bottle.

Elena, my tubby hostess – fortyish, with frizzy black hair and an unhealthy pallor – was elated to meet a foreigner. Her grey-blue eyes glittered excitedly as she joined me by the high tin woodstove, inviting me to relax on a beer crate which at once drove a needle-like splinter into my left thigh. Between strenuous bouts of mastication, I answered her questions as best I could with the aid of two mini-dictionaries. Meanwhile Ion – her burly, balding husband, polite yet much more guarded than she – was studying a smudged ledger, breathing heavily and whispering to himself.

10

For some time the shop remained customerless, though its long shelves were stocked from floor to ceiling. It can serve as the prototype of all Rumanian shops during that period. Three items were on offer. One set of shelves held the Aperitif – which, time revealed, had sinister after-effects, explaining the presence of so many hundreds of bottles. The other shelves, behind Ion, held rusty-topped jars of off-colour tomatoes and whole pears floating in some greyish-green chemical. The only other food for sale was a powdery substance, allegedly flour, and two old men eventually rambled in to collect their meagre rations in cloth bags. Wistfully they asked for sugar and salt but neither was available. Probably they spread the news – 'A foreigner is here!' – because soon the shop began to fill up with young men and teenage boys who at first feigned to ignore me, while thawing hands at the stove or horse-playing on the wide open spaces of the shop floor. Then, reassured by Elena's intimacy with me (Rumanians are compulsive huggers and kissers), they became cautiously friendly.

The atmosphere changed when a Fat-Cat entered, expensively dressed and already, at noon, smelling strongly of Scotch – a luxury not available to honest Rumanians. His smooth round face didn't seem to match thin lips and narrow, fast-blinking eyes. Curtly he demanded to see the ledger – whereupon Ion slammed it shut, thrust it beneath the counter and shouted 'Ceausescu is dead!'

The young men cheered and clapped and laughed derisively; when Elena joined them so did I. In response to a quick signal from one youth she produced a grimy, tattered 'Ceausescu flag' with its Communist emblem intact – which the youth used to wipe Fat-Cat's supple Italian boots. Then all the young men ritualistically used it on their own (mostly disintegrating) shoes, before passing it to me. Exhilarated by this symbolism, I vigorously rubbed my muddy boots, deliberately meeting Fat-Cat's eye. I won't soon forget his expression of baffled hatred as he left the shop.

Moments later – there was no time for collusion – two female Fat-Cats entered, heavily made-up and wearing nylon 'fur' coats. Again the atmosphere changed dramatically. Now a hush fell: plainly everyone was scared. One woman opened a file of documents and spread them on the counter while the other challenged

Ion about something. The instant these two appeared Elena moved away from me, back to her position behind the counter, and thereafter she refused to catch my eye. Abruptly one woman turned to me, asked quite civilly to see my passport – and at once pronounced my visa invalid. It should, she asserted, have been issued for only fifteen days, not thirty, and I should have paid £20 (the fee pre-revolution) not the £8.50 requested by the Rumanian embassy in London. How had she come to know so much about visa charges? Who was this termagant? Could she be bribe-hunting? Given courage by the previous incident, I emerged from under the shadow of deportation and boldy followed Ion's example. 'Ceausescu is dead!' I declaimed, stretching a hand towards my passport. The visa expert stared at me with such venom that for a moment I regretted my daring. Then I chose the most appropriate weapon and steadily held her gaze. Seconds later she swung away, threw my passport on the counter and resumed her harassment of poor Ion.

I left immediately, feeling bad about not saying goodbye to Elena; but plainly she wished to avoid giving any impression of having 'cultivated' me. And it would have been imprudent to linger within reach of those mysteriously potent females. Afterwards, I realised the value of that encounter; having survived it, I no longer felt afraid of Rumanian officialdom.

The sky was cloudless and the sun almost warm as I followed the valley of the Mures – 'between the woods and the water'. I hoped Patrick Leigh Fermor would never be rash enough to revisit this area. Trekking in June 1934, he described 'the trees of the foothills ... with sprays of wild lilac scattered among the branches ... The women in the fields wore kerchiefs on their heads under hats of soft plaited straw as wide as cart-wheels ... Pale cattle with wide straight horns grazed by the score ... Wherever horses and mares with their foals moved loose about the grass, a few ragged tents were sure to be pitched. Everything in those reedy windings was inert and hushed under a sleepy spell of growth and untroubled plenty'.

My memories are of fast, tormenting trucks trailing eye-stinging fumes. On this main but narrow highway I was re-peatedly forced to take refuge in the ditch. Few of the trucks were Rumanian; they came from all over Europe – there was even one from Albania – and included a convoy of six snow-white gigantic refrigerated Red Cross vehicles from Luxembourg. The occasional local motor-car, old and overcrowded, was only recently back on the road after years of severe petrol rationing and proudly flew that strangely poignant post-revolutionary flag with its holed centre.

During a seven-mile walk I saw only one vestige of the Starkie/ Leigh Fermor era. A shepherd in an ankle-long fleece cloak, wearing a high black conical hat, leant on his crook as he stood with his back to the rapid raucous traffic, contemplating his flock. They were nibbling between tree stumps on eroded forestry wasteland and, though fleeces are deceptive, one could detect their emaciation. Where would that shepherd's grandfather have been grazing his sheep in 1929 or 1934? Not, assuredly, on wasteland.

Another sort of gloom assailed me when indigo clouds swarmed suddenly and spat coldly. This was crunch-point. I couldn't afford to get wet, having nothing to change into and no possibility of drying sodden garments. But, *sans* waterproofs, I couldn't avoid getting wet ... As the cold spits became sleet a tractor drawing a load of firewood overtook me and stopped to offer a lift. It was awesomely ancient – in Ireland people pay good money to witness such machines in action – and already had two passengers in the cab, one of whom sat on the other to make room for me. Jolting towards Birzava, I decided a tip would not come amiss; as a newcomer, I still had much to learn. When I offered 100 lei – more than a day's pay for a state farm tractor driver – my rescuer flushed with insulted embarrassment. In rural Rumania, humans helping humans is not yet a commercial enterprise.

The big village of Birzava was half-hidden by soft, slowly swirling snow. Having forgiven my attempt to pay for an act of kindness, the driver indicated a café where I might – he didn't sound optimistic – find sustenance. The street door led directly into a small low-ceilinged room where an elderly widow, dressed all in black and wearing too-loose wellingtons, peered doubtfully at me through the early twilight. She had nothing to offer, not even herbal tea or acorn coffee, and seemed slightly scornful of my naïve hopes. Suddenly I felt the effects of having walked so far after a sleepless night. Collapsing into a wobbly easy-chair, I took out my last mini-cigar – provoking a yelp of horror. The widow indicated a 'No Smoking' notice, referred agitatedly to the police, beckoned me to the door and pointed out a nearby restaurant.

My arrival caused a *frisson* of alarm among the thirty or so men hunched over stained tables fiddling with empty coffee glasses. (The supply of ground acorns had just run out.) Everyone stared silently at me – except two army officers, sitting by the long street window where there was still enough light to play backgammon, with the collars of their greatcoats pulled up and the ear-flaps of their fur hats pulled down. Choosing an empty corner, opposite the door, I wondered if the Boss had a room with bedding to let. By now I had identified my sleeping-bag as my single greatest loss, on the practical level. With it, I could survive a night in a barn, a stable, an outhouse; without it, I might not survive a midwinter night in this unheated restaurant. But of the Boss there was as yet no sign.

Then a dark-skinned young man stood up, unsteadily, and lurched towards me, drawing a bottle of home-distilled *tuica* from his pocket and pulling off his scarf. '*Frig!*' (cold) he mumbled, thrusting the bottle into my hands and draping the scarf around my neck. When someone behind him sniggered he quickly turned, his face transformed to a snarl – and fell heavily as he moved to attack the sniggerer. Simultaneously the Boss appeared, a handsome, well-built, neatly-dressed man in his thirties. He kicked my prone would-be benefactor – hard, on the buttocks – and shouted something that made all the men laugh. Appalled, I laid a restraining hand on his arm. As he impatiently shook it off the street door opened and three Gypsy women entered, their long swirling brilliant skirts seeming to light up that dismal cavern. The Boss looked from them to me to the groaning drunk. '*Tigani!*' he explained, loading the word with the accumulated contempt of centuries. In 1950 I would have tongue-lashed him in a white-hot rage, regardless of the fact that he couldn't understand me. In 1990 I merely turned away and took a swig of whiskey, cannily keeping the bottle concealed in its plastic bag. Meanwhile the Gypsy trio – hefty women, though low of stature – had got their man to his feet and were half-carrying him to the door, ignoring everyone.

14

The Boss sat opposite me, apologising for the lack of coffee and alcohol and offering his cigarette packet. Plainly he felt no embarrassment and had we met in normal circumstances I would have thought him an affable fellow, as no doubt he usually was. He had no room to let but looked genuinely concerned about my accommodation problem and at once sent his wife out into the snow to look for suitable lodgings.

During the next half-hour, as though the Boss's talking to me had lifted some embargo, the village men crowded around, asking to see my passport, leafing through my notebooks and poring over my road-map of Rumania – a fascinating novelty – their horny unwashed forefingers jumping excitedly from one familiar place name to another. Several of them were animated by more than curiosity; evidently not only Gypsies carry *tuica* in their jacket pockets.

Wife returned from her quest accompanied by Livia, the café widow, who now greeted me like an old friend, and an extravagantly obese woman with fair hair pulled tightly back from a round weather-beaten face dominated by a hooked nose. Anna's close-set hazel eyes were tired and sad; soon I learned that her husband, a chemical factory worker, was dying of cancer in an Arad hospital. For some time a leggy fourteen-year-old remained invisible behind Mamma's vast bulk. Anna was eager to entertain me but Livia, claiming prior knowledge, insisted that she should enjoy that privilege. A cynic might have thought them greedy for dollars; in fact they were greedy for a foreign presence. When the Boss adjudicated in Anna's favour it was agreed that Livia should join us later.

We hurried up the main street through a swaying curtain of light snow. Anna's flat was on the ground floor of one of several oblong four-storey mini-blocs that fifteen years ago had replaced rows of village houses. The unlit alleyway approach to the rear flats – between two blocs – was so narrow that my hostess had to compress herself before squeezing through. Then we stumbled over rough slushy ground in total darkness, Anna leading me by the hand, and climbed six concrete steps – two perilously unstable – to a warped door leading into a minute hallway. There eighteen-year-old Bogdan, lanky and spotty and grinning from

15

ear to ear, pumped my hand wordlessly while drawing me into an overheated bed-sitter; two divan double beds took up most of the floor space.

Uncle had followed us in – he lived next door – bearing a bottle of his own excellent wine, full-bodied and warming. As he opened it, Anna fetched an earthenware platter on which were artistically arranged discs of salami, chunks of beef sausage, thin slices of *slanina* (smoked raw bacon fat) and cubes of a fetta-like cheese. Ada followed, carrying bowls of pickled mushrooms and cucumber and a plate piled with bread. Everything was home-made and delicious, except the sour sticky grey-brown bread; it's anybody's guess what substance was then being used to adulterate Rumanian flour. One didn't expect such a spread in 'starving Rumania', yet its instant appearance proved that villagers, even then, had their resources: though almost certainly this was not the family's daily fare. Unluckily, I was just then beginning to feel the drastic purgative effects of the Aperitif and my lack of appetite caused general disappointment and concern.

A wide, six-foot tiled stove – creamy porcelain – occupied one corner and was too regularly fed with logs from a neat pile. In another corner a walnut china cabinet contained orange glass fishes standing on their tails, green glass sitting ducks, pink glass begging poodles and red glass running rabbits. (Uncle worked in a glass factory.) Behind this menagerie could be glimpsed some attractive Czech cut glass and my admiring it caused Anna's eyes to fill with tears; it had been a wedding present, twenty years ago. A large solid wireless stood beneath an outsize television set – identical to all other Rumanian television sets and not expensive, that medium having been Ceausescu's favourite propaganda tool. Above the beds hung shiny tapestries, some four feet by two, depicting the Last Supper (which it would be blasphemous to describe accurately) and a romantic mountain scene – brick-red deer drinking from an electric-blue lake surrounded by lime-green trees under a salmon-pink dawn (or sunset?) sky. The adjacent room was much bigger and also overheated, for my benefit. Near the stove stood a double bed; eight simple, monastic-looking chairs circled a fine oak dining-table; the handsome matching sideboard held a long row of empty Scotch whisky, English gin and French brandy bottles.

Only the cramped bathroom fitted one's image of 'Ceausescu's Rumania'. Green-black mould grew on the naked breeze-block walls; all the paint had long since peeled off a small rusty bath full of dirty garments; the stained loo had never worked; the wash-basin taps were immovable; the iron stove's cracked chimney pipe had blackened the ceiling. Bogdan – whose self-taught English was impressive – explained that for fifteen years the residents of these blocs had been awaiting running water, while continuing to fetch their daily requirements from the nearest well.

A snow-loaded Livia arrived in time to watch Mr Iliescu talking persuasively on The Box. Everyone stared worshipfully and applauded at the end. He was, they assured me, a *good* man who had delivered the nation from the Ceausescus, provided normal heating and lighting, unbanned foreign television and raised the wages of many workers – including Bogdan.

By then Dorana had also joined us: a trim, vivacious neighbour with brassy dyed hair. She set about solving the mystery that had been bothering my new friends all evening – why did I have no baggage? And no headgear, gloves, scarf, warm socks, water-proofs, nightwear? Had nobody told me about Transylvania's winter climate? Was Ireland always warm? My sad story provoked shame and sympathy but little surprise. Everyone nodded som-brely, agreeing that police and customs officers are very bad men – which sweeping statement I did not feel moved to contradict.

Ada got out her homework as Uncle and Bogdan settled down to watch a Western. Already I was almost asleep but Dorana insisted that we womenfolk move to her flat to sample something special: double-distilled apricot *tuica*. In design this flat was identical to Anna's but seemed more spacious because Dorana lived alone. Her two sons worked in an Oradea factory; her husband had recently run off with a glamorous young woman from Bucharest who had been compelled to teach in Lipova. Husband's photograph still adorned the TV: he had a treble chin, a down-turned mouth and a crew-cut. The glamorous young woman must have been desperate. But possibly an accommoda-tion problem, rather than other needs, had fuelled this romance. As an engineer working in Lipova, husband was entitled to a flat there – a better flat than any fledgling teacher could ever hope to get.

That *tuica* was indeed something special; I have rarely tasted its equal. As it flowed, I found it increasingly difficult to keep awake – especially as Dorana, obsessed by my inadequate clothing, had ordered me to recline on the bed, against a pile of vividly embroidered cushions, wrapped in a soft homespun blanket. Yet it was my duty to remain alert, striving with dictionary aid and sign language to understand and answer countless questions about the trivia of daily life in the Occident.

At last Anna suggested that it might be my bedtime. Dorana then insisted on presenting me with new socks and a pair of slacks that, though well-worn, were soon to prove invaluable. This was a hard-to-take irony, my having crossed the border laden with thermal socks for the deprived natives. But being so dependent is a good lesson in humility. And, at least among the Rumanians, it quickly shows you the best side of the national character.

My walking-therapy worked well. That night I slept for ten hours: a deep sleep, not rucksack-haunted.

2

Hospitality from the State

Anna served my ideal breakfast: a vast dish of cabbage and carrot stew, reinforced by chunks of tender beef. Two tumblers of very sweet herbal tea followed. Also, as a parting gift, my plastic bag was loaded with half a kilo of pickled cucumber, a kilo of cooked beef sausage – deliciously spiced – and a loaf of stale bread.

Then came what I knew would be an awkward moment, but I had planned ahead. No one could object to Ada's being tipped . . . She was packing her satchel – school started at 8 a.m. – when I surreptitiously transferred dollars while shaking hands. She however refused to co-operate. Opening her fist, she stared at the money as though it were some noxious insect – then looked, aghast, at her mother. Swiftly Anna stepped forward, seized the bill and thrust it into my pocket with angry violence. (After that, I devised a more cunning ploy; the youngest member of the family would find an envelope addressed to him/her when I had long since departed.)

Freezing fog had replaced the evening snow; it felt so much colder than the day before that Dorana's slacks were soon being pulled on over my own. The map showed a route leading north into the mountains and before long I was in a region outwardly unchanged since the Starkie/Leigh Fermor era. And this rough earth track, its surface now solidly iced, was traffic-free.

For unpopulated miles I was gradually climbing, on my left dense beech woods, on my right open pastureland sloping down to an invisible river. Beyond rose another steep wooded ridge, each leafless tree silvered by hoar-frost and strangely incandescent beneath the low dull sky. Only the occasional squabbles of jays, and a few subdued notes from goldfinches and blackbirds, broke the midwinter hush.

The sun struggled through as I descended to river level; this mountain stream was almost iced over despite its speed. Here I

19

was in hilly farmland – too hilly to have been 'collectivised'. The several villages were long rows of sturdy one-storey dwellings, freshly painted in contrasting combinations of colours. The design of these homes – self-built of wood and stone, or wood and brick – showed endless variety and considerable imagination. Rumanian peasants are proud individualists, which partly explains Ceausescu's compulsion to herd them all into soul- and mind-numbing blocs. In front of each house on my right, beyond the river, an old tree-trunk bridge spanned the water. Elegant wrought-iron gates led into tidy yards where – as in the fields between the villages – maize stalks were stooked and conical hay-ricks woven around tall poles. The doors and windows of barns and stables (some brand-new) were finely carved, as were the roofs protecting each family well. Every yard had vines trained over trellises; in summer these provide cool awnings beneath which to drink the wine from last year's crop. Carefully pruned fruit trees – apple, plum, apricot, cherry, pear – flourished in gardens where enough vegetables could be grown to allow a surplus for bottling. There were however a few ominous new dwellings which suggested that a milder version of the Irish bungaloid blight could soon hit Transylvania.

There is no need to rise early in midwinter; only when the sky became blue did incense-like pine smoke begin to mingle with the pungency of steaming dunghills. On these, turkeys were energetically breakfasting, the cocks often pausing to display magnificent quivering fans. Then, from yard after yard, came flocks of shrill guinea-fowl and a superb variety of hens and richly plumaged cocks. Grey and white geese halted on their way to the frozen river and hissed aggressively at the stranger – then waddled frustratedly over the ice, thrusting long necks this way and that like caricatures of disapproving school-marms. A shrunken old man, tripping over a patched army greatcoat several sizes too large, led a bony cow to the river's edge and smashed the ice with an axe. At once geese and ducks came quacking and flapping from every direction and I too stopped to drink from cupped hands – which within seconds were numbed. The old man responded to my greeting with a scared glance and a mumble; seemingly he had not divined my foreignness till I spoke.

20

From the larger homesteads animals were being released by elderly scarved women, wearing striped aprons, calf-length full skirts and embroidered sheepskin bodices. One woman herded a few brown or white sheep, and new-born lambs, to a nearby sheltered corner where the sun was beginning to defrost short wiry yellowed grass. When she left a white woolly sheepdog in charge I wondered if he could be trusted to remain on duty. I didn't yet know how highly developed a sense of responsibility has been bred into Rumanian sheepdogs.

Black and white piebald pigs, with distinctively short snouts, wandered along the track finding improbable things to eat, like bits of rotten wood and scraps of rope. But Rumania has never seriously attempted to get rid of the class system, and there was a local porcine élite: three half-grown boars guzzling from an eight-foot-long carved wooden trough, burnished with age. Their squeals and snorts of ecstasy were audible thirty yards away.

Little work could be done outside and I saw only two men labouring – one stooking wine-red willows, grown in clumps by the river, the other spreading muck from a cart drawn by two glossy fat ponies. A few weeks previously, Rumania's revolution had ousted even the US invasion of Panama from the world's headlines. But what, I wondered, had it meant to those peasants?

Beyond the last village I was climbing again, towards a knot of smooth-crested, pine-dark mountains. The sun shone brilliantly on a slightly snowy landscape of steep, tree-edged fields, some scattered with haycocks, others ploughed. Pausing for a snack, hypothermia seemed an imminent risk; after a swig of whiskey – a rapidly dwindling asset – I marched on.

Then the track became a precipitous path through a forest of oak, sycamore, birch, beech and the dignified, towering spruce fir which bears no resemblance to its puny commercially cultivated cousin. I savoured the illusion of remoteness created by ancient forests, even where one knows villages to be close. On this sheltered slope the path had turned to thick black mud and only my own squelching footsteps broke the silence. On my left, as I followed a narrow ridge, lay a long shadowy gorge. On the other side was brightness; the wide snowy expanse of a thinly forested mountain. Then there was brightness ahead and soon I was on

21

the pass – an open saddle, broad and sunny, its crisp dazzling snow criss-crossed with the footprints of foxes or wolves. (Only experts can tell the difference.)

I lingered, enchanted, reluctant to descend. Clumps of briars – blackberry and wild raspberry – were still russet-leaved between hazel groves and spindly dwarf elders and a gnarled pear tree. The slopes ahead, carpeted in beech leaves, glowed red-gold in the noon sunlight. Beyond them, a dark green density of firs stretched to the silver-grey summit of a craggy mountain. The air tasted of snow and resin, of purity and peace. I wanted to make no sound; the silence was an integral part of this beauty. Almost seventy years ago, an Inuit shaman told Knud Rasmussen: 'The best magic words are those which come to one when one is alone, out among the mountains. These are always the most powerful in their effect. The power of solitude is great beyond under-standing.'

The descent – much steeper than the climb – was difficult. Here the track, following a deep gulley between broken slopes, had become a frozen torrent some three yards wide. Aesthetically this was a pleasing sight, with its translucent loops and whorls and corrugations of ice sparkling where the sun shone through. But it forced me onto the high ground and that evasive action involved some tough climbing; to choose the easiest way forward would be to risk losing sight of the path.

Where the gulley ended – on the banks of a frozen river – a motorable track appeared and gradually descended, through a widening valley between beechy slopes, to a hamlet of wooden foresters' shacks – wretched dwellings, compared with village houses. Then, as on the previous afternoon, dark clouds suddenly threatened sleet.

As I sprinted for shelter a motor vehicle slowly jolted into view: something long, though not immediately recognisable as a bus beneath its mud coat. Three young women came running through the sleet from the shacks but I got there first and, when the door opened, stood aside to let a mother with baby descend. The driver shouted a question at me – then, recognising a foreigner, made it plain I must not board. Feigning obtuseness, I entered and held out a 100-lei note. He scowled, struck my hand quite hard and pointed to the door. I shrugged and took the seat behind his as the other women entered. Accepting five-lei fares, the driver attempted to enlist their support; but they merely glanced at me sideways, uneasily, before retreating to back seats. When my passport was demanded I showed the visa page; the driver frowned at it, then stared searchingly into my face. Wagging a reproving forefinger, I said sternly, 'Ion Iliescu gave me this visa'. The name-mantra worked. Turning away, the driver slammed the door and started the engine. But he rejected my five-lei fare, muttering something about 'the military'.

As a connoisseur of beat-up vehicles, I appreciated this bus. We lurched from crater to crater at walking speed, while the loose seats rattled, a free-swinging roof panel threatened to guillotine me and mud sprayed my legs through a gaping hole in the floor. At two villages, barely discernible through whirling wet snow, we picked up three more passengers. In Buteni, a large village on a tarred road, I made to get off – thereby reducing the driver to apoplectic anxiety. His agitation was so obviously genuine that I agreed to continue to the town of Sebis; it seemed he wished to hand me over to the army.

We filled up in Buteni, where an old woman embarked with her pet goose, snug in its travelling basket and clearly used to bus journeys. It was a strikingly handsome bird, wearing a tiny pink bow in its contrived top-knot: but it had a hidden vice. When its owner lifted the basket high, while negotiating a pile of sacks, it took a fancy to my right ear and nipped it sharply, drawing blood. This greatly diverted all present, including the driver. Much to my surprise, he bellowed with laughter; I had not hitherto thought of him as a jovial fellow.

Our arrival in Sebis coincided with an immense crimson post-storm sunset. Having shed the other passengers, the driver delivered me to army headquarters, a pleasant old building – once a Magyar mansion – flying Rumania's holed flag but not otherwise militarised. Leaning out, my captor summoned the conscript on sentry duty who summoned a junior officer who summoned three senior officers. I was then allowed to disembark and the driver sat nervously awaiting developments.

The officers greeted me politely and an English-speaker asked, 'Can we help? What is your problem?' I denied having any problem, but explained that the driver seemed to need some sort of reassurance. Whereupon he was dismissed with a contemptuous gesture and the English-speaker directed me to a hotel. Then the trio shook hands and retreated from the rapidly dropping temperature to their doubtless overheated mess.

But for a plaque by the entrance, one would never suspect that Sebis's tall grim hotel is Class I, Category A. Standing in the doorway, I was unnerved to see eight soldiers armed with sub-machine-guns occupying the otherwise empty lounge. Could it be that the counter-revolution was about to start in Sebis? Then I realised that they had not even noticed me, so absorbed were they in a television programme: the Wales versus France Rugby match. Later these teenage conscripts admitted that their formidable weapons were unloaded; they just carried them around to get used to the feel of them.

My companions' rapt expressions owed less to the quality of the Rugby than to the fact that they were watching Western television, a novel experience for their generation. At intervals the English-speakers turned to me and exclaimed, 'We're *free* now!' Or, 'This is our liberty!' Or, 'Now we can watch the whole world!' They were not drinking their beers, which had evidently been bought as an 'entry fee', and when one youth offered me his bottle I understood why. At that date Rumanian beer (five pence a litre at my rate of exchange) was a flat acidic abomination, laden with sharp bits of grit, virtually non-alcoholic and tasting of soap powder – perhaps added in an abortive effort to make it foam.

Soon after the final whistle my companions stood up, adjusted their weapons awkwardly, doffed their fur caps and filed past me to say goodbye, each bowing respectfully and kissing my hand. They were gentle youths; it upset me to think of them being trained to kill.

At the far end of that vast, cold, dimly-lit lounge I thumped repeatedly on Reception's high counter. Eventually diminutive Irina appeared. Only her fur-hatted head and enshawled shoulders were visible as she gazed up at me in wordless astonishment, before accepting my passport and scuttling away into a back room. Long minutes later she returned and said in precise English, 'Welcome to our country! But I am sorry, we must charge you 300 lei for one night. It is too much, but that is the rule for tourists. I am sorry again that the restaurant has no food. This is not a good time for tourism. But your room will be warm. Since the revolution, our Front for National Salvation has given us more heating.'

Irina looked miserably guilty as I paid my 300 lei: three days' wages for the average Rumanian. Then a weedy uniformed figure – one of the hotel's many surplus lackeys – drifted out of the gloom to conduct me upstairs. 'Let him carry your luggage,' urged Irina. On hearing that I had none she laughed nervously; evidently this confirmed her original impression that there was a lunatic on the premises.

My warm double room boasted bedside lamps, television, telephone and an *en suite* bathroom. But the lamps lacked bulbs, the television and telephone didn't work and the only water came from the wash-basin cold tap in an intermittent trickle. However, the loo did flush, if one experimented patiently with its hydraulics. And for me, *sans* sponge-bag, the water supply was unimportant; I simply wiped my face with a dampened end of the grubby little hotel towel.

I was supping off Anna's bounty when a knock on the door heralded two worried-looking young men. Liviu was dark and stocky, Gabi tall by any standards and freakishly so for a Rumanian. They were worried because the hotel had charged me the tourist rate. Gabi returned my 300 lei while Liviu explained, 'You must be the guest of Rumania because Ceausescu exploited tourists, so now it is our duty to make them welcome.' Ignoring my argument that 300 lei was a reasonable charge, they bowed and withdrew. Later Irina informed me that they were Timisoara students who had 'helped to make the revolution' and were now 'serving on the Committee' in their home town. 'The Committee' was defined as a spontaneously formed group which had in effect replaced the local Party bosses; hence Irina's acceptance of the young men's decision that I should be given free accommodation. Such Committees were most influential in small towns but did not last long anywhere; their practical know-how fell far short of their idealism.

At eight o'clock next morning Irina thought breakfast might be served some time after ten but she couldn't *promise* ... I assured her that I had ample food and was hoping only for a glass of herbal tea or a cup of acorn coffee. She grovelled:

neither was available. Then she grovelled again because of the weather. Usually, in January, it was much colder with heavy snow and then hours of bright sunshine. Together we stood peering through sheets of sleet at Sebis's 'systematised' town centre, which even on a balmy spring day is uninspiring. 'You cannot walk on now,' observed Irina. Agreeing, I returned to my room.

Since leaving Arad my action-packed life had protected me from booklessness. Now the full horror of having *nothing* to read, for the first time in my life, induced panic. Then I remembered the pocket diary given me as I left London: it contained printed matter. Seizing it, I found numerous gardening-related quotes and was musing over the potted biography of Sir Joseph Paxton when Liviu and Gabi reappeared, to assure me that my second night in Sebis would also be on the state. As it was Sunday they were free to relax and talk. Gabi commented, 'There is much to be done, reorganising things, even on a Sunday. But in this country it is hard to get people to work on any day and impossible on Sundays!'

My friends were curious to know how the outside world had viewed Rumania's revolution – a widespread curiosity at that time. I reported our astonished admiration for the bravery of the unarmed young and our elation at the apparent triumph of People Power.

'But why were you astonished?' asked Gabi. 'If *you* were young and lived in Rumania under Ceausescu, wouldn't *you* be willing to risk your life to change things?'

Liviu added, 'And it had to be the young who acted, the others were too worn down and terrorised. But people who didn't live under Ceausescu couldn't imagine it, that's why they were astonished.'

As I later realised, both these young men were much more politically astute than the average Rumanian. They felt pessimistic about the immediate future, believing their country needed at least a year to prepare for its first attempt to organise democratic elections. 'At best,' said Liviu, 'it can only be an *attempt!*'

We parted after a few instructive – I hoped for all of us – hours. At supper-time we were to meet again in the restaurant; there might be no supper, but there would certainly be a Gypsy band

and a popular local singer of post-revolutionary ballads.

The sleet had stopped but a low sullen sky made noon seem like dusk. As I rambled around the town a distant choir, sounding more fervent than tuneful, drew me to the little Orthodox church where a funeral service was following the Sunday Mass. Recently the building had been redecorated; its walls and ceiling were covered with bright stilted murals on conventional Byzantine themes. All Rumania's Communist rulers secured the support of the Orthodox church by lavishly funding restoration work and new building, as well as paying local popes 2000 lei a month, by way of supplementing their other sources of income, and paying senior clergy a great deal more.

The overflowing congregation included all age groups but had a predominance of wizened women in black headscarves. Soon after my arrival the mourners uncovered baskets of large buns, or unwrapped huge circular loaves, and for some ten minutes ritualistically raised their offerings – each with a lighted candle on top – high above their heads, then lowered them, then again raised them. Meanwhile, the pope in gilded vestments, and two adult acolytes who wore only slightly less gorgeous robes, were swinging censers and solemnly singing in the centre of the church. There tall candles surrounded an ornate brass table supporting two gigantic pottery basins full of some dark brown gooey substance. The ceremony concluded with the distribution of bread and goo; within moments I had received a dozen buns and several dollops of sticky stuff wrapped in paper napkins. The accompanying smiles and handshakes were heart-warming; unfortunately I could converse only with the pope, who too closely resembled the worst sort of Irish parish priest: plump, complacent, calculating and sure of his power over his people. Those buns proved just edible, though of a weirdly rubbery texture. But the goo – different versions of some anti-human confection – could not possibly be forced down. Immediately after the revolution, the sheer repulsiveness of most Rumanian food and drink was beyond exaggeration.

Sebis – not to be confused with the much bigger Sebes, near Alba Iulia – lies on the banks of a polluted river at the base of a long, forested, wolf-infested ridge. During the night I had heard persistent howling: to me the eeriest of sounds, arousing an

27

absurd atavistic fear. According to Gabi, the 'simple people' (a Rumanian euphemism for peasants) suffer from chronic wolf-phobia though no local adult has been killed since the winter of 1962–3. Then three foresters disappeared, in separate incidents; the simple people couldn't understand why their boots were eaten but their scalps discarded, a detail which for them greatly magnified the horror of the tragedies. During the past few decades small children have occasionally been attacked in midwinter, but for that Gabi and Liviu blamed careless parents rather than hungry wolves.

I spent that cold dark afternoon walking briskly around Sebis and its environs, adjusting to Ceausescu-scarred Transylvania. This process was helped by my having acquired two good Sebis friends who tentatively hoped, if all went well politically, to visit me quite soon in Ireland. Already my focus of interest was shifting from the Transylvania of my dreams to the Transylvania of today.

Before its cruelly enforced transformation into an 'agro-industrial complex', Sebis was a small attractive town surrounded by prosperous farming villages. Now the whole area is ugly, impoverished, dispirited, its handsome sturdy village dwellings replaced by dreary rows of jerry-built farm-workers' blocs. No one was around, on a Sunday afternoon, to hinder my probing the scandals of 'collectivisation'. Wading through ankle-deep liquid manure, between a score of broken-down rusted tractors, I found animals being kept in Belsen conditions. An Irish farmer who inflicted half as much suffering would be jailed. But then, no Irish farmer would be so improvident; Irish livestock make money for their owners. To console myself, I reflected that farms never look their best in midwinter.

Over supper my friends declared that the new regime should at once return the land to private ownership. To us this sounds trite; one tends merely to nod before raising some more debatable point. Yet how can the return of village collectives to the original owners (or their descendants) be fairly organised after the passage of forty socially deforming years during which the land has been consistently abused and most of the younger generation have migrated to the cities? All their lives the peasants have been paid only a slave-wage, apart from the élite corps of state farm

28

tractor drivers and mechanics, who were paid more than academics. So how can individuals afford to nurse sick fields and animals back to health? And how can the younger generation be persuaded to exchange steady urban jobs, with regular hours and wages and mod. con. flats, for the unpredictable incomes, long hours and material discomforts of private farming? When collectivisation began, thousands of peasants who refused to co-operate were arrested and punished. Forty years later, will it be necessary to arrest and punish their children and grandchildren for refusing to return to the ancestral fields?

Another problem: who is to decide how to share out the vast state farms, expropriated from the nobility? Should those millions of hectares go to peasants who have never possessed land, the descendants of the poorest serfs of the feudal landlords? (Feudalism lasted longer in Rumania than anywhere else in Europe.) Poetic justice suggests that, but could such people cope? Might it not be wiser for the state to lease those potentially fertile hectares to the most prosperous and dynamic villagers, those who were best able to manipulate the black market under Communism?

Romantic city-dwellers, Gabi said, argue that the mere possession of land would trigger an instant chemical reaction in most peasants, stimulating hard work and efficiency. This might well be true if the majority were not geriatric. Throughout the Communist years, village families put much energy and initiative into producing the maximum of food in the minimum of space; otherwise Rumania would literally have been famine-stricken during the 1980s. But Liviu and Gabi feared that those whose homes have been razed and gardens lost might be irredeemably demoralised. As unthinking cogs in the collective wheel they have become reluctant to assume responsibility for anything outside the narrowest circle of domestic concerns.

In the crowded hotel restaurant each customer could have only one portion of leathery beef kebabs with stale bread. There was nothing else, not even pickled cabbage or cucumber though the local shops were packed with those delicacies. The hotel had used up its pickle allocation, my friends explained, and rations are not transferable, however embarrassing the shops' surpluses. An *alimentara* gets its quota, a hotel gets its quota – and that's *it* . . .

'But,' I protested, 'you've had a revolution! For how much

29

longer must this lunacy go on?' They exchanged gloomy glances. 'Who knows?' said Gabi. 'Where can we begin?' said Liviu. More than any other eastern bloc country, Rumania seemed unable to find the answer to that question: or was, for reasons that gradually suggested themselves to me, unwilling to seek it.

The Gypsy band failed to turn up; having played elsewhere at lunchtime, they had been too well rewarded with *tuica*. However, the ballad-singer – dark-skinned with mischievous laughing eyes and wavy shoulder-length jet-black hair – arrived only an hour late. He wore the sort of jeans that threaten emasculation and an 'I LOVE JESUS!' T-shirt over a polo-neck sweater. His grinning blonde girl-friend accompanied him on an ill-tuned piano in a corner of the dining-room; her black tracksuit was decorated, fore and aft, with a skull and crossbones. The anti-Ceausescu ballads were wasted on me but evoked semi-hysterical giggling and tumultuous applause and foot-stamping from the audience – including a group of hitherto sombre-looking army officers, sitting close to our table.

In the middle of the room three youths were equipped with a full-sized 'Free Rumania' flag, tied to a shepherd's crook, and at intervals they waved it joyously. I found the prevalence of those triumphantly mutilated flags curiously moving. They flew from offices, army and police barracks, churches and schools, private houses, bloc balconies – and, in miniature form, from trucks, tractors, buses, trains, trams, motor cycles, cars and horse-carts. That neatly-cut hole then seemed to symbolise, most powerfully, Rumania's sudden change of fortune. When I suggested it as an appropriate permanent national emblem the young men remained silent. Then, looking down at the table, Gabi slowly said, 'But maybe . . . one day it will be patched?'

A waiter passed us, bringing labelled wine bottles to the officers, and I at once became over-excited. (During our forenoon session we had emptied the whiskey bottle.) However, my suggestion that we too should indulge was scorned – 'That is not real, it comes from a laboratory. All our real wine goes abroad, except what we make at home.'

Despite the alcohol drought, and my companions' underlying pessimism, I suddenly felt intoxicated. A month previously, this scene would have been beyond the imagination of the most fanciful Rumanian. I looked at the crowd; years of malnutrition had left people abnormally susceptible to cold, and all were wearing woolly caps or fur hats, and sheepskin jackets or heavy drab anoraks. Yet to me the room-temperature seemed just right – and ecologically much sounder than our Western hot-houses. Many faces showed signs of long-term exhaustion and strain but now were relaxed: even, in some cases, serene. On one level this revolution had been totally successful. After decades during which only silence was safe, all Rumanians now felt free to express themselves loudly, as individuals, in public – and in the presence of members of the security forces. So completely do we take this freedom for granted that only then did I fully appreciate what it must mean to those to whom it is new.

My impression in Sebis, and during the next fortnight, was of a dazed and grateful people celebrating their escape from a diabolically efficient terrorist state which had used a tiny minority to repress a stoutly anti-Communist majority. This, like many political first impressions, was misleading – as Liviu and Gabi could have told me. Perhaps they were superstitiously reluctant to be explicit, lest voicing their fears might help to fulfil them.

After my friends' departure I lingered, hoping for further interesting encounters. Rumanian is not an insurmountable barrier, if both sides are keen to communicate, but no one else wanted to become involved. All along my route, during that significant period, my appearance in a restaurant or other public places caused atmospheric crackles; the simple people were still uncertain about responding to friendly overtures from an inexplicable solitary stranger. Yet their reaction was never hostile; in some villages my reception incongruously recalled Ethiopia's Simien region, where the local headman would courteously offer me hospitality while everyone else backed off.

Before departing, my friends had warned me that the sleety weather would continue and, intuiting that I had exhausted Sebis's charms, suggested my going north to Maramures by wheeled transport. There the weather was likely to be more seasonable: real snowstorms interspersed with sunny days conducive to trekking. They arranged for me to be given a lift to Oradea early enough to catch a train to Baia Mare. From there, weather permitting, I could walk over the mountains to Maramures.

31

3

Disabled on the Road

Twenty-four hours later I was lying on my bed in a Satu Mare hotel room with a plum-sized lump on my skull, a sensational headache and an area of agony at the base of my spine. I could remember the bald-tyred Sebis car sliding slowly off a steep icy road – so slowly that I had time to ask the driver, 'Is there something wrong with the steering?' Then came a moment of incredulity (incredulity, rather than fear) as the car went over the edge.

When I came to I was lying on sacks in the back of a state farm grain truck. It had been closely following us and was wearing snow-chains, a luxury not then available to private vehicles. The car driver lay beside me, still unconscious, with blood oozing from both ears. We had been covered with fleeces. It was snowing lightly. The truck driver's mate sat between us and when I opened my eyes he gently stroked my hair and said *'spital'*.

I only vaguely recall my fellow-victim being admitted to the hospital where (it later devastated me to learn) he died within a few hours. I was refused admission, apparently because I could walk – albeit with difficulty. The truck driver and his mate then helped me find a bus for Oradea; inexplicably, they were very keen on my not being interviewed by the local police. From Oradea, where no hotel would accept lei without an exchange certificate, I caught a train to Satu Mare. I vividly recall walking to the *gara* and queueing for my ticket – but, curiously, as though it were an ordeal I had read about rather than a personal experience. The bus and train journeys are both blanks: and on arrival in Satu Mare I must have been still semi-concussed; when revisiting the place in March, again arriving by train, I had no recollection of getting from the *gara* to a Centru hotel.

That evening I told myself I'd feel better in the morning. In fact I felt worse, so painfully stiff that I could drag myself to the bathroom only by hanging onto the furniture. My lower back was hotly throbbing but Adrian, the young waiter who came to my room yearning to change dollars, laughed at my fantasy about finding pain-killers in Satu Mare.

Lacking anything to read, I spent most of that day writing a concussion-blurred description of my misadventure for Rachel's entertainment. This was composed in as light-hearted a vein as events warranted but alas! it failed to amuse my daughter, then in London. She shared the news with her godfather (my publisher) and the pair of them colluded in a most shameful exercise which caused me exquisite embarrassment when, much later, they confessed their indiscretion. Alarm signals were sent out in every direction: to the Foreign Office, the British Embassy in Bucharest, the Rumanian Ministry for Culture, the International Red Cross, the British Council ... *Please*, could somebody find me and provide appropriate aid and comfort and let London know where and how I was? For someone who believes that when travellers get themselves into trouble they should, if at all possible, get themselves out of it, this was the ultimate humiliation. I don't of course take independence to extremes; in Quito, as already recorded, we benefited from diplomatic cosseting. And when we were arrested near Lima by Peru's sinister Political Police, in 1979, we at once sent an SOS to the British Embassy and were promptly rescued. But such appeals should, in my view, be reserved for major crises.

By evening, solitary confinement in a bookless room had caused me to develop piteous print-withdrawal symptoms. Observing these, Adrian was puzzled. 'This is good!' he assured me, switching on the television and demonstrating its versatility; Satu Mare receives Hungarian, Czech and Russian programmes. 'You can watch all day,' he consoled me. 'Here! Look! A funny show from America in English!' As he turned up the volume I shuddered and begged him to switch off. 'Is there an English teacher in Satu Mare?' I asked desperately.

Adrian considered. 'Maybe one old lady, finished work – you want her? I can find.'

'Please do!' I said. 'And explain that I need to borrow some English books.'

An hour or so later Adrian returned with Agnes, a dynamic

elderly Magyar lady married to a Rumanian teacher of Russian. When she drew from her shopping-bag two Iris Murdoch novels, bought in Moscow in 1980, I almost sobbed with relief. Gratified by my reaction, Adrian beamed and slapped me vigorously on the shoulder: in the circumstances, an unfortunate gesture of affection. Seeing me wince, Agnes investigated my injuries, then resolved to seek pain-killers. She had a contact . . . But for once *ciubuc* failed.

Ironically, Agnes and her circle of gregarious friends were so attentive that I had time to read only one novel before moving on to Baia Mare. Although the hotel larder happened to be going through a fecund phase of its allocation cycle, my friends insisted on providing all my meals, including breakfast. For them, my foreign company was a precious commodity. For me, their Magyar views on the peculiar problems of Transylvania were no less valuable: at once illuminating, saddening and worrying.

My Satu Mare conversations suggested that the Magyars' post-revolution euphoria was tempered by fear – an impression repeatedly reinforced elsewhere. The political boat had been rocked and, though it was a hated prison-vessel, the Magyars had learned their way around it. Now, after the rocking, they were confused and nervous. Whether or not this reaction was reasonable is, in a sense, irrelevant; the emotions aroused were real and troubling. Agnes and her friends tended to convey these emotions indirectly, despite their assumption that I, as an Irishwoman from the Latin West, would of course be pro-Magyar.

Forty-year-old Eva, a fluent English-speaker, channelled her anxieties into the effects on 'the common people' of access to Western television. 'The revolutionaries see this as an important symbol of liberty, but it could unsettle people before the Front can satisfy their new demands. It could cause terrible discontent and riots. A month ago most people didn't know how deprived they were compared with any other Europeans, East or West. Now every day they see films about normal life, so they begin to realise their situation. And they may not have patience to wait for the economy to be reformed, which will take a long, long time! Soon they could become dangerous. Rumanians are very fiery people, very wild and impetuous . . .'

I remarked that, judging by what I had seen of Rumanian

34

television sets in action, they seemed unlikely to reveal enough of the outside world to inflame the multitude.

This feeble witticism was taken seriously. 'So they will want better sets,' said Eva grimly. 'They will feel thwarted because the good films are there but they cannot see them. Then they will make trouble.'

Eva's sister-in-law spoke up; she and her family were about to migrate to Hungary. 'You don't understand', she said, 'how *violent* Rumanians are. Quickly they can become like savages. And they hate *us*! If they become angry, for any reason, they will attack *us*. And now there is no government in this country, not even a bad one. The police and army do not know what they should do, in a crisis. They have no boss. For us this is a very dangerous time. Transylvania is my home, my only home – I belong here, I don't belong in Hungary. But I have two children to protect, so we must go . . .'

As time passed, and blood was shed in Transylvania, and I investigated some of the background to that bloodshed, it seemed to me that the phrase 'they hate *us*' revealed an unhealthy projection. The fanatically nationalistic Ceausescu regime did indeed hate Magyars and tried to suffocate their culture. However, Rumanians, Magyars and Saxons suffered equally under Ceausescu, with the important difference that Magyars and Saxons could – as many thousands did – get permission to migrate. Unfortunately Ceausescu's anti-Magyar campaign was helped by both the Hungarian government and the ex-patriate Magyar lobby, who tirelessly disseminate tendentious accounts of 'the Transylvania Problem' throughout Western Europe and North America. This naturally angers ordinary Rumanians, who have no comparable international network to present their side of the story. Thus the post-revolution heightening of Rumanian–Magyar tension was partly an outside job, though with many insider accomplices.

At noon on my third convalescent day I gingerly emerged, leaning heavily on a beautifully carved walking-stick – a gift from Eva. Before the Treaty of Trianon in 1920 Satu Mare was Szatmarnemeti, capital of the Hungarian county of Szatmar and a major trading post on the river Szamos. The Magyars claim that since being deprived of its natural hinterland across the border it has lost not only its prosperity but its character: which may well be true. Yet I enjoyed my first glimpse, despite every step provoking red-hot twinges. The architectural flavour of the city centre remains Magyar, as does a big minority of the population – though *how* big I couldn't discover. The lack of reliable figures is a handicap all writers on Rumania must accept. Unreliable figures of course abound; statistics on everything from agriculture to zoology poured from Ceausescu's presses, all designed to prove how singularly blessed among the nations was the Socialist Republic of Rumania.

Near the three conspicuous but unmemorable basilicas – Orthodox, Roman Catholic, Calvinist – several maimed beggars were sitting on wet cold pavements: discarded citizens who seriously damaged the image of a blessed Socialist Republic. But naturally Ceausescu had never been allowed to see beggars. This was the first city I had explored and it distressed me to observe how many passers-by looked malnourished to a Third World degree, their faces recalling photographs of starving European refugees at the end of the Second World War. Yet the majority were adequately dressed and all those unhealthy bodies, normally attired, underlined the fundamental insanity of Ceausescu's dictatorship. There had never been an extreme clothing shortage, my friends explained that evening. The manic 'save energy' campaign was accompanied by exhortations to dress warmly and, since there was so little food to be bought, people could afford to spend on their wardrobes. But many garments were 'seconds', unimaginatively designed, drably coloured and of poor workmanship. 'Firsts' were, at least in theory, for export only.

Petrol was still very scarce and the city's buses ran on gas, contained in huge, torpedo-like cylinders on the vehicles' roofs. Motor cars were far outnumbered by rubber-tyred carts; the glossy (uncollectivised) horses or ponies had their tails neatly plaited and tied up short, to avoid muddying, and wore long anti-evil-eye red tassels on their head-collars.

Most of the shops were three-quarters empty; when I asked for a toothbrush people laughed – derisively or sympathetically, according to temperament. The customerless *alimentaras* were however crammed as usual – here, with giant jars of pickled apples, tins of blackberry jam and bottles of murky 'carrot-juice'.

Bread was plentiful; within hours of taking control, the Front had ordered the release of extra flour for domestic consumption. I paused outside one small shop to admire some rare delicacies: a little pile of shrivelled spotty apples, four bunches of sprouting onions and a few coarse beetroot. Then a collective truck pulled up beside me and two men delivered two sacks of half-rotten potatoes. A moment before the street had been almost deserted, now scores of panting men and women converged on the shop and at once formed an orderly queue. Its logic was beyond me, so many people had arrived simultaneously; but the Rumanians had perfected the art of fair queueing and everyone seemed satisfied with their placing. They had also devised an informal rationing system; on such occasions, it was not done to seek more than one's share. Observing that scene, it struck me that Rumania could probably survive for quite some time without a government, proceeding under the momentum of forty-five years of regimentation.

Food for the mind was equally scarce. Four bookshops had tellingly bare shelves which a month earlier would have been laden with the spurious works of Nicolae Ceausescu. A month later, Rumanians rejoiced to see on television tons and tons and tons of those phoney volumes being pulped to provide paper for, they hoped, real books – or politically independent newspapers and journals. Meanwhile, Satu Mare's citizens were virtually restricted to the complete works of Mihai Eminescu (1850–89) in a fine centenary edition of twelve *Encyclopaedia Britannica*-sized volumes. One French grammar and three German engineering textbooks provided links with the outside world.

Next morning, feeling slightly more flexible, I hitch-hiked to Baia Mare: a test to determine whether or not my trek should be abandoned. After a five-mile walk, in the shadow of squalid tower blocs or through disintegrating industrial estates, I reached the wide level fields of a state farm. Here a relentless wind from Russia – some twenty miles away – went through me like a rapier, despite the cloudless sky, and in an hour only three trucks passed, each with an overcrowded cab. By then my back was protesting yet I dared not rest, in that temperature. I was regretting not having taken the train when a decrepit motor van stopped, the driver assuming me to be Rumanian. (My build, colouring and attire often fostered that illusion.) Momentarily he seemed non-plussed, but when he noticed me painfully struggling to embark – my back having suddenly become inflexible – he jumped out to help and provided a thawing swig of *tuica*.

Gheorghe, a jolly young man with a chubby ruddy face and oily dungarees, spoke two words of English: 'private enterprise'. These he proudly repeated, several times, while jerking his thumb towards his load – hunks of rusty machinery which had come from a Satu Mare factory and were to be sold to Gypsies in Baia Mare for Gheorghe's benefit. It seemed unlikely that he had bought them, but I suppose the Free Market has to start somewhere.

During our fifty-mile drive Gheorghe gloated over the Ceausescus' executions, turning to me and putting two fingers to his temple, then simulating sudden death and laughing uproariously. At intervals he flung back his head and chanted triumphantly, *'Jos Communismul! Jos Communismul!'* (Down with Communism.) When we stopped to buy cigarettes he took from his wallet a blurred newspaper photograph of Iliescu and stroked it affectionately: a *good* man was now leading the country ... Then he presented me with an ID-card-sized photograph of himself, having neatly inscribed his name on the back, and requested one of me in exchange. I obliged, wishing I had brought a bigger supply; exchanging photographs, it was becoming clear, is an important ritual among 'the simple people'.

Abruptly, across the wide ploughed plain, dark blue mountains bulked against the northern sky, their slopes only slightly snowy. My pangs of frustration were sharp. It had taken me four hours to walk ten miles on the level road from Satu Mare, yet my back had resented even that gentle exercise. Clearly trekking was out for some time to come.

Crossing a ridge, we saw Baia Mare far below. Gheorghe superfluously informed me that it is a very big city with many factories; he seemed inexplicably proud of it. A mining centre (on and off) since pre-Roman times, it has lately become a grotesque agglomeration of pollution-wreathed high-risery on the banks of the poisoned river Sasar. Because one tries to avoid looking at them, one can't afterwards describe such places in any detail. However, I should record that *The Rough Guide* lists several minor tourist attractions which I was in no state to be attracted by – the house of Iancu de Hundeoara, a Baroque cathedral, Stephen's Tower, a Mineral Museum and a Village Museum.

Gheorghe insisted on delivering me to the city centre Hotel Carpati, built for hypothetical tourists on the chemical-scented Sasar. I didn't argue; the idea of lying down, immediately, was appealing. But Fate had other plans for me. As in Oradea, my lei were rejected for lack of a bank exchange certificate, and the hard currency charge for a single room was $50. (An interesting post-revolution change: *The Rough Guide* gave the 1988 charge for this hotel as $28 single.) I protested that in Sebis and Satu Mare no such certificate had been demanded. The young woman at Reception looked apologetic and sad as she explained, 'In this city we have not been told to make things different.' Apparently Rumania was then being governed by autonomous local factions, some adhering to the old rules, others discarding them – others again modifying them for personal gain.

Retreating to the enormous crowded restaurant, I took the last empty table and wondered what to do next. The four good-looking young waitresses were beaming and efficient and had time to exchange semi-flirtatious jokes with 'regulars'. The table-linen, as in most such hotels at that time, was crisp and spotless. Then gradually Ceausescu's terror-influence waned and standards declined; when I revisited the Carpati in March everything looked perceptibly scruffier.

The restaurant was crowded not because of lunch-time – few were eating – but because of a tolerable-looking beer. As I ordered two bottles, three men at a nearby table heard my foreignness and eagerly invited me to join them. French is Rumania's first foreign language but – to counterbalance my various misfortunes – I chanced to meet an extraordinary number of English-speakers.

Mihai and Justinian were in their early thirties but looked older; life under Ceausescu was ageing. Tiberiu – tall, too thin, with a long pale sensitive face – had just left university. All three worked in local factories but now Tiberiu was hoping to be able to do a post-graduate course abroad. 'I have my passport!' he said elatedly, taking it from his jacket pocket and waving it above his head. 'Yesterday I got it – now we can all get passports! Tell me,

39

please, which is the best university in Europe for chemical engineering?'

Before I could reply Mihai said impatiently, 'But you have not enough wages to buy dollars – and you have no one living in the Occident. For you it is impossible to leave, to be abroad without dollars.'

Justinian nodded and remarked, 'It's bad to give everyone passports they can't use. It makes people discontented and angry.'

'But in a democracy,' I said, 'people must be free to travel, if they can find the means. That's their problem, but it's the government's duty to provide passports.'

Justinian looked puzzled and Mihai shook his head and said sombrely, 'We have much to learn about democracy – everything! Can you send us some books when you go home? We need to *study* democracy. No one in Rumania can understand what is it, really . . .'

I promised to do what I could and didn't say what I thought – that the practice of democracy cannot be learned from books.

The atmosphere in that restaurant, at lunch-time on an ordinary working day, was exuberantly festive. And not because of the liquid intake; Baia Mare's flowing beer, though just drinkable, was scarcely two per cent alcohol. When I remarked on all the jollity in the air Tiberiu said, 'The Ceausescus are dead, so we are happy all day and all night!' He finished his beer and took another bottle from the bucket on the chair beside him.

Justinian clinked glasses with me and said, 'We are *free*! I think in the West you have a problem to understand what means freedom, because always you have it. It means for us we can shout *"Jos Ceausescu! Jos Communismul!"'* – and he did joyously shout those words, and at other tables young men and women laughed and echoed them, and the waitresses clapped and one grinning old man threw his fur hat high in the air.

'Six weeks ago,' said Mihai, 'if we spoke those words the Securitate would come and beat us up and take us to prison. Or if we talked to you for five minutes, they would force us to repeat what we said to you and you said to us.'

'And if you didn't tell them the truth . . . ?' I wondered.

'We *must* tell true,' replied Justinian. 'Maybe they knew already,

40

they had so many listening machines. Then if we don't tell true they beat us even more.'

'What about the future?' I asked. 'Is it good to have elections so soon? Can the political parties get organised in a few months?'

They looked at one another, doubtfully, and hesitated. Then Justinian said, 'We must have a government and order. Now no one has no one to obey. That is not good, but it would be worse if we didn't have Iliescu. He is a strong, honest man. He can keep the country safe until the election, so we are lucky. And Petru Roman also is good. But we have too many parties – eighteen!'

Mihai frowned. 'Now anyone can have an idea and not know what to do with it except make a new party. I don't like this way of politics, but we are told it is democratic.'

(That was in January. By 20 May – Election Day – the Rumanians had lost count of their parties. There were rumoured to be seventy-five, or perhaps seventy-eight? And three months later there were 102 . . .)

Suddenly Mihai was angry, his fists tightly clenched on the table. 'Foreigners think our democracy will be a joke! Why are so many reporters and television men coming and treating us like animals in a zoo? We have pride and dignity, we are not crazy lunatics for Western people to stare at!'

'Maybe Western people think we *must* be crazy', said Justinian, 'to have waited so long before killing the Ceausescus.'

'And maybe', said Tiberiu, 'we *are* crazy!'

Mihai scowled. 'We are *brave* people, our revolutionaries had no weapons, only they were *brave*, to go out and get thousands killed to get freedom for us all.'

The long silence that followed was vaguely uncomfortable. Tiberiu broke it: 'No one was killed here, in Baia Mare.'

Mihai abruptly got up and went to the telephone. Justinian went to the *'toaleta'*. Tiberiu said, confidentially, 'It is hard in places where no one is dead. We are free without fighting. We have bad feelings about that.'

'You mean you feel guilty?' I asked. 'Or ashamed that you didn't all go out on the streets to defy the Securitate?'

'Yes, guilty!' said Tiberiu. 'That is the right English word which I could not remember.'

41

When the others returned Justinian repeated, 'We are lucky to have Iliescu, when he got rid of the Ceausescus he gave us everything next day – more food, heat, light, passports. And liberty to have many newspapers saying different things, and bigger wages and pensions for miners and farm-workers. And every day foreign films on television.'

Mihai agreed. Tiberiu twiddled his beer glass and said nothing. I mentally noted, not for the first time, a certain confusion in the Rumanians' perception of their revolution. Many seemed to believe, simultaneously, that it had been brought about by 'thousands of brave unarmed heroes' and by 'strong, honest Iliescu!'

We talked for over four hours. My friends should have re-turned to work soon after our meeting but were so excited by their new freedom to talk openly to foreigners that they found me irresistible: the first foreigner they had seen since the revolution and the only foreigner with whom they had ever held normal converse. At intervals one or other would dash to the telephone to make flimsy excuses to some boss, then hurry back, eagerly demanding 'What were you saying? Tell me what I didn't hear!'

I then mistook this casual opting out of the afternoon's work for a symptom of the general post-revolution euphoria, a natural reaction against a lifetime of regimentation. To the wandering foreigner it seemed at first attractive and convenient – everyone everywhere dropping everything to talk, advise, guide. But I soon realised that this feckless attitude to work is among Rumania's most ominous problems, which becomes deeply worrying once the implications have been seen. Either people are in phoney jobs, as is often the case, or they regard their work as supporting a system they despise and thus get some satisfaction out of neglect-ing it. Which under Ceausescu too many could do with impunity, if they took care to keep their political noses clean.

This form of corruption is recognised as such by those who call themselves 'intellectuals' – the university educated, though in our terms not necessarily 'intellectual', new middle class. One mid-summer morning I was sitting in a friend's kitchen, far from Baia Mare, having an absorbing discussion about the differences between police and Securitate corruption. Suddenly my friend looked at her watch and exclaimed, 'It's 10.30! So I'm corrupt too,

I should have been at work two and a half hours ago but I prefer talking to you. In this country we're all corrupt – you know that?'

I felt no need politely to demur. By then numerous Rumanians, of every condition, had explained that no one could have survived the past forty-five years without jettisoning normal standards of honesty. Clearly this was so; but as one historian bluntly told me, and several other friends coyly hinted, the Rumanians found it not too difficult to practise those habitual dishonesties essential for survival under Communism. The historian said, 'We are a half-Oriental country. In Wallachia and Moldavia, for centuries, Ottoman standards prevailed. In Transylvania, under the Magyars, the Rumanians were outcasts, so discriminated against and deprived that any cheating of the rulers seemed justified. We have no tradition of *not* being corrupt.'

By sunset the Carpati's beer quota had long since run out and the restaurant was almost empty. My back objected agonisingly to the short walk to the loo; a quest for pain-killers in the capital seemed the logical next move. But when I announced that I was going to Bucharest on the night train Tiberiu exclaimed, 'That is not possible! First you must buy where to sleep in the train. Now you come to my apartment and early tomorrow buy for tomorrow night.'

Mihai drove us through long, wide, straight boulevards, feebly lit, to Tiberiu's bloc. Cranes surrounded it: sinister angular shapes against the night sky. Tiberiu explained, 'Ceausescu came over here in a helicopter and saw little bits of ground left between the blocs. He said they must be filled up with other blocs for people from villages around – then the villages could be cleared away. So now no one in any bloc will have any light or air or space. In the Occident do you know he was mad?'

Alina was awaiting Tiberiu, looking tense. They had their own problem, quite apart from state terrorism. As partners outside of Holy Matrimony, they could not live together; Alina's parents insisted on her always being home by midnight, though she was twenty-two, and so they had to be consistently deceived. Luckily Tiberiu's parents, who would have been equally awkward, lived far away and were not a complication.

Alina looked tense because Tiberiu was late and she had plotted a pleasant surprise which required his immediate co-operation.

She would be able to spend the night in his apartment, having had an invitation to stay with a girl friend in Satu Mare and told her parents she was accepting it. However, to prevent any burgeoning of parental suspicion Tiberiu must now ring a friend of his in Satu Mare and ask him to ask his sister to ring Alina's father at his factory – he was on the evening shift – and enquire about the train's exact time of arrival.

I have never felt so *de trop*. This tiny apartment, though adequate for one person, could not possibly accommodate a pair of lovers plus guest. As Tiberiu hurried down six flights of concrete stairs, to the public telephone by the entrance, I glanced at my watch and remarked that I mustn't stay long as I hadn't yet booked my hotel room.

Alina stared at me, aghast, and for a moment it seemed she was about to cry. 'But Tiberiu said you were staying with *us!*' She pressed her hands together as though in prayer and begged, 'Please, please don't go!' She was small and already tending to dumpiness, with a broad, pleasant, too-pale face and wide rather sad brown eyes, now pleadingly fixed on me.

When Tiberiu returned I was persuaded that the privilege of having a foreign guest really did outweigh all else. It felt oddly touching to have my company so valued – and its value doubled when my profession emerged. Authors, I was to discover, are much respected in Rumania. And books are often regarded as an individual's most precious possessions: especially foreign books, it being some time since volumes uncontaminated by Communism were published within the country.

Alina's English was more fluent than Tiberiu's; she had wanted to study English and French at Cluj university but her father had a flawed file – he had been involved in a factory dispute in 1986 – so she had failed to gain a place.

These two were the first of several young couples who befriended me and then revealed that for them the path of true love was strewn with multiple obstacles, personal and official. Under Ceausescu unmarried couples were forbidden to cohabit, which partly explains a high divorce rate in the under-thirty age group. On the family level, it baffled me that so many parents retained rigidly puritanical views though religion is no longer a dominant force.

As we ate our supper of scrambled eggs and stale bread, I asked Alina, 'Why are your parents so strict? Are they very religious?'

She looked down at her plate and prodded her food irritably before replying. 'They believe in God and go to church at Easter. But I think they are strict not because of God but because our friends and relatives would think I was a bad woman if they knew about Tiberiu – I mean, that we go to bed. It is just the old custom, not the religion.'

During the months ahead, I was frequently given this explanation for parental inhibitions.

'The biggest problem', said Tiberiu, 'is that we *love* our parents, very much. We can't make them sad. They have worried and suffered to feed us, when we were growing up – going without enough food for themselves. So we must respect the way they think, even if it is very troublesome.'

Alina said, 'Both our families would be happy if we married and last year we wanted to – but it would be wrong to have children while there is no good food for them. And we couldn't afford the tax punishment for not having them.'

'Next June', said Tiberiu, 'I will be twenty-five and under Ceausescu I would then have to pay the same fine for *not* being married. But now Iliescu has stopped all those laws so maybe we can marry soon.'

'Why "maybe"?' I asked.

'Because of where to live,' replied Alina wearily. 'If we marry Tiberiu will lose this apartment – it's for one person *only*. But it's hard to get a bigger place so maybe we must live for years in my parents' little house. And we don't like that although we love them.'

'Perhaps Iliescu will also change the housing laws,' I suggested. 'Then you could both live here.'

Tiberiu shook his head. 'No! He is changing only the laws that people outside have made trouble about – the baby tax, illegal abortion, contraceptives banned. People outside never heard of all the other bad laws, like not having freedom about where to live and other things – many other things! So those he won't change. But maybe after the elections our new government will be more kind . . .'

Alina flared up. 'Iliescu is a good man! He hated Ceausescu and

Ceausescu was afraid of him and punished him!'

Tiberiu shrugged. 'What punishment? To be Director of a publishing house! I would like that punishment! Iliescu is a friend of Gorbachev, they studied together in Moscow and ever since are friends. So always he is under Russian influence, which for us means our enemy's influence.'

There is no evidence that Gorbachev and Iliescu were acquainted as students, yet throughout Rumania I heard this rumour frequently repeated. I asked, 'Don't you believe Gorbachev is a new and different sort of Russian? Didn't he make possible the collapse of Communism throughout Europe?'

Tiberiu smiled at me tolerantly. 'People in the Occident can't understand. You get confused because Gorbachev is a different sort of *Communist*. But he will always be a Communist, and Iliescu the same. *Perestroika* and *glasnost* are only new sauces on the same poisoned food.'

This was a standard 'single' flat, with hot water for two hours both morning and evening since the revolution. The little kitchen had an aluminium sink and three-ring gas cooker but no refrigerator. Food was stored, when there was any to store, on the balcony, to which there was access from both rooms through french windows. The bathroom, to the left of the entrance door, was a windowless cubby-hole with space for only one person to stand between bath, lavatory and hand-basin. The hallway, though not big enough to hold a bicycle, provided extra storage space for – in Tiberiu's case – books. In Poland and Moscow I have seen whole families living in flats no bigger than this; by Communist standards, most Rumanians were not ill-housed.

On the bed-sitter walls every available space was covered with pop-star portraits, sent from Austria by Alina's *émigré* cousin. But there was room for only half a dozen, one wall being occupied by a typical piece of Rumanian modern furniture, some six feet high and eight feet long. This incorporated bookshelves, clothes drawers at floor level, food and china cupboards, knick-knack alcoves and a narrow wardrobe. On top were displayed the sort of things more fortunate people put on their mantelpieces. Most of these plywood conglomerates look attractive enough but many have tiresome defects; sticking drawers, loose door knobs, hinges that break and cannot possibly be replaced. All the best Rumanian furniture, which is very handsome indeed, was of course exported, mainly to the USSR – like the best Rumanian everything.

It was after midnight when we retired. News of a foreign body had spread fast and relays of excited neighbours arrived to present me with gifts and beg me to stay with them on my next visit. The conversation was mainly political, in the widest sense. Tiberiu's anti-Iliescu stance was generally deplored, yet many doubts were expressed about Rumania's ability to 'go democratic' within months of the revolution.

I slept uneasily, being often awakened by agonising spasms, and during the small hours came to a decision: should Bucharest fail to yield up effective pain-killers, that quest must be pursued in Belgrade.

At breakfast (more scrambled eggs and stale bread) Mihai reappeared, having already been to the *gara* to buy my tickets for the night train. In honour of the foreigner he, Tiberiu and Alina had reported 'digestive trouble' to their respective bosses – a plausible Rumanian complaint, for obvious reasons. It was a brilliant sunny morning but when Mihai offered to drive us to Baia Mare's various tourist attractions I had to admit to being in too much pain to enjoy sight-seeing. Whereupon Mihai and Tiberiu, looking genuinely stricken on my behalf, rushed away to search unsuccessfully for a remedy.

Alina asked probing questions, then advised me to go straight home and have my pain investigated. I explained that I couldn't bear to leave Rumania as yet, having just arrived after a fifty-year wait. And as I spoke something bobbed to the surface of my consciousness.

'It seems to me,' I said – astonishing myself – 'that I'm going to want to spend much longer here than I'd planned. In fact . . . well, I've just realised this. I want to write a book about Rumania.'

4

Bucharest under Black Ice

On the crowded train to Bucharest two of the three young men sharing my sleeper spoke some English. The third, a rosy-cheeked conscript from near Sighet, wept quietly while hanging out of the corridor window waving goodbye to his parents. Having failed to get into university, he was doomed to fifteen months' hard labour on a state farm – or similar unpaid work. Student conscripts were required to do only nine months.

After my physically inactive Baia Mare day (mentally it had been quite strenuous) I was able to stand in the corridor for a few hours, sharing in the prevailing effervescence – an atmosphere of elation so infectious that to some extent it acted as a pain-killer. Wild rumours were being exchanged and, usually, believed. Nicu Ceausescu, though imprisoned, was said to be organising a counter-revolution for the following day (26 January) to mark his father's birthday. Thousands of Libyan mercenaries were said to have been flown to Yugoslavia in disguise and were about to cross the border. And so on and on and on ... This predisposition to credit absurdities, especially those designed to transfer blame to non-Rumanians, then seemed to me merely pathetic. Later I saw it as a dangerous weakness, leaving the simple people (and many others, too) wide open to manipulation.

Between rumours, everyone was loudly proclaiming their hatred of Communism, their trust in Iliescu, their incredulous joy at being *free*. Long after I had stretched out on my clean, comfortable couchette, '*Libertate!*' was being toasted in *tuica* up and down the coach. It was one month, that day, since the Ceausescus' executions.

During an almost sleepless night I began to suspect that Alina's advice might have been sound. When we arrived in Bucharest, punctually at 7.30, bending to put on my boots presented a major problem and I had to be helped to descend from the high coach.

48

Rumanian trains are peculiarly unkind to the disabled – as I had occasion to notice again, months later, after my next disaster.

On that grey, foggy, far-below-freezing morning, Bucharest looked not at its best. Even in the Centru, streets and pavements were treacherously covered by mounds of dingy packed snow and the sheets of black ice almost broke my nerve. A fall on ice seemed just what was needed to finish me off. In the only open pharmacy a skeletal sallow woman with a severe squint laughed sardonically when I asked for pain-killers. All the hotels demanded an exchange certificate; without one, the cheapest charged $40 a night. That grotty old building must once have been quite beautiful; now it had a stained and ragged carpet in the foyer, a truculent unshaven man on duty at Reception and stinking blocked lavatories.

As I moved from district to district on the Metro, seeking a non-tourist hotel, people stared at me; despite my inadequate garments, I was visibly sweating with pain. There were few places to sit; most restaurants and cafés had been closed since the revolution, even in the main railway station, and the atmosphere in the hyper-luxurious Intercontinental Hotel felt unendurably sleazy. This was one of America's Ceausescu-boosting investments during the early 1970s. To make way for it, the architectural heart of old Bucharest had to be torn out; little remains now of a capital once known as 'the Paris of the East'. As I passed through the swing doors, an ostentatiously-uniformed porter hastened to eject me; socially deprived Rumanians are not permitted to sully this temple of affluence. The man's expression was comical when I told him to get lost; clearly he was unused to coping with socially deprived foreigners and didn't know the rules. He hesitated, glanced nervously towards Reception, then allowed me to proceed into the foyer where I sat for a few nauseated moments before ejecting myself.

During that first visit to Bucharest I experienced the city on two levels which, in retrospect, seem curiously separate though at the time they overlapped. On one level I was coping with my own physical suffering, on the other I was responding to the citizens' emotional suffering. Rumania's then state of collective shock was most starkly apparent in the capital. Here the revolutionary price had been paid and many were jumpy and/or slightly aggressive.

49

The feeling was quite different from anywhere else I had been.

Emerging from the Piata Universitatii Metro not long after dawn, I immediately got the churchy whiff of melting candles – and then through the freezing greyness saw them warmly flickering in their hundreds, encircling the long pile of evergreens and wreaths and frost-bitten bunches of flowers that marked the spot where many had died. Simple wooden crosses, embedded in the evergreens, bore photographs of the dead, and messages from their families – often 'To The Rumanian People' – and commemorative poems carefully handwritten, mounted on wood and protected by transparent plastic. People of all ages, on their way to work, were crossing the wide streets to light candles and stand by this memorial for a little time. No doubt some were relatives or friends of the dead and the majority still looked traumatised. Many crossed themselves repeatedly and prayed before one of the icons, kneeling on the ice. A few added new inscriptions, tying them to the fir branches with numb, fumbling fingers. Some leant forward, their faces taut, staring intently at the photographs as though striving to reinforce their own courage by recalling the courage of those heroes. The silence was complete; no one spoke, or prayed aloud, or sobbed – or even looked at anybody else.

All around that area, up and down the wide boulevards, were similar though smaller memorials, and fir tree saplings planted on the kerb where someone beloved had been shot. Every few hours, new 'political statements' appeared pasted on walls, or in the windows of shops or offices – handwritten, or typed, or crudely printed. Then at once a crowd would gather to analyse passionately every sentence of the latest 'proclamation'. I was naïve enough at the time to be impressed by the surging fervour of these spontaneous public debates – which made all the sad memorials easier to accept.

At last I came to a semi-sympathetic hotel where the haggard young woman at Reception assured me that the Front for National Salvation – the interim government: FSN to Rumanians – was issuing documents to foreigners cancelling the exchange certificate requirement. This was the first time the FSN had come to my attention as a real live government. 'You mean the Front is actually organising things?' I said – with perhaps an involuntary note of scepticism in my voice.

Reception looked huffy. 'Our leader Iliescu is organising *every-thing* and making improvements for everyone', she coldly informed me.

It seemed unlikely that the FSN would concern itself with my petty affairs yet the notion of seeing it in action tempted me. 'Where is the Front?' I asked.

'In the Piata Gheorghiu-Dej', Reception said '– two or three kilometres away.' She added that there were no trolleybuses and I'd be very lucky to find a taxi. I was not very lucky; it took me more than an hour to walk there, mincing ultra-cautiously over the black ice.

Manned tanks still stood around that devastated war zone; bullet and shell holes marked every wall in sight. Passing the fire-gutted University Library, I gazed at the infamous balcony of what used to be Party Headquarters and at the sinister façade of the nearby Securitate base; that menacing structure would look sinister even if one knew nothing about its function and history. Two undersized conscripts, with frost-bitten noses and rotten teeth, were leaning wearily against a tank under the balcony. They informed me that the FSN headquarters had moved the day before to the Piata Victoriei, some two kilometres away in the direction from which I had come; there was a Metro stop in that Piata, they added.

Emerging from the Metro, I saw five or six hundred soldiers, in full combat gear with weapons at the ready, surrounding the old Ministry for Foreign Affairs which had just become the Front's main base – a long, bleakly austere building. Twenty tanks also ringed it, belching black fumes, which one somehow felt was not what they should be doing if in good working order. There were no civilians visible and five or six hundred pairs of military eyes curiously followed my slow progress from the Metro exit across the empty, icy width of the Piata. Reminding myself that the army was, at least in theory, pro-democracy, I tottered boldly towards the centre of the cordon and casually said, *'Permiteti-mi'*, as though moving among a supermarket crowd. Without hesitation two bemused-looking soldiers stood aside to let me through. But as I made for the central entrance, some fifty yards ahead, a senior officer came hurrying after me.

'Welcome to Rumania!' he said earnestly, seizing my hand. 'You are British?' On discovering his mistake he seized my hand again and this time held it in both of his. 'So you are *Irish*! Then you must very well understand our problem because you have a revolution all the time!'

I felt too frail to embark on contemporary Irish politics but asked, 'Why did you think I was British?'

He laughed. 'You look unusual, not like French or Germans or Americans. And after reading many English books I think all the English are *unusual*. So I made a bad mistake and I am sorry!'

Encouraged by all this affability, I enquired, 'Why so many troops around?'

'Just a precaution,' replied the colonel soothingly. 'Last evening a big crowd of young came here – impatient, wanting democratic elections *now*. Some were very angry against the Front. Also, there are little rumours about a vendetta attack on this building today, to celebrate *his* birthday. That is not true, I think, but to be prepared is better – like British boy-scouts!' He beamed, proud of this allusion, then added, 'Of course you are very welcome to visit the Front right now, they always make foreigners welcome – foreign aid is so important for us now . . .'

Being already pain-demoralised, I momentarily felt unkeen about hanging around in a building that might at any minute be attacked by the resurgent Securitate. Then common sense reasserted itself and I allowed the colonel to escort me to the entrance, where he handed me over to a stocky lieutenant armed with a sub-machine-gun, a long pistol and an unsheathed *kukri*-type knife.

New partitions divided an enormous high-ceilinged hall into small rooms or offices. Expensively dressed men hurried to and fro looking preoccupied/irritated/angry/exhausted/frightened or just generally harassed. But these civilians were far outnumbered by the armed soldiers on guard and the unarmed senior officers who seemed to be present in a political consultative capacity. As elsewhere in Rumania at that time, relations between the two groups were warmly friendly – even affectionate. Later I saw several soldiers being spontaneously embraced by strangers on the streets or in the Metro.

There was much tension in the air: understandably so, given the Rumanians' vulnerability to rumour. Far from being welcome, the foreigner was, as I had expected, ignored. The Front after all had a countrywide post-revolutionary upscuttlement on its agenda and could not reasonably be expected to attend to the trivial request of a dishevelled wanderer. For want of a chair, I perched on a little table in a corner; to be sitting was such bliss I hoped no one would focus on me for some time. Then suddenly I fancied that I was glimpsing history in the making; all around was, apparently, chaos, yet out of it would come – surely – a new order for Rumania.

After half an hour I began to feel slightly unreal. I might have been invisible ... Easing myself off the table, I presented my passport to the stocky lieutenant at the entrance-desk who spoke no English or French. He studied my visa closely, then summoned by telephone a tall young man with narrow grey-blue eyes, wearing a pin-stripe suit and highly polished tan shoes.

'Now we have separate departments,' he said. 'Today you are not in the foreigners' department. Yesterday it moved to a building near the Piata Gheorghiu-Dej – do you know where is that?'

'Yes,' I said sourly. 'I've just come from your old headquarters there.'

'So now you return to a street not far from there,' said the young man, 'and that department will help you.'

'Could you', I pleaded, 'ask the lieutenant to call a taxi? I've damaged my back.'

The young man, looking down at me with a mixture of scorn and animosity, said, 'In this city it is not possible to call taxis.' And then he strode away, with no word or gesture of farewell. He was the most unpleasant of the few rude Rumanians I met.

Outside, the colonel mercifully reappeared and sent three of his men in different directions to requisition one of Bucharest's elusive taxis.

Twenty minutes later, it did not surprise me to find the department for helping foreigners firmly closed, though guarded by a squad of conscripts. Their CO – a beardless youth – was apologetic; the rumoured vendetta attack had made it seem expedient not to open ancillary departments but to concentrate military protection around the Piata Victoriei.

As this conversation ended – it took place on the pavement – an

American accent sounded in my ear. 'You have a problem?' asked Vicki.

'Two problems,' I said. 'Medical and accommodation.'

Instantly Vicki adopted me; having recently returned from a four-year exile in Florida, she too had a problem – culture shock. She needed me, it soon transpired, as much as I needed her. 'I'm a dentist,' she said, 'so I can figure how to get pain-killers. Come on, keep going! It's not far to the drugstore and then you'll be fine!'

Turning a corner, I recognised the pharmacy and wailed: 'This is no good! I've tried here already, they've nothing.'

'But they can find something', said Vicki, 'if they want to.' As she bullied the skeletal woman I sat on the floor, not to make a point but because by then I could no longer tolerate the pain of standing, which had become much worse than the pain while walking. Eventually a girl assistant was despatched to some mysterious source of Piofen and Mydocalm, one of each to be taken every four hours. I had been prepared to pay whatever number of dollars might be demanded but those 200 pills cost a total of thirty lei – about twopence. In certain contexts the Rumanians are singularly free of corruption.

Within fifteen minutes I was sufficiently pain-free to be able to think of other things, like food. When I suggested lunch Vicki was decisive: 'Let's go to the Intercontinental, we can't get a real meal anywhere else.'

'But it's horrendous!' I protested. 'This morning I looked in – it's unbearable. There must be food somewhere else, even if not as good.'

Vicki stared at me, baffled. 'All foreigners like the Intercontinental, it's the only civilised place in this shitty dump!' Plainly she longed to escape into that oasis of cosmopolitan vulgarity. So we made our way to a restaurant on the twenty-first floor (or was it the twenty-second?) and were served an excellent meal, with a bottle of superb Rumanian claret, for a total of £2.90 at my rate of exchange.

I asked our smarmy young waiter where the crisp lettuce came from – the first lettuce I had seen in Rumania. 'From Holland, madame – Aid flown in this morning.' And the tender juicy beef? 'From Ireland, madame. Many gift tons come in refrigerated trucks.' And the perfectly ripened blue cheese? 'From Italy, madame – all foreign countries are very, very kind to Rumania.' He obviously saw nothing wrong with a state-owned luxury hotel commandeering food donated for free distribution among the deprived. Nor, depressingly, did Vicki. 'It's all helping Rumania,' she argued. 'Otherwise how could we look after the foreigners who've been here since the revolution? They're used to good food, they expect it – and we should give it to them.'

Vicki ate like one starved; she admitted that this was her first 'normal' meal since leaving Florida three weeks previously. Yet being in this Americanised refuge from the realities of her native city was obviously as important as having a square meal. The Intercontinental symbolised what had become her preferred world. 'I need to be able to spend time here,' she said, 'but I have no money so I can't. You must be able to buy something. The staff watch people like me and if I don't buy I'm thrown out.'

'So why did you come home?' I asked.

'Because I'm Rumanian and I love Rumania. We make bad exiles, we're always homesick, even after a lifetime abroad. When the revolution happened I thought it would all be different and rushed home. Now I see it will take years for anything to change, if it ever does. I planned to practise here – in Florida I couldn't, my degree wasn't recognised so I had to work in all sorts of crappy jobs. But it was crazy to come back and spend all my savings on the fare. Now I'm stuck, living off my mother who hasn't enough for herself. Or off my brother, who needs all he earns to get black-market food for two kids . . .'

Vicki's immediate dilemma was painful; she yearned for foreign companionship and felt deeply ashamed of her home. After much prevarication, she blurted out an invitation to stay the night '– if you don't mind a really beat-up place? It's my mother's house – my father's dead – and it's just a shack . . . D'you figure you can take it?'

To reassure her I gave a graphic description of my own home in Ireland, stressing its more primitive features.

'We're a long way out,' said Vicki, 'and the buses are too crowded and smelly and slow – let's take a taxi!'

That eight-mile ride, in a battered Dacia along back-jarring streets – all potholes and ridges of packed snow – cost less than £2.

On the way we passed what was to have been the Ceausescus' new residence, designed to out-palace all Europe's royalty. The clearing of the site had involved the razing of hundreds of substantial, beloved homes.

This provoked Vicki to an anti-Communist frenzy and she tended to sulk when reminded that in Rumania such vicious extravagances pre-date Communism. King Carol II had ambitions to outdo Buckingham Palace and on the way to fulfilling them he too ruthlessly razed the dwellings of the *hoi polloi*. Vicki was only one of many friends who disliked being encouraged to look farther back than the Communist take-over in their analyses of Rumania's present problems.

Most of 'the shack's' tiny snow-filled garden was occupied by a rusty car skeleton, proof that before his sudden death in 1980 Vicki's father had been a car-owner. Status symbols, I was discovering, are extremely important in Rumania; but this squalid heap of scrap seemed to be taking the preoccupation rather far. Crunching through deep snow, we were greeted with joyous wags by Goofy, a shaggy white sheepdog permanently chained beside his commodious wooden straw-carpeted kennel. Although rarely exercised and never allowed into the house, he had inexplicably remained good-tempered and loving. Then Mango appeared – sleek, smoky-grey and plump – an ever-purring bundle of frisky affection. As Rumania knows nothing of feline birth-control she had produced twelve litters in her nine years but seemed not at all worn down by family responsibilities.

The solid, red-tiled, five-roomed cottage, built a century or so ago, was one of a few score strung along the roadside, each in its own garden. This had once been a prosperous farming village, now it was about to be engulfed by Bucharest. But still it retained a village peace and that feeling of neighbourliness which is so threatened by bloc life – though not always conquered by it, in Rumania.

During winter only one small room was used, as a shared bed-sitter; wood for the tall tiled stove was expensive and scarce. Vicki apologised for not lighting the stove. 'My mother does it when she gets home at 6' – it was then 3.45 – 'because I've lost the knack of making fires. Americans don't have them.' That was a cheerless, impoverished room, half filled by a double divan bed on which Vicki said we could all three fit – if we slept across it, with our feet resting on chairs. (How I grieved for my lost flea-bag, on such occasions!) The television set had been broken for years but an old wireless was at once turned on and left on all evening, though no one was listening.

Vicki sat on the divan, wrapped in a blanket, and offered me one. But I was warm enough in my padded jacket, sitting at a small table by the window with Mango on my lap, looking out over flat snowy fields that had, Vicki said, belonged to her paternal grandparents. Her parents were *not* peasants; Father had worked in an *alimentara* and just been promoted to manager when he died. Mother had been a cashier in the same *alimentara*, retiring two years ago at the age of fifty-five. Vicki's brother, a year her junior, was a nuclear physicist married to a chemical engineer. Every day Mother went to the far side of Bucharest to look after their two small children.

Vicki's culture-shock was worryingly severe. Rocking to and fro on the edge of the divan, she burst out: 'If only I hadn't seen our revolution on TV! I could still be in my lovely Florida apartment ... I got carried away, I figured this was a real revolution, that all those brave heroes dying must make a new country for all of us – all the blood and sorrow ... And I wanted to be part of *creating* the new Rumania. Now I see the truth. Goofy's been seven years tied to his kennel, he doesn't know anything about freedom. If I let him loose he doesn't want to run away, he turns round and goes back into his kennel. And that's what Rumania is going to do, though most people don't see it yet. They're muddling the Ceausescus being got rid of with a real revolution. They're ignorant about freedom and democracy and they don't know how to begin to learn.'

'But you've experienced freedom,' I remarked, 'so perhaps you can help people to learn? And there aren't many Rumanians who speak three major European languages fluently – you could be an invaluable link with the outside world.'

Vicki gestured impatiently. 'Now *you're* talking like we've had a real revolution! With Rumania back in its kennel, what role will there be for people like me? Except as a prisoner, good fodder for the Securitate when they surface again ...'

As the light faded I went out to the squat-over earth closet in a 'sentry-box' wooden shed beside the kennel. Since Goofy was emotionally dependent on people going to the loo, I stopped to fondle him; his thick coat was well groomed – by Mother, it later emerged.

It was pitch dark and freezing hard when Mother arrived, a woman as cheerful and relaxed as her daughter was gloomy and tense. Quickly recovering from the shock of my presence, she gave me a typical Rumanian welcome: hugs and kisses and exclamations of worry about my inadequate garments. Briskly she lit the stove, before taking an ironbound wooden pail to a deep well behind the house – evidently another chore her daughter had lost the knack of in Florida.

'My mother knows nothing about *enjoying* life,' observed Vicki peevishly. 'It's all work, work, work – non-stop, from dawn till dusk. She doesn't understand any of my attitudes. She's never made the most of her opportunities.' ('What opportunities?' I wondered privately. She was still a child when the Communists took over.)

For supper Mother had the hard end of a grey loaf, smeared with that ubiquitous blackberry jam and helped down by two cups of sugarless herbal tea. There was no other food in the house and she rejoiced to hear that we had lunched well. Her appearance suggested that she never lunched well; although a year my junior, she looked at least seventy-five.

'They say we've more food now,' observed Vicki, 'but to get it you've gotta queue half the day in the snow. I'm not used to that, I can't take it . . .'

There are disadvantages in not having peasant parents; among Rumania's urban millions the first-generation city dwellers had least difficulty surviving Ceausescu's Dark Age.

At 8 p.m. I curled up on my part of the bed, explaining that the previous night had been virtually sleepless. Before dawn Mother would escort me to the Centru; every day she had to be with her grandchildren by 7 a.m. Vicki said she never rose before noon – and even then the day was too long . . .

The radio woke me at 5 a.m., announcing Bucharest's temperature: minus three degrees centigrade – a mild January morning by local standards. But to me it felt otherwise as Mother and I walked a mile to the trolleybus terminus, negotiating by the light

58

of my torch fearsome hillocks of newly-iced snow. Although I felt quite supple, as compared to twenty-four hours previously, any incautious or involuntary movements were punished. My revised plan was to spend the next week among the painted churches of Moldavia; now I would go straight to the *gara* to book a couchette on the night train to Iasi. Within a week my nameless injury should either be on the mend, or decisively not on the mend, making a return to London inevitable.

In Baia Mare I had begun to keep a detailed journal and part of my entry for that day records:

> The metal seats of our trolleybus were so cold my bum ached. At the terminus it filled up with wretched workers: faces sad, worn, bewildered, resigned. No conversation. Bucharest seems not to be feeling its fair share of post-revolutionary euphoria. Too many people look trapped in their own day-to-day miseries, plus perhaps personal grieving for people dead or injured – and/or acute anxiety about the future. Yet many others are in a political fever, or as though drunk on Freedom of Speech. Up and down the wide boulevards, or in Metro stations or shop queues, strangers suddenly form groups to debate – loudly – what should or should not be done, and by whom and how and where and when: with 'when' often the most crucial issue. Riveting though confusing for me, hearing so many differing views vigorously expressed. English-speaking students always appear, eager to translate. These groups, sometimes swelling to small crowds, are mixed: all sorts and ages and both sexes. Four more people have begged me to send them a 'book about democracy'. Among the youngsters, especially, there's a healthy apprehension about this country's having suddenly been pushed off, in a frail vessel, onto a rough political sea – and without a compass.

> There's much fear in the air. Not of the Securitate (most seem confident they and the immediate Ceausescu mafia have been effectively dealt with) but of the essential immutability of 'The System'. Several people asserted that millions of Rumanians have a vested interest in 'no change'; the only change they wanted was to get rid of the Ceausescus. A

regime so corrupt, cruel and cynical leaves a scary residue of vicious racketeers at every level all over the country. One young woman said, 'All the world thought our revolution was a glorious thing, an inspiration – and it was, our young people were brave like mythical heroes. But we've taken only the first step of a thousand-kilometre walk to *real* freedom, stability, prosperity.'

The main fear is of the Front rigging the elections and retaining power. Yet few dispute the need for an election soon; this self-appointed interim government is too unsettling, something more noticeable in Bucharest than elsewhere. Here many shops, hairdressers, hotels, offices, pharmacies, restaurants and so on have closed, or open only briefly and irregularly, and there is a general sense of passive anarchy – of a society close to collapse. I find the city unexhilarating despite 'Incredible!' being constantly in use to express the joy of being free to display and discuss political documents stating precisely what the individual thinks, wants, believes. Too much violence and terror, too many deaths and injuries have left the citizens with long-term shock in their eyes. And there's an odd hush over Bucharest, apart from those geysers of political debate. People queue or walk, or ride on the Metro or trolleybuses, in silence and unsmiling. When a whole city is behaving thus, the feeling is quite eerie.

Today, as yesterday, four young soldiers guard each Metro ticket-barrier. Their rumoured function is to deter any homicidal remnants of the Securitate from taking revenge on platform crowds – surely an extreme improbability? But doubtless that rumour is contributing to the atmospheric unease.

At dusk, as the workers were going home, many gathered around the main memorial near the Intercontinental and just stood there, with bowed heads, for some minutes – then lit a candle and went on their way. This strong communal emotion is all the more overwhelming because so muted.

After dark, a young couple invited me to accompany them

60

to the Piata Victoriei where there was another anti-Front student demo confronting a double line of troops and tanks. This was a small crowd, no more than twelve or fifteen hundred – waving placards, chanting enthusiastically and, despite their anger, somehow creating quite a *jolly* atmosphere. I suspected them, and their many senior allies, of demonstrating just for the hell of it – to flex their liberated muscles rather than to make an ideological point. But my companions foretold that much more would be heard of student-led opposition to the Front.

During the forenoon it occurred to me that I should inform my long-suffering publisher of my intention to write a book about Rumania. (He then had other plans for me.) Finding it impossible to ring London, I went to the British Embassy to look up the Murray telex number – little guessing that as I sat anonymously in the hallway, under the disdainful gaze of a porter (it was then some considerable time since I had changed my clothes or washed), the Embassy's higher echelons were diligently battling with Rumania's telephonic eccentricities in a vain attempt to establish my whereabouts and state of health. I watched my message being telexed from the nearby Hotel Dorobanti and was given a copy and a receipt for my $5. But it never made it to London.

In that oppressively gloomy hotel foyer, while writing my journal, I noticed a grey-faced, well-dressed elderly man sitting opposite, staring fixedly at a newspaper cutting. His hands were trembling and he looked so forlorn that I spoke to him. He beckoned me to his side; the cutting was a photograph of his twenty-five-year-old son – his only child – taken the day before in hospital. His mother was bending over him and he was giving the V-sign with his left hand. On 22 December his spine had been fractured and his right arm so bady smashed it had to be amputated. He was an architectural student, in his last year at university, and will never walk again – and perhaps, without adequate physiotherapy, will never draw again. Two small tears trickled down his father's face as he said, 'Mamma and Pappa cannot accept this, but Gheorghe can. He has a vision of what

Rumania can be – and must be. Now we hope the future will not betray him. Mamma and Pappa must pray to God to give courage. We cannot have enough ourselves.'

Gheorghe was one of more than a thousand victims of the revolution incapacitated for life; other thousands were seriously injured but will recover. As Nothern Ireland has long since taught me, we too often tend to forget the permanently disabled (physically and/or psychologically) while mourning the dead.

Arriving early at the *gara*, I added to my journal:

Rumanians are shocked to learn that the Irish language ceased to be generally used early in the nineteenth century. I can understand why. Imagine a Rumania in which everyone spoke Russian or Hungarian or Turkish – could it *feel* itself to be an independent nation? Granted, all Austrians and most Swiss speak German, and many Belgians speak French; but they didn't abandon their own languages, with all that that implies. However, Britain did give us something very valuable, something none of Rumania's conquerors or exploiters knew anything about. And that genuine respect for democracy preserved the new Irish state during our post-Independence civil war and the uneasy decades that followed. Rumania's pre-war pseudo-democracy was proved a mere pretence on many occasions. I fear Rumanians won't be greatly helped by 'books about democracy'. It's not after all a mechanical political technique, but a collective state of mind that takes a long time to evolve.

5

Indirectly to the Painted Monasteries

Oradea – if you look at the map – is not on the way from Bucharest to Moldavia. Yet I travelled via Oradea; apparently fate had decreed that for me in Rumania nothing was to be straightforward. At 7 a.m., all seats on the night train to Iasi were already booked. Then I met Paula, who had been unsuccessfully trying to book a couchette to Oradea. She explained: 'Since the revolution, half the population is travelling all over the country every day to visit families and friends. It's one way of celebrating liberty. But it's not very good for the economy – they just make a silly excuse and stop working, or go without saying anything. And their bosses feel they have no authority over them. That's one bad result of not having a real government – this feeling "there's no one in charge, we can do what we like, the police are afraid of us". And of course now our trains are heated and comfortable. Before, they were so cold in midwinter a long journey could be dangerous. People often died of hypothermia in the carriages.'

Paula and I immediately took to one another and she suggested, 'Why not come to Oradea with me tonight? Seats are still available and from there you can get on the Timisoara–Iasi express. Then we'll have all night to talk – and I want to talk much more with you. OK?'

I agreed; as this first-class ticket cost £1.25, no great squandering of funds was involved. Paula beamed, hugged me, booked my seat – then hurried away to spend her day translating from scientific texts at the university.

Fourteen hours later we were settled in our numbered seats in a modern(ish) wagon with open coaches, the only one of its kind I saw in Rumania. Loud complaints about the tropical temperature were general; Paula deduced the staff had forgotten how to

63

regulate the heating system. Then she exclaimed, 'I'm so happy! It's always nice to leave Bucharest! That's where you see the worst of Rumania – is it the same in all capitals?'

'I'm prejudiced,' I confessed. 'Most big cities switch me off. But today was fascinating, just wandering around talking to people – all congenial, apart from tourist hotel staffs. Is it true they're mostly Securitate ex-informers?'

'Wise people', said Paula, 'don't believe they're "*ex*".'

Already our fellow passengers, stripped to shirt-sleeves and blouses, had embarked on serious, sustained political arguments. I remarked on how attentively they listened to one another, how orderly these conversations were, as compared to a coach-load of Irish political debaters.

Paula smiled. 'These are all intellectuals who *respect* our new freedom of speech. Six weeks ago they would have travelled in silence, afraid to show their thoughts. Now we all discuss everything with everyone, which is natural for us – we're spontaneous open people, not secretive or suspicious.' Then, overhearing some remark with which she disagreed, about the free market, she quickly turned and plunged into economic waters too deep for me. As always in Rumania, everyone politely translated for the foreigner's benefit, and on finding this 'capitalist' an economic ignoramus they looked both incredulous and disappointed.

When our sweating companions had at last slumped on each other in uneasy small-hours slumber, Paula fell into a gloom. 'All this unorganised foreign aid, thousands of tons of it coming every week – who distributes it? You must have seen what happens to some – *how much?* – of the food aid. OK, we need aid – especially medical aid, and lots of it. But that needs to be watched, too. Rumanian doctors can be very corrupt – if you meet a poor one you know he's honest. There's a rumour the International Red Cross will give us thirty million dollars' worth of sophisticated hospital equipment, but that's no use without people trained to use it. And will all this aid encourage us to work even less? Foreigners can't reconstruct Rumania, that we must do ourselves. Now we're in a self-pitying mood, which isn't healthy. I notice it even in myself and my friends – I suppose it's part of the reaction, after so much stress and strain. But other countries shouldn't encourage it by being sentimental about "poor Rumania". I come from Timisoara, I only moved to Oradea five years ago. And I think you'll find Timisoara people more realistic and objective – we've always been mentally closer to Western Europe. Bucharest likes to think it's cosmopolitan, but historically Timisoara is Rumania's only cosmopolitan city. Bucharest still lives under two shadows, the Ottomans and imported royalty. Another mistake foreigners make is about our workers. They think it's so simple: oppressed workers liberated from Communism can now live like Western workers. They don't understand that our workers can *only* think Marxist. Now everyone says they're anti-Communist because they see Ceausescu as the symbol of Communism. But while they're saying that they're still thinking and feeling and reacting one hundred per cent Marxist, the way they've been trained from age seven. How could they suddenly become different just because the Ceausescus are dead? They're mentally maimed, probably for life. This generation will always fear freedom because it goes against their mind-set. Most workers in every country are simple people. Aged twenty-five, thirty-five, forty-five, they can't throw away their conditioning and follow new paths. We mustn't expect real change until the next generation is in control – the children now at primary school, whose brainwashing stopped one month ago . . .'

In Oradea, at dawn, Paula booked me a seat on the 9.50 a.m. to Iasi and reminded me to get off at Gura Humorului. 'You should arrive about supper-time but there may be no supper – try to buy some bread here.' Given the taxi shortage – because of the petrol shortage – her bloc was too far away for me to breakfast with her.

Seeking the station restaurant, I had to push my way through a dense throng including many Gypsy trader/smugglers on their way to or from Hungary. (Oradea is close to the border.) No 'tea' or 'coffee' was available because the water heating system had broken down; the packed restaurant was simply being used as a waiting-room. Along one wall yards of food display cabinets contained a single plate on which reposed three of those too-familiar grey-brown 'meat'-rolls. When I asked a cheerful waitress if these were '*bun*' (good) she flexed her biceps and grimaced – by way of warning me 'too tough to eat'. That little pantomime brought smiles to many faces; despite the grimness of daily life, most Rumanians laugh readily. When I bought a roll – the

65

pain-killers didn't function on an empty stomach – several men cheered and clapped sardonically, then watched with a sort of awed admiration as I gnawed my way through some unidentifiable strip of offal. I was not, I noticed, becoming accustomed to the food shortage. Personally it didn't bother me too much – I carry plenty of spare fat – but it enraged me to contrast restaurants like this with the choice always available to rich Rumanians (and foreigners) in tourist hotels.

Outside the grimy, twilit station – smelling strongly of unwashed garments and stale urine – it was a clear sunny morning, only invigoratingly cold. My bread hunt took me down the Calea Republicii to the Piata Republicii; all very Austro-Hungarian Baroque and neo-Classical, which seems quite beautiful in contrast to Ceausescu cityscapes. The many *alimentara* stocked the usual thousands of repellant jars, tins and bottles. The general *magazins* displayed four saucepans in one twenty-yard-long window, two jackets and a few shirts in another, six leatherette belts and an umbrella in a third – and so on. A fast-moving queue signalled the presence of bread; having secured a stale kilo loaf I did not have to queue for the tin of blackberry jam bought to enliven it. On my way back I passed a Gypsy girl peddlar standing on a street corner calling her wares – 'Antibebi pills! Antibebi pills!' I lingered at a little distance, wondering who might be her customers; but all the young women passing on their way to work had too much sense to risk a purchase.

Paula had advised me always to travel first class, to increase my chances of meeting English-speakers. In Oradea we were too late for that, but my luck still held. Liana was beside me – a stunted young woman who could have modelled for an anti-Ceausescu poster, with her unhealthy pallor, dull splitting hair, decaying chipped teeth and cracked finger-nails. A faint colour came to her cheeks when she discovered my Irishness; she had never before met a native English-speaker. She came from Brasov, was now doing her 'compulsory service' in a Banat village school and had taught herself English from her mother's old school-books, with World Service help. At first she was painfully inhibited. 'I have spoken no English since my mother died five years ago – because they made her wait till next day for an operation. So now I'm not sure you can understand me?'

66

In fact Liana's grammar and vocabulary were so polished that I had no problem with her pronunciation. She described her years of travail as a World Service listener in a Brasov bloc. 'I only switched on late at night because we knew the Securitate were lazy!'

'What would have happened, had they caught you?'

Liana shivered. 'We would all be punished, all the family, my sister too. I don't know how – nothing was certain, that was part of the fear. It could be big fines, some imprisonment, losing jobs or apartments, no promotion ever for any family member – it was different in different areas, or under different Chiefs. Some you could bribe, if you had lei enough. Others not – if you tried your punishments would be even worse. But informers frightened us more than officers. If new people came to an apartment near us it was terrible. For months we felt fear, until something happened to show they were safe – though you could never be *sure*, about most people, even friends, because of intimidation or black-mailing.'

'But what could people inform *about*, apart from your radio?'

Liana smiled a little, sadly. 'You are lucky, not to understand! Every day we had to break some law, to survive. Mostly about food, or medicines if someone was ill. My father's parents are peasants and he would bring from the village food they stole from their collective – just a little, but without it we would become sick of hunger. We could get no meat, cheese, milk, eggs, butter – even ordinary Party members couldn't, during the past few years.'

'Were your local Securitate officers identifiable? And were they *all* bad?'

'Yes, they were obvious – but not all were completely bad. Some we knew were a bit on our side, especially since 1986. Then the law was passed that we could only have four hours' heating in twenty-four, and six hours' light with a forty-watt bulb. All the Securitate didn't use their right to enter any home any time to check. But some did and people went to prison for using oil stoves smuggled from Hungary or Yugoslavia. Sometimes the informers would smell those and report and get their money and privileges. Then, if the Securitate officer was a bit sympathetic and did not punish, the informer would report on *him* and get more money, and the officer would be punished. *All* the informers were very bad. And there were thousands of them – millions, maybe, all over Rumania. We wonder what will they do next, because they are used to extra money – how will they make it now? I know one who informed on my sister is interpreting in Bucharest for French journalists, getting a hundred dollars a day! He reported my sister had damaged her bedroom by making holes in the floor. She had to put up a tent for their two children – when it was closed up they got warm inside. This is not our normal winter – then you would *die*, wearing so few clothes!'

I asked Liana, as I had asked many others, how it came about that there were so many AIDS victims in Rumanian orphanages – which are not genuine orphanages, most of the inmates being abandoned rather than parentless children. She looked puzzled, she hadn't heard about this ... And anyway what exactly *was* AIDS?

When I left home, 'Children-With-AIDS' was the aspect of newly exposed Rumania engaging most popular attention. Yet during January 1990 I met no one, outside of Bucharest, who was aware of this most shameful feature of their own society. In June 1989, the Bucharest Institute of Virology had reported that almost one in five children from various 'Homes' were HIV-positive. Ceausescu then asserted that only capitalist countries suffer from AIDS. The report was banned and the doctors concerned were ordered to misinform the World Health Organization, which they did. In an interview with Christopher Walker of *The Times*, Dr Gheorghe Jipa, Director of the Victor Babes Infectious Diseases Hospital, explained: 'This is the direct result of the dictator's cruelty. He prevented measures being taken to test blood products and his policies caused the malnutrition which was the reason many of these children had blood transfusions in the first place. The tyrant spent more on feeding his dogs than he did on these children. He just did not want to know about them. We were told that if we spoke out we would die. The Securitate was everywhere, even here in this hospital.'

There was a complete lack of interest when I volunteered information, to Liana and others, about the Children's Homes in general and the AIDS epidemic in particular. Everyone gave the impression of having too much on their personal plates to be concerned about the fate of discarded children – most of whom are alleged to be Gypsies, though this is wildly improbable both demographically and psychologically.

By June 1990, knowledge of this ultimate horror of the Ceausescu legacy – though not of its Rumanian cause — had spread quite widely. Yet accurate information remained scarce. Grave-diggers were refusing to bury the bodies of infant victims – seventy had died since 1 January – and some parents were refusing to respond to official requests that they should collect their children's corpses. But still the subject was never referred to unless I brought it up, not even by those most addicted to dwelling on the many other horrors bequeathed by the Ceausescus.

Beyond Cluj – where Liana disembarked – the train gave up pretending to be an 'express' and became a fifteen m.p.h. inter-village conveyance. Soon my carriage was full of characters recalling nineteenth-century illustrations of Balkan brigands – bearded men in heavily embroidered homespun clothes with long knives in their belts and huge gnarled hands and strong bony faces and deep-set eyes. They smelt even more pungently than I did; otherwise you couldn't have more agreeable travelling companions – gentle and courteous and warm-hearted. They too ceaselessly talked politics, as the train very, very slowly climbed up and up and up, between snowy forested hills, stopping for fifteen or twenty minutes at every tiny village. Lacking an interpreter, I could only glean that they were unanimously pro-Iliescu, though far from unanimous about how he should run the country.

At one stop a burly forester and his weedy teenage son settled opposite me, then took out their lunch: a brittle loaf and a slab of *slanina*. Father sliced the bacon fat thinly, with a knife that was half-way to being a sword, while son struggled to cut the loaf. When I politely declined to join them, though my mouth was watering, they both looked so upset that I had to accept an unwieldy but delicious sandwich; then only *slanina* made Rumanian bread edible. For pudding we had juicy apples with an old-fashioned flavour; the semi-sword was used to peel, core and slice mine, a superfluous concession to assumed foreign fastidiousness. Then father and son wiped their greasy hands on the

69

window curtain and urged me to do the same; but, absurdly, my adaptability couldn't stretch that far.

Soon after, I moved to stand by an open corridor window, thereby importing the image of 'the mad Irish' into the Carpathians. We had reached the provincial border zone, an apparently uninhabited region of steep, densely-forested mountains and deep narrow gorges fringed with twenty-foot icicles. Every tree was snow-laden; pure, wind-moulded drifts towered by the track; every stream was solid ice – and high on a cliff a frozen waterfall, reflecting the vast red sunset, briefly became a pillar of fire.

Here the temperature must have been at least minus thirty. Yet at half-mile intervals (approximately) I counted eighteen solitary soldiers on duty in open sentry boxes atop tall metal stilts that brought them level with the track. At first I wondered if they were dummies; it seemed impossible that humans could long survive such exposure. But then I saw a few moving slightly. They may have had stoves beside them, though I doubt it, and I later discovered that the guard changes every two hours. But maintaining it, in 1990, was symptomatic of a dangerous global disease: military paranoia. Even then, some off-the-wall Generals in Bucharest must have been taking seriously the 'threat' of a Soviet invasion.

When darkness fell the train slowed almost to walking speed, as though it couldn't see its way, which may indeed have been the case; I had long since ceased to marvel at Rumania's mechanical handicaps. At the last stop before Gura Humorului a weary-looking couple appeared, father carrying a skinny toddler. Wife and I pooled our pidgin German; she was a doctor, from Sibiu, enduring three years 'exile' in Moldavia. Her husband and son had come for the weekend: she hardly ever saw them, her mother looked after the boy. But perhaps soon the Front would set people free to choose their own jobs ... Her bed-sitter was too cold for a child so they were going to stay with a friend in Gura Humorului who would of course drive me to the hotel, some two miles from the pitch-dark *gara* on the town's edge. This chance encounter saved me from wandering for hours through streets unlit and deserted at 7.30 p.m.

The non-tourist hotel was a dreary 1960s bloc run by a small square peasant woman permanently wrapped in a brown blanket and wearing a fur hat over her headscarf. She greeted me with astonished disapproval; the hotel restaurant had been closed for three years, Gura Humorului had *no* food to spare in winter, why had I not come in summer when many tourists pass through? (Those 'many' tourists – mostly ex-Communist country coach tours – pass through only because two of Moldavia's most famous painted churches are nearby.) On the first floor my large, clean, frugally furnished room was suffocatingly overheated and the big window proved immovable – not only by me but by Alex, my one fellow guest, a sturdy young construction engineer from Constanta. He it was who directed me to the *toalet*, down a wide corridor with ominous cracks zig-zagging all along the walls. He cautioned me to stand far from the lavatory when pulling the chain; sometimes the tank provided a cold shower. And then he warned me against the locals. 'These Moldavian people are wild and rough, all smugglers and robbers – take care!'

At sunrise I went food-hunting; improvidently, I had eaten all my Oradea loaf for supper. In its original incarnation, as a compact logging town on the banks of a swift mountain river, Gura Humorului must have been attractive and lively – the market centre for many modestly prosperous villages in the surrounding valleys. In its Communist reincarnation it is an industrialised shambles, where ex-farmers make unwanted goods in jerry-built factories. Near my hotel, a row of solid, brightly painted farmhouses was being bulldozed to make way for yet another factory and monster cranes were erecting yet another prefabricated bloc. Mindlessly the building juggernaut rolled on, oblivious of the revolution: to me a frightening symbol.

The several restaurants were closed – not unreasonably, so early on the Sabbath, but none looked likely ever to offer sustenance. Then a functioning café appeared, built on that grandiose Communist scale – seventy yards by thirty, its frontage glass – which somehow makes the chronic shortage of everything all the more exasperating. Trays of pastries, buns and colourful little iced cakes were on display but experience had taught me not to rejoice at the sight of food. Availability signified inedibility. A dozen men, women and children – dull-eyed, hollow-cheeked, blue with cold – were sitting at rusty metal tables drinking ersatz

71

fruit juice from unlabelled bottles. Although starved-looking, none was attempting to ingest the solid matter on offer. They stared incredulously as I made a bed for my pain-killers by eating a bun and a cake – or rather, gulping them like a greedy dog, since they discouraged retention in the mouth. Now I regret not having taken samples of Ceausescu-fare to London for analysis; it would be fascinating to know exactly what went into those synthetic substances on offer to Rumanians in January 1990. And this in a country naturally self-sufficient in every basic foodstuff.

Despite the pain-killers, my back resented the five-mile walk to Humor Monastery, up a wide shallow valley through long villages. In most gardens tall crucifixes, under peaked wooden shelters, had bouquets of plastic flowers at their feet. The several little churches were packed to overflowing with congregations of all ages and both sexes. This is one of the few corners of Europe where peasants still dress traditionally every Sunday, and the women wore brightly striped knee-length swinging skirts, brown sheepskin bodices, homespun stockings and kerchiefs. The men – young and old – gained dignity from their tight pure white trousers, of finely woven wool, with long matching tunics, dazzling white sheepskin jackets and high black lambskin hats. Every garment was exquisitely and brilliantly embroidered – an endangered art, dependent on indifference to the cash economy.

Moldavia's painted churches, post-dating the fall of Constantinople by at least fifty years, have been described as 'a posthumous child of Byzantine art'. The blizzards of some 450 winters have almost completely erased the frescos from northern and north-eastern walls but of the survivors Josef Strzgowski wrote in 1913, 'No other country in the world offers us anything similar' – a statement never since disputed. The still-glowing colours are believed to have been derived from madder; ochre or unripe wheat ears; indigo plants or lapis lazuli; charcoal and soot; gold dust. Before its application to a plaster base containing lime and sand, each paint was mixed – experts surmise – with weather resistant egg-yolk and cow's bile. One wonders – whoever first discovered that cow's bile was weather resistant? And how did it come about that so many of these esoteric technical discoveries were lost during subsequent centuries?

At the head of its valley, Humor Monastery stands alone, few traces remaining of the original fortifications. It is a long simple building with a steeply pitched roof and no tower, surrounded by level grassland – that morning covered in sheet ice. Nearby, a protective semicircle of spruce-clad peaks and ridges rose darkly against the deep blue of the mountain sky. There was no one in sight – nothing moving, no sound – as I sat on an old wooden bench in the warm sun and gazed at Humor's south wall.

Those frescos break the time barrier; one is prepared for their beauty, but not for the anonymous artists' eerie ability to communicate, across four centuries, the emotions and concerns of their own day. For illiterate peasants – forbidden to enter churches and unable to understand what they could hear of the Slavonic liturgy being chanted within – this 'mass medium' provided the only religious education available. For us it still provides much gloriously exuberant comedy, often revealing direct links between the humour of sixteenth-century Moldavia and the abundance of sly black jokes which now serve the Rumanians as safety-valves. Most memorably, at Humor, all twenty-four stanzas of a hymn of praise to the Virgin Mary are illustrated in minute and entertaining detail. This hymn commemorates the legend that in 626 AD Mary personally intervened to rout the Persian and Arab armies then besieging Constantinople. The besiegers, however – last seen being flung into a demon-infested inferno – are depicted as contemporary Turks and Tatars. These artists' princely patrons expected them to keep up the level of popular anti-Ottoman feeling, an urgent political need during that crucial century in Moldavia.

Humor replaces an older church, destroyed in the early 1520s, and was partly subsidised – to placate certain hostile Orthodox clergy – by Petru Rares, an illegitimate son of Stephen the Great. In 1527, after a long exile at the Polish court, Petru was manoeuvred onto the throne by a process even more devious than usual and his subsequent career prompted the following judgement from R. W. Seton-Watson:

> It cannot be denied that the kaleidoscopic character of his perfidy is almost unique even in the annals of the sixteenth century. It is impossible to admit that he was in any way fitted for the role which a modern Rumanian historian has treated

as feasible – namely that of rallying the Rumanian masses under the Habsburg banner and playing them off against the Hungarian nobility, which was using the dire anarchy of the times to strengthen its feudal power.

That was written in 1933; Communism does not deserve all the blame for the present sad state of Rumanian historiography.

Some twenty yards from my bench stood Humor's high belfry, an open wooden platform under a shingle roof. Suddenly an elderly man appeared, clad all in black, and climbed the ladder-like stairs to ring the changes on seven mellow bells – from a sweet tinkle to a sonorous bass. At intervals he paused to drum, very fast, on a suspended length of wood which reminded me of the hanging stones used to summon Ethiopia's Coptic Christians to prayer. That was an interlude 'soothing for the soul', as my Rumanian friends would say: just me and the mountains and the vivid sunlit frescos and those ancient rhythms, their undulations seeming to take possession of the whole still valley.

My return route to the town – west of the river Humor, avoiding the road – took me through several straggling hilly villages where everyone seemed wary of me. Perhaps they had not yet got the message that talking to foreigners was allowed. Or perhaps history has left them with a permanent distrust of all outsiders. Mercifully Gura Humorului's industrialisation is not – or was not then – of the sort that uglifies the surrounding countryside by being visible and smellable for many miles. Here nothing marred my enjoyment of the astonishing creativity expressed in the original designs and decorations of these peasants' wooden dwellings, each with its eaves-high supply of firewood symmetrically cut and stacked – obviously another local art form. The rough lane ways were thronged with flocks of geese, turkeys, ducks. And a 'rare breeds' buff would have swooned over the variety of hens and cocks: crested, trousered, ruffed, some jet black, some a shimmering peacock green, others a rich blend of every possible colour. In each yard were tethered a few pigs or sheep – or both – and the dog: either a large white sheepdog or a small personable mongrel, the majority looking better fed than the average local human.

Back at the hotel, I found the blanketed one and her friends huddled on an uncomfortable sofa in the lounge – no more than a hallway, leading off the street – watching television. Alex and I joined them for the news, which was followed by a Czech film of the aftermath of the revolution in Bucharest. All of it was disturbing and the final scene showed hundreds of corpses piled in mortuaries, being identified by stricken relatives – usually parents. Typical was a peasant mother struggling to drag her stark naked son from a roughly-made coffin while another son, his schoolboy face contorted with grief, tried to persuade her the youth was really dead. By the end all the viewers, men as well as women, were in tears.

Alex turned to me and asked, 'Do you think it's good to show such films, now? What is the motive? All these simple people here are weeping, made sad, agitated. Why do this to them? For what purpose? Why not give this time to teaching about democracy, about election systems, about the free market, about all the changes we hoped the revolution would bring? That film was only anti-Ceausescu. When will we have some anti-Communism on our TV?'

I deduced, 'You're pessimistic about the future?'

Alex stood up and frowned. 'You think I'm pessimistic? But you are a visitor, knowing nothing about Rumania. *I* think I'm realistic. *Noapte buna!*'

At intervals throughout the night my back reproached me for having walked some fifteen miles that day. The writing was on the wall, though my eyes remained averted from it.

Early next morning – it was cloudy and slightly less cold – I found a loaf and took it back to the blackberry jam; I had given up uselessly yearning for tea or coffee. Then I made my slow way to Voronet, shuffling along like a patient in a geriatric ward.

This most lovely village is hidden among steep, then snow-streaked, forested hills, three miles from the town. Scores of houses line the road, many two-storeyed and each in its spacious yard-cum-garden with superb barns – several brand new – their doors, windows and eaves finely carved. Even the iron-bound pails over the wells – recalling *Little Grey Rabbit* illustrations – were decorated, to match the lattice-work walls and roofs of the wells themselves. But alas! garish paint, instead of creosote or stain, is everywhere coming into fashion. I paused to watch two new dwellings being built: all of wood, including the roofs. No foundations are dug; the frame goes up on a four-foot-high substructure of large mortared stones. Here the ancient tradition of craftsmanship in wood seems safe; it was good to see youths working beside their grandfathers, creating beauty.

Voronet's reputation as the 'Sistine Chapel of Moldavia' has brought about a car-park, a tourist-trap hut/shop – not too offensive in winter, when closed – and a ticket barrier beneath the handsome entrance archway. Previously, according to the *Rough Guide*, this archway sheltered an enormous photograph of Ceausescu conducting 'lofty foreign guests' – the Shahinshah of Iran and Empress Farah – around Voronet. Happily, though the gate was open there was no one about to give me one of those guided tours that drain the joy from every aesthetic experience.

Voronet celebrated its quincentenary in 1988. All Moldavia's fortified monasteries, which served both military and spiritual purposes, were founded by boyars or princes in the fifteenth or sixteenth centuries and endowed with vast estates and swarms of serfs. Inexplicably, they survived unblemished the gradual Ottoman conquest, which coincided with the painting of the frescos. Why did the Turkish troops, who left few fortresses standing, spare these churches on whose external walls they were depicted as the very epitome of evil?

Stephen the Great built Voronet in a few months, to commemorate one of his numerous military victories, but the frescos are later – between 1547 and 1550. The ghoulish comedy and agile inventiveness of the Last Judgement on the west front must have terrorised all True Believers – as undoubtedly it was meant to do, by way of keeping the serfs docile. My favourite figures were ferocious semi-mythical beasts in the process of regurgitating human bodies, very much in the manner of a cat who has hastily gulped too big a fish-head. Less amusing, given the subsequent history of anti-Semitism in Moldavia, were the Jews seen writhing in company with the Turks.

On the way back I was offered a lift by an elderly man in traditional garb: not spotless as on the Sabbath but frayed and farm-stained. He had a kind smile, merry blue eyes, long white whiskers and shiny red cheeks. His red-tasselled, smartly-trotting bay also shone and was drawing a long, narrowish wagon, beautifully proportioned and – of course – elaborately carved. I longed to be able to climb aboard but was too stiff even to attempt such a feat.

At 2 p.m. the town was surprisingly crowded, mostly with shabby, unshaven, hungry-looking men just hanging about. Many wore baggy homespun trousers and fleece cloaks, or calf-length homespun overcoats edged with leather all around – including the pocket-flaps. But again those friendly vibes I had come to associate with Rumania were absent.

Hunger drove me to explore the enormous new market, opened only a few months previously on the edge of the town – an attractive traditional market-place, built not of the usual concrete but of red brick. Only three of the one hundred numbered stalls were in use, presided over by ancient grim-faced peasant women offering a few braids of garlic, five rotting cabbages (literally rotting) and a small mound of marble-sized onions.

Turning towards the hotel, I realised that a truck-load of alcohol was being distributed among Gura Humorului's restaurants – which event is everywhere guaranteed to bring Rumania's males into the public arena. As my own alcohol level had fallen dangerously low during the past several days, I hastened to the nearest restaurant. The delivery had been of something described as 'cognac'. It looked like real cognac, and was warming, and tasted like a cocktail of poteen and arak. Everyone had ordered three or four glasses simultaneously, one of the many bizarre customs evolved in Ceausescu's Rumania where supplies so quickly ran out. When I did likewise the genial waitress, while arranging my four glasses in a neat semicircle, murmured that I could have a *bottle* of cognac for one dollar. '*Bun!*' said I. Moments later a newspaper-wrapped bottle was slipped into my Hatchards plastic bag – which by then looked not at all West End-ish.

This crowded, filthy, noisy restaurant had a brown tiled floor, a low nicotine-discoloured ceiling and dark green walls. It also had food: gristly minced meat balls (*what* had been minced?), squidgy tinned peas and pale pink puffed-up discs which were, I suppose, potato crisps Ceausescu-style. I was devouring a double helping of these horrors ('Hunger's good sauce!' as my mother used to say) when Lilia shyly approached. Her English was poor but adequate; would I join her when I had finished? Her friends would like to buy me a cognac – she pointed to a table in a far corner, where two men sat staring at me.

Lilia had just qualified as a vet and was from Suceava. She was in Gura Humorului on her first job – bovine TB eradication. One of the men was her husband, a pale skinny twenty-one-year-old with carroty hair; he was trying hard to grow a beard to make himself look older. They had a two-month-old son; it had been a shot-gun wedding. 'You sell me anti-bebi pills?' Lilia pleaded wistfully. I tried to explain that anti-bebi pills without medical guidance (or even with it) are dangerous; but Lilia's English wasn't equal to that ... She was however eager to work at communication and her companions had a lot to say about the new feeling in northern Moldavia, where most people have relatives beyond the Prut. The possibility of eventual reunion with an ex-Soviet Moldavia was of much more interest than the day-to-day machinations of politicians in distant Bucharest. Yet here too Iliescu was much admired.

The older man, Petru, was a charmer – in his forties with a long narrow sallow face, fiery brown eyes and thick drooping black moustaches. When Lilia gave me her home address, urging me to come to stay *soon*, he slipped the piece of paper into the top pocket of my jacket – then took it out to add his own address in a village almost on the border. Petru agreed with Lilia that Bucharest had never done anything for Moldavia – 'under kings or Communists all the same no good'. I never discovered Carroty's name but he was adamant that 'Here we're much closer to our own people over the Prut. Chisinau (Kishinev) is *our* capital, the capital city of our souls.' English-speaking Rumanians use the word 'soul' with interesting frequency.

We left the restaurant together, then paused to say goodbye on a wide terrace where overflow customers – dozens of men – stood around clutching glasses. When Petru suddenly put his hand in my jacket pocket I assumed he wanted to add something to his address. Instead he whipped out my Swiss knife and said, 'For me!' His face was transformed; now he looked like the nastiest sort of bandit. Momentarily I was too taken aback to react. Then I made to grab the knife and he transferred it to his other hand, yelling abuse. Enraged, I struck him hard on the shin with my stick and, as he doubled up in pain, prised the knife from his loosened grip. I felt slightly scared of the possible reaction of the half-drunken crowd all around; it seemed ominous that Petru had felt free to rob me in public. As quickly as my condition permitted – not even glancing at Lilia and her husband – I descended the steps and made for my hotel in a state of mild shock.

Lilia soon overtook me, in tears and looking quite scared. She insisted that Petru was drunk, though at no stage had he shown symptoms of even mild intoxication. She begged me not to change my mind about staying with them in Suceava. Petru was not her real friend – she was not that sort of bad person – her husband was afraid of Petru, which was why he had not helped me ... I soothed her as best I could and invited her to the hotel that evening for another chat. She said she'd come, but she didn't.

Later, as I was writing in my room, the bulb died and could not be replaced. Alex explained, 'This town is waiting for the next lot of smuggled goods from over the Prut. Already some local people get rich on free enterprise. In Russia they buy cheap in bulk – bulbs, salami, cooking oil, electric kettles and batteries – then sell very dear.'

'But,' I said, 'aren't the Soviets short of everything?'

'Compared to us, *now*,' replied Alex, 'they're affluent! But ten years ago it was another way – then we had many Poles coming to Moldavia to buy food.'

That evening the writing on the wall had to be read. My plan was reluctantly to catch the Iasi–Timisoara 9.15 a.m. 'express', *en route* for Belgrade and a cheap flight to a London doctor. There were then no cheap flights from Bucharest.

6

A Nasty Video in Timisoara

Much to the astonishment of the natives, I was becoming quite an admirer of Rumania's railway system. Admittedly, many of the trains are disintegrating; sometimes gaping holes in the corridor floors allow one to study the state of the sleepers (poor) as one chugs along. The carriages are usually filthy and the *toalets* always catastrophic – in fact unusable, unless one can tolerate wearing shit-clogged boots. But everything is relative and thus far I had found the trains astoundingly punctual, starting and arriving not even one minute early or late. They are also, on the whole, less slow than Yugoslav trains and much better organised. When you buy your ticket – sometimes, conveniently, in a main urban Post Office at a special desk – a second ticket is provided giving coach and seat numbers; and there is no reservation fee. In my experience this system never fails. My seat was always vacant, even when I joined a train midway on its journey and found a dozen seatless passengers in the corridor nearby – those who had bribed their way on without reservations.

There are no long-distance intercity bus services and some of the scenes in urban stations reminded me of India – minus the colourful clothes and baggage, and the variety of food and drink on offer. At village stations many passengers board with turkeys and geese in baskets, or lambs and pigs in sacks, or hens under arms. Second-class journeys are often enlivened by pan pipes and folksongs, the musicians recklessly stamping on the unstable carriage floors as they play and sing. It is pleasing to be in a region where folk music just happens, where it is still the peasants' way of avoiding tedium. This will soon change; 'trannies' and Walkmans are already regarded by Rumania's youth as symbols of liberty and sophistication.

From Gura Humorului I travelled second class, opposite an endearing old couple with quite a large pig in a poke on their adjacent laps. He slept in transit but woke at each stop and squealed most piteously – causing his owners to stroke him through the sack while crooning a sort of lullaby.

One dramatic symptom of that winter's climatic moodiness was visible for hours as we traversed the Carpathians at less than cycling speed. February was only beginning, yet a recent thaw had broken the frozen river Dorna into mighty chunks of ice. Then a flood from an even warmer spell, farther upstream, had tossed those chunks about; and then again it froze hard, welding the weirdly misshapen slabs of ice one to another, at improbable angles – turning the wide river bed into a freakishly beautiful polar landscape. For much of the way a main road accompanied the railway, carrying scarcely any traffic.

Beyond Vatra Dornei I invaded the first-class corridors, in search of an English-speaking smoker. As smoking in carriages is forbidden, and most Rumanians of both sexes are hopeless nicotine addicts, many passengers spend much of their time in the corridors.

Soon I was talking with Camil, a young chemistry lecturer at Iasi university. Noticing my discomfort while standing, he obligingly moved to second class – then horrified me by berating the old couple for inflicting their porcine companion on the travelling public. To me he complained, 'These people are too primitive, they give you a very bad idea of Rumania!'

'On the contrary,' I said, 'I feel an affinity with people who have meaningful relationships with their pigs.'

Camil looked at me suspiciously; unlike most Rumanians, he didn't have much sense of humour. He did however share in his compatriots' tendency to exaggerate the length of the Ceausescu nightmare. For twenty-four years, he asserted, Rumanians had been allowed to read only Communist propaganda. I made no comment; it was certainly true that Rumanians had been isolated for long enough to cause an alarming unawareness of and indifference to the rest of the world. I met no one who was even slightly informed about Yugoslavia's current problems; the two countries might have been on different continents.

Camil smiled scornfully when I mentioned that Gura Humorului's cinema was advertising, for the coming week, British, West German, Swedish, French and American films. 'That is the new policy,' he said, 'to show everyone life in the West. But what will those primitive peasants understand? From foreign films they will get more bad influence than education. And they will be very confused – all they see and hear will contradict all they have been trained to believe and feel. Our revolution was so sudden we have no good plans for dealing with its success. It was unique because Ceausescu was unique. Now he is compared to Hitler, which is stupid. Nazi paranoia was more healthy. The Ceausescu mafia used Rumania like a personal estate, they were only interested in their own gain and for that they took Rumania to hell. But they didn't want to conquer the world. The Nazis were inspired by a sort of idealism, they weren't only criminals.'

Involuntarily I shivered; this was the dark aspect of the Rumanian psyche, which I had already glimpsed on a few occasions. It is one more measure of (among other things) the Rumanians' isolation, that many people so unselfconsciously reveal their prejudices. Plainly they cannot imagine the effect, on a 'normal' Western European, of remarks such as 'I *hate* Jews!' Or, 'Gypsies are *below* human beings! Here we have millions and they breed very fast – somehow we must get rid of them...' Words with a dreadful resonance: first you convince yourself that the people to be somehow got rid of are not human beings...

Camil, unusually, did not give me his address before he left the train at Cluj; there had been a mutual failure to recognise a soul-mate.

When darkness fell, soon after, no lights came on. The system had failed – a common occurrence – and for five hours everything happened in pitch darkness, the ticket collector operating with a dim torch hung around his neck. To me there was something surreal about passengers plunging deep into conversation with people they had never seen; many familiar words rang out – democracy, economy, liberty, Ceausescu, collectives, election, Iliescu, Securitate.

At Oradea, a young couple boarded with difficulty; ours was the last coach and so beyond reach of the feeble station lights. They found their seats with the aid of my torch and, on discovering that my Jimbolia train left Timisoara at 1 p.m. next day, at once invited me to stay the night.

'Tomorrow', said Maria, 'I can show you where the revolution started. I am angry because now the Front tries to make people believe the revolution was made in Bucharest. They want all the honour for themselves, to have it looking like somehow *Iliescu* organised everything!'

Hours later, on the platform at Timisoara, we looked at one another with open curiosity – then simultaneously laughed. 'Only in Rumania', said I, 'could a wandering foreigner be invited to stay by a hostess who hasn't yet seen her!' Maria – short and wiry – had curly black hair, large luminous brown eyes, a quick generous smile. Radu was tallish and frail-looking, his mousy hair thinning, his voice gentle; at thirty-four he looked nearer forty-four.

On our overcrowded tram, Maria proudly told me that Timi-soara was among the first cities in the world to run trams; in 1864 the horse-drawn version appeared. Twenty years later it became the first city in Europe to install electric street lighting. Ironically, its street lights are now conspicuously few and feeble, even by Rumanian standards.

High in a bloc, an ample meal was swiftly served: salami, sheep cheese (Radu's parents were peasants), home-pickled forest fungus, white bread brought from Hungary by a Magyar friend and a hearty red village wine.

Like many of their generation, Maria and Radu had married as students; 'shacking up' was illegal. 'We've been lucky,' said Maria. 'It went one way or the other – either very young couples couldn't cope, given all the daily problems, or they made a *special* marriage. Our baby came nine and a half months later – an accident, but without contraceptives we didn't know then about managing. Nobody blamed us, but bringing a baby into such difficulties made me feel guilty.'

For that baby – Mihai, now aged ten – not only his parents but Maria's parents and her brother (five years her junior) sacrificed much; if there were only six slices of salami, Mihai got them. So effectively was he protected from the worst deprivations that he wondered why the Ceausescus had to be executed – indeed, why there had to be a revolution. Politics had never been discussed in his presence; as the child of 'unreliable' parents he was likely to be under special surveillance at school.

Maria and Radu had both acquired bad files by refusing to

become Securitate informers. Therefore Radu was made to work in a distant factory, getting up at 4.30 six days a week and arriving home fourteen hours later. And Maria had to teach in an even more distant village school, leaving home at 4 a.m., changing slow buses twice and returning, shattered, at 5 p.m. Living nearer their workplaces would have meant meeting only on Sundays, if then, and they would have seen even less of Mihai. But because they worked outside their city of residence they were not entitled to accommodation there and for five years shared Maria's parents' standard three-room flat, where her brother needed one room in which to study. Then their period of punishment was over. Both were allowed to work in Timisoara, where they soon bought a flat with financial assistance from both sets of parents. Even then, however, Maria's parents had to continue to look after Mihai, the customary role for accessible grandparents. Often a widowed grandmother (or grandfather) lives in, or close by, and this inter-dependence of the generations has forged powerful family bonds just as these are weakening in the Occident.

After too little sleep and too much wine, we were bleary-eyed at 6 a.m. Radu had to fetch Mihai from his grandparents and take him to school before going to work. Maria was determined to introduce me to 'the revolution's birthplace' before starting her job. The sun rose over a frost-bound Timisoara as we stood in a packed tram, swaying towards the central Piata Huniade. Maria pointed out a huge banner, proudly welcoming people to the 'First Free City of Rumania'. Then she began to air a complicated hypothesis about the forty mysterious corpses forcibly removed from the city morgue on the night of the 17–18 December by Securitate officers – while the Director in charge of post-mortems, Dr Milan Leonard Dressler, was held at gunpoint. As we walked towards the splendid Opera House – an Austro-Hungarian legacy – Maria paused by a wall-poster display. 'See this!' she exclaimed. 'All is uncertain – listen!' And she translated a poster which accused Dr Dressler of having collaborated with the Securitate to conceal the number of those killed during the revolution – and which threatened his life.

Timisoara's Orthodox Cathedral is a 1930s hybrid which not unsuccessfully combines neo-Byzantine and traditional Moldavian influences. In its shadow, on 17 December, many young demonstrators were killed. As we stood beside the piled wreaths and fresh bouquets, watching the prayerful candle-lighters, Maria asked, 'Do you feel very emotional? Often foreigners come to this spot and weep – *they* know our revolution started *here!*'

I replied honestly, 'If I'd come here first, after crossing the border, I'd probably have felt more emotional. Now, I see too many question marks . . .'

'Is that why you're coming back?' probed Maria. 'To look for the answers?'

'Not really, because I don't expect to find them. I'll only find more question marks.'

'So you're coming back because you like places with many question marks?'

'Well, yes – I suppose I do, now you mention it . . .'

When Maria had reluctantly left me (she could have taken the day off but on principle wouldn't) I soon sensed quite a strong anti-foreigner undercurrent. Several young men, of whom I asked the way, snapped at me in English – and revealingly.

'Why no camera?' 'Reporter go home!' 'You're late, there's no blood left!'

Plainly Timisoara was reacting strongly against its recent over-exposure to the global media. Thrice I was abused for being English but when I showed my passport two of the young men apologised and one befriended me – and succinctly explained the anti-British vibes. 'We know how much respect the Ceausescus got, all over the Occident, because the Queen of England gave *him* an important medal – the one she gives her own ambassadors. Then a few hours before we shot him she took it back, to try to save England's reputation. She didn't want a man executed for terrorism, by his own people, to go down in the history books as Elizabeth-decorated!'

Ion was pitifully undersized, with a shocking crop of boils on his neck and a longing (very common among young Rumanians) to go to Australia. 'I'm a well-trained electric engineer, I want to work hard and have good schools for my little sons – they are aged one year and two years. And here is a bad future for them. Now so much aid comes from all over Europe – hundreds of trucks day and night. And who gets it? Ceausescu's mafia, who could fool the foreigners! And that is a sign of how our life will be.'

Ion urged me to go with him to visit a friend in hospital who on 17 December had lost both legs. 'If you are writing about Rumania you must *see* our hospitals – all the reporters want to see them. In the Occident you have nothing like our primitive ,conditions.'

I thanked Ion but could not bring myself to visit a legless young man in the role of 'reporter' gathering 'material'. My virtue, if such it was, later had its own reward when Fate organised an opportunity for me to study Rumanian hospitals at first hand.

Then Ion noticed that I was flagging and invited me to his apartment in a semi-derelict bloc conveniently near the *gara*. Some of the apartments had been abandoned – damp seemed to be the main problem – and this was the most impoverished Rumanian home I had yet seen, apart from Vicki's cottage. It was however glutted with expensive electronic equipment, doubtless 'perks' accessible to any enterprising 'electric engineer'. No one was at home; the boys were in a state crèche, their mother at work. To entertain me, Ion showed a video of the Ceausescus' trial, execution, and burial – the most horrible film I have ever watched. That evening I wrote in my journal:

> Ion's video was shattering, not least because of my own reactions to it. Despite knowing the denouement, an extraor-dinary tension built up within me as N.C. was dragged from an armoured vehicle to face his judges. And despite knowing that E.C. was dead, a no less extraordinary fear – a primitive sort of terror – gripped me as I gazed at her face. (I'd never before seen *Her* and had only glimpsed *Him* during the revolution.) Whereas N.C. looked not only bad but mad, *She* looked completely sane – and utterly evil. One sensed in her case no extenuating circumstances, such as the paranoid megalomania that so clearly afflicted *Him*. As the film con-tinued (it seemed agonisingly long-drawn-out) I found my hands sweating and felt a churning mix of emotions: a squeamish distaste for the violence of the imminent execu-tions but also a longing to *see* the Ceausescus' corpses. Part of

me wanted to experience vicariously the awful savage exhilaration of taking revenge. It shocked me badly to be taken over, for the first time in my life, by pure hatred of fellow beings. (*Hatred*, as distinct from fierce antagonism to the policies of certain governments, or angry contempt for the cruel greed of certain corporations.) During the past few weeks of exposure to the grievous sufferings inflicted on the Rumanians, I've been uneasily aware of this hatred smouldering within. Yet when it burst into flames today I was appalled, not only on my own behalf but on behalf of the Rumanians – because I knew I was then feeling what so many of them have been feeling for years. And hatred, however apparently justifiable, excusable or inevitable, always damages the hater.

On 25 December the Ceausescus had to be killed without delay and the entire population had at once to be convinced that they were dead. As long as they remained alive, everyone would have felt threatened, fearing that at any moment the Securitate might rescue and reinstate them. This I fully understand, after watching that film and myself experiencing an irrational but real fear of the dead E.C. (Or was it irrational? Obviously I feared not the dead woman but what she represented: the power of evil manifestly to control an individual.) It seems fitting that the nation was persuaded to believe in the tyrants' deaths through a video film, television having been one of their favourite propaganda weapons.

The trial's aura of unreality also seemed fitting. Of course whoever was taking decisions at that time (Iliescu & Co?) erred badly by staging such a phoney trial and producing the absurd charge of genocide. It would have been more honest and equally forgivable had the two been shot on 23 December 'while trying to escape'. But what the trial lacked in legality, according to international law, it made up for in poetic justice. The Ceausescus had created a state in which 'a fair trial' could not even be imagined; it was a concept belonging to another world. And they died by the standards they had set. If it is true that they rejected the offer of a 'civil trial', in which their defence could have been insanity, that was the only constructive thing they ever did for Rumania.

Some outsiders thought it gratuitously barbarous to show the corpses in such gruesomely minute detail, with close-ups of both faces immediately after death, while the blood was still streaming from E.C.'s body and N.C. lay looking like a discarded rag doll, his legs folded back under him. But for the Rumanians to credit the apparently impossible, it was essential that they should see every move of the doctor's post-mortem check, establishing that life was extinct. In Rumania, for at least half a century, all official statements have been lies. Without that brutally graphic film, many would have continued to suspect or believe that somehow the Ceausescus had been rescued, that the executions were fakes and the corpses mere dummies.

The cameraman had a duty to linger for long minutes on those bodies, and especially on the faces, both immediately after death and when they were being coffined for burial in a 'secret' spot in Bucharest. Allegedly they had prepared for themselves coffins of solid gold, but they ended up in crude wooden paupers' coffins and again the camera lingered on their faces, showing them from every angle, and remaining steadily focused on each coffin while a white cloth was placed over the inmate and the lid was firmly closed. The scene then shifted to the burial site – evidently the corner of a cemetery – where large snowflakes were swirling softly. When the Ceausescus had been laid in shallow graves, a tall burly man stepped forward (Ion didn't know who he was) and threw a handful of earth onto the coffins. The incongruously familiar noise recalled that both were born into peasant families in a Christian country. Each grave was then sealed with massive stone slabs. And the final shot showed a young soldier plastering cement over the cracks between those slabs.

Ion grinned as he switched off the video machine. 'Good sport! But better if we didn't shoot them – too quick. I would like to see them dying very, very slowly – maybe starving to death, the way they tried to kill us.' He was only one of many Rumanians who made similar remarks to me – and looked puzzled when I didn't enthusiastically echo them.

The train to Jimbolia, on the Yugoslav border, moved at

walking rather than cycling speed. I shared my carriage with an elderly couple recently retired from their factory jobs, two sisters in their mid-twenties and an exhausted-looking mother who sat with her head on the shoulder of her nineteen-year-old son. As a political debate raged, I noticed again how attentively – often respectfully – many of the older generation listened to their juniors, as though aware that National Salvation depended not on the Front but on the young. (Women, interestingly, are no less assertive in public than men: possibly a beneficial side-effect of Communism?)

Andrei, the young man, spoke English idiosyncratically but uninhibitedly. He too longed to go to Australia and when I asked why so many young Rumanians regard Australia as Utopia he replied, 'We don't like America so much because it has too many Jews and negro people. And we would like to be in a big country where we could have land to farm – we are mostly peasants, we like to have land, not to live in the dirty city. I tried all is possible to leave Rumania and go *somewhere*. In Australia they don't receive me because I have no money and no any friend there. In June they will call me to the army and my mother will be crying all the time. My father is dead, my mother has only me. Please forgive me for my English is not good – they did not teach me at the school. But I learn myself, to give me more chance if ever I can leave this country. Can you help me? Can you take me to Ireland? I can do any work, I will be your servant! Please, try to help me! When you return to Timisoara, please come and be our guest. We are poor people but we have rich hearts!'

In Belgrade that evening I completed the first part of my journal:

Poor Andrei! Indeed he is right – 'We have rich hearts'. Now I realise that what has kept me going since the crash was falling in love with Rumania – always an invigorating experience, whether with a person or a place. How have so many Rumanians, despite their history, retained so much generosity, wit, vivacity?

I didn't expect such a marked temperamental affinity between Irish and Rumanians. Also, many details – positive and negative, trivial and important – remind me of Ireland forty years ago. The way women dress and their crude make-up; children's acceptance of parental discipline and authority; the eager unsophistication of adolescents; the lack of luxury consumer goods; the light motor traffic, even on main roads. And, most significantly, the brand-mark of centuries of oppression – a half-apologetic, half-defiant national inferiority complex.

On my arrival in London, after a series of nightmare hassles at Belgrade airport, I felt sufficiently like an 'emergency' not to protest when my friends rushed me to a casualty department. A fractured coccyx and torn back ligaments were diagnosed and a fortnight's immobility was enjoined. I spent much of that time telephoning bookshops in search of the numerous volumes I had promised to provide on my return to Rumania – books in English and French on democracy, books in English on Rumanian history and politics, books in Rumanian by exiles and a wide selection of school textbooks for teachers of English, physics and mathematics. It pleased me to have this task, to be able to repay some fraction of the Rumanians' touchingly generous hospitality.

7

Jimbolia, Jollifications and Forebodings

All those rashly promised books complicated my return journey at the beginning of March; bossy friends protested that it would be ligament-endangering to haul a mini-library single-handed to Timisoara. Rachel therefore came from her temporary Skopje home to meet my National Express coach at Zagreb and porter me, via Belgrade, to the border post near Kikinda.

When we left Belgrade, at sunset, I was beginning to feel the effects of two almost sleepless National Express nights. Few were travelling on our stop-at-every-village tube-type train to Kikinda – a journey quite short in miles but four hours long. Soon after 10 p.m. we alighted at a deserted station. It was pitch dark and very, very cold; there were no street lights; not a mouse stirred – it might have been 2 a.m. Silently we turned towards the distant town centre, stumbling over enigmatic chunks of concrete. On my homeward journey I had become only too familiar with this dreary spread-out town of long straight streets that seem to lead nowhere.

Ten minutes later I muttered desperately, 'There *must* be a hotel somewhere!'

'Why?' wondered Rachel.

I stood still; that was a good question. Who in their right mind – or even out of it – would ever for any conceivable reason want to spend a night in Kikinda? When I suggested camping Rachel grunted assent and we turned back. Not far beyond the station starlight revealed a level patch of land on which stubble concealed embedded, sharp-edged broken bricks. It was quite a challenge to have to erect a new tent for the first time (apart from a trial run in a Clapham garden) with numb fingers, by torchlight, on singularly inhospitable ground. Watch-dogs in three nearby farmyards

91

barked hysterically as we pitted our exhaustion-blunted wits against 'the very latest thing' in light one-person tents. At any moment I expected a suspicious farmer to appear, but none did. Our mastery, within ten minutes, of strange hoops and loops – instead of poles and guy-ropes – boosted morale. Then it sank again as we discovered that this was a strictly one-person tent – not, like my stolen treasure, a single into which two could just squeeze, side by side. We took it in turns to lie on top. The under-person, being pressed onto jagged bits of brick by ten and a half stone (Rachel) or eleven and a half stone (me), suffered extremely. At dawn, as we shook the tent free of its coating of ice, we agreed that that had been our most uncomfortable camping night ever – which, as Rachel noted, is saying something.

By 7 a.m. Kikinda was coming to what passes locally for life. Groups of workers with closed faces trudged glumly towards the day's toil. Two policemen stared at us as though we were objects fallen off a garbage truck. A few little shops were open but sold only bread. If anyone knew when the next bus was leaving for the border they weren't telling. 'What's *wrong* with this place?' demanded Rachel peevishly.

I sat chewing dry bread on one of a row of tree-stumps, thinking how much less dire the street would look had those trees not been felled. 'At least', I said, 'the bread is fresh here.' Then I added, 'Perhaps history is what's wrong – this whole Banat region too messed about for too long – like three thousand years. For centuries Timisoara was the capital, now poor Kikinda is a spoke without a hub.'

We mooched on up the street, between weather-beaten red-tiled two-storey dwellings and bleak four- or five-storey office blocks. Kikinda looks as though built by and for dispirited people. Outside a petrol station stood a bus, about to leave for Belgrade. Its driver thought a bus might leave for the border in an hour or two.

'We could hitch?' I suggested, impatient for reunion with Rumania.

'*I'm* waiting for the bus', said Rachel. 'Who's carrying the books?'

A long, low building, near the bus-stop, proved to be a 'supermarket' offering unalluring edibles but tempting beer. We bought six large bottles and sat in the sun – already warm at 8 a.m. – in the middle of an adjacent half-acre of wiry yellowish grass. 'Just like Cameroon,' recalled Rachel. 'Beer for breakfast . . .'

By 9.30 we felt more cheerful. 'OK,' said Rachel, 'let's return the empties and hitch – I've lost faith in that bus.'

Across the Banat's insipid flatness, our narrow traffic-free road was discouragingly visible for miles ahead. In relation to the population there was an astonishing amount of litter by the wayside. An hour later the bus overtook us and stopped in response to frantic signals. A squat scowling woman conductor abused us stridently as we strove to fit our load into the bus's already packed belly. But her bark was worse than her bite; she gave us a free ride because we were foreigners going to Rumania – evidently, in her estimation, an act of lunacy and one mustn't take advantage of lunatics . . .

Soon we were on the last lap, a two-mile walk from a straggling, muted village to the frontier. When I saw the Rumanian flag on the horizon my spirits soared and I began to chant sentimentally – *'Olé! Olé! Olé!'*

'And what about poor little me?' said Rachel. 'How do I get back to ghastly Kikinda?'

'Easy!' I replied with callous cheerfulness. 'It's just noon so you've six hours of daylight and no books to carry.'

We parted on the Yugoslav frontier line and when I looked back from Rumania, down that long straight road, my daughter was a dot in the distance. Later she reported more favourable second impressions of the Banat. An ancient shepherd riding a moped transported her to Kikinda on his carrier, then invited her home for a meal with his wife before escorting her to the 4.30 bus for Belgrade.

It would have been easy to leave Yugoslavia unobserved; I had to knock on a door and yell loudly before an irritated-looking officer slouched out, glanced at my passport and waved me on. A hard-currency shop – no more than a big shack – occupied the narrow no-man's-land and in February had been doing a brisk trade; now it was closed. Then – perhaps because it was a Saturday afternoon – there had been much cross-border traffic.

My re-entry formalities were speedy enough but rather nasty. Two truculent customs officers, redolent of *tuica*, roughly unpacked everything before leafing through the Rumanian volumes and pronouncing them confiscated. Promptly I produced a letter of introduction to a senior member of the Front – a household name in Rumania, someone who not long after became disillusioned and resigned. When I claimed, untruthfully, that those volumes had been requested by him, the officers both changed colour; one went red in the face, the other white. And at once the books were thrust back into my mega-briefcase. Meanwhile a third crook – this one very grandly uniformed – had been going through my plastic carrier-bag. As I turned away from his colleagues, I saw him strolling into an office openly clutching my precious bottle of duty-free Scotch. When I shouted indignantly the others hastily retrieved it, muttering about 'a mistake'. Without that letter, I might have again entered Rumania as one of the dispossessed.

I had almost finished repacking – a wearisome process – when a rusty, much-dented Yugoslav car came through. The scruffy middle-aged Kikinda couple immediately offered me a lift to Timisoara. They were small-time smugglers, a common local occupation, and on excellent terms with the customs officers.

Five minutes later, at a traffic-lights stop on the outskirts of Jimbolia, we were suddenly surrounded by a dozen shouting young toughs waving fat wads of lei and demanding 'Change! Change!' They banged on the roof, shouldering each other out of the way, yet co-operating to prevent the car from moving as the lights changed. *'Tigan'* (Gypsy), explained the driver unnecessarily. When he dismissed them in Rumanian, revealing that he was a local, they kicked the car, hard – then withdrew looking sulkily frustrated. It would have done me no good to encounter them alone and on foot, wearing a brand new rucksack and dragging heavy cartons.

In the middle of the town we turned down a side street and stopped outside a disintegrating school. This was evidently a routine; at once a mob converged on the car, looking almost as threatening as the Gypsies. Frantically they swarmed as the smugglers got out, opened the boot and began to sell – for enormous sums in lei – Yugoslav cigarettes, toilet soap, condoms, toothpaste and tiny gimcrack combs. I too got out, my luggage being exposed in the boot; and as I stood poised to foil a thief one sneaked up behind me – a small boy with a filthy pinched face, red-rimmed eyes and an air of savage desperation. He tried to pick my jacket pockets while my hands were in them. Meanwhile several adults, also with haggard faces and wild eyes, were physically fighting over bars of soap and packets of cigarettes. Jimbolia is not recommended for a first crossing into Rumania; there one would be unlikely to fall in love with the country.

A few sad-looking Swabian villages lined the road to Timisoara. These had once been exceptionally prosperous; the detached dwellings were roomy and solid, often with the German family name and date of construction (I noticed 1897, 1908, 1922) over the main entrance. When this region went from Turkish to Austrian ownership, in 1718, thousands of Swabian peasants were 'relocated' to farm the Habsburgs' new and very fertile territory. Like so many of their Saxon cousins in Transylvania, an unre-vealed but disquieting number – also subsidised by the Bonn government – migrated to Germany during Ceausescu's 'Golden Age'. Rumania will soon notice their loss; as peaceable, hard-working, intelligent farmers, they formed part of an unusually productive community.

In Timisoara, at 1.30 p.m., the kind smugglers offered to find my friends' bloc – though the address meant nothing to them. But no one would be home before 3.30 so I asked to be put down in the city centre. My first thought was, 'How quiet it is!' Certainly the traffic was heavier than on my previous visit – some petrol for private use had just become available – yet it remained soothingly light compared to any other European city I can think of. Slowly I dragged my load through the spacious sunny square overlooked by the Orthodox Cathedral; all the seats were occupied by citizens visibly luxuriating – like cats – in the spring warmth. Since last I saw it the horticultural shrine to the martyrs of the revolution had been elaborated on and much expanded. Now the stylised carved wooden crosses were almost buried under mounds of evergreen branches, plastic blooms, lovingly renewed fresh wreaths and enormous black nylon bows that from a distance looked discon-certingly like monster bats. Hundreds of thin orange candles still flickered steadfastly and yards of melted tallow made solid pools around the fir branches. In the middle of the square, facing the cathedral steps on which many died, a high metal archway

95

surmounted by a cross had become the centre of the shrine. Panels on either side supported life-sized paintings of the Crucifixion: the work, I was told later, of a Maramures village artist. These were strangely moving, unlike the conventionally correct paintings by the state-subsidised artists who during the past few decades restored many Orthodox churches. Around and above them were smaller depictions of Christ crowned with thorns, the Virgin Mary and a dreamy-looking Pantocrator; from Maramures had come a weird but forceful merger between the Byzantines and the Impressionists, with a touch of severe El Greco mysticism.

Two solid, cheerful-looking peasant women, wearing long skirts and striped aprons, and dirty sheepskin jackets and black kerchiefs, were amiably competing as candle-sellers. The many other faces around the shrine wore varied expressions: sad, thoughtful, stern, puzzled. And some were still anguished and shocked.

For how long, I wondered, would (or should) this intense public commemoration of the dead continue? Was it perhaps in some danger of becoming an unhealthy cult, a retreat from reality, a substitute for organising coherent political action (as distinct from having political discussions) because the sacrifice of those being mourned had *not* made it easy to be free? Another key was needed to unlock the door to liberty, an intricate key that could not be cut in a few days of reckless, despairing heroism. Then I reproved myself for being too insensitive to the inner needs of a city that so recently had suffered so much – perhaps mentally even more than physically. Yet it worried me that the Rumanians may – like the Irish – be dangerously prone to martyritis. The political martyr syndrome, based on a natural impulse to honour and seek inspiration from brave patriots, too often breeds myths that mislead and paralyse whole generations.

In a small foodless dingy restaurant there was no choice of drinks; the waiter brought a tumblerful of something known as 'bitter' which tasted unique and looked like stale blood. At the next table three shabby unshaven men were fervently debating the trial of four senior Securitate officers which had opened in Timisoara a few days earlier. Then I noticed Gheorghe, a well-built youth with light brown hair, dark brown eyes, rosy cheeks and an open expression. He worked in a shoe factory and had taught himself a rudimentary form of English. By one of those happy coincidences that littered my Rumanian paths, he lived in the bloc behind my friends' – some two miles away – and was returning home. So he became my porter and we arranged to meet again at 7 a.m. next day. 'Tonight I make a programme for you!' said Gheorghe. 'You are like the radio for me, giving a lesson in English!'

Vintila and Elise lived in a standard three-room apartment (plus kitchen and bathroom) on the top floor of a ten-storey bloc overlooking similar blocs in every direction. Elise was Paula's sister – Paula with whom I had travelled overnight from Bucharest to Oradea. Both she and Vintila were by now vehemently anti-Front, though they admitted to having been pro-Iliescu for a few weeks after the Revolution – 'Before we had time to observe and deduce...' Their two sons, aged thirteen and eleven, were scandalised to find me devoid of opinions about Ireland's chances in the World Cup. They had no doubt about the real, central significance of the Revolution: now they could watch *all* the World Cup matches.

Conversations in English are made no easier for anybody by the Rumanians' reluctance ever to silence the monster in the corner. However, that evening two illuminating programmes followed one another – illuminating both in their content and in their wider political significance, as interpreted by my friends. The first showed, with a plethora of technical detail, exactly how the state – in the Bad Old Days – had bugged telephones, homes, offices, factories, shops and collective farm buildings. The police officers demonstrating these countless arcane electronic wonders wore expressions of righteous indignation which failed to impress my companions. Vintila commented that three months ago the same officers were probably using those very gadgets and tricks which they now regarded with such virtuous disdain. Elise added, 'And in another three months they may be using them again!'

The next documentary illustrated how Ceausescu's manic industrialisation had polluted Rumania's air, soil and water to a homicidal degree. Elise frowned and cracked her finger joints. 'All this is too clever! It is a campaign to make us think only about *Ceausescu* – how wicked and cunning he was, how much harm he did. Then people will feel more and more grateful to Iliescu and the Front for our "national salvation". And because the Front allows such anti-Ceausescu films to be shown, and the simple people think "Ceausescu equals Communism", they will believe the Front is anti-Communist – so it will feel safe and right to vote for them!'

Vintila, like many others, worked hard though unsuccessfully to convince me that 'Rumania has *never* been a Communist country, most of us *never* supported Marxism!' Not surprisingly, Rumania's sordid inter-war political scene had created a substantial number of Communist sympathisers. These were mainly miners, and oil and transport workers, who tried to organise protests against avaricious foreign companies and their corrupt Rumanian allies – including King Carol II and his mistress (much later his wife), the notorious Magda Lupescu. The army, backed by the then ostensibly governing National Liberal Party, dealt ferociously with all protests and strikes. (In fact the king was governing, in so far as anyone was at that date.) The army's worst excesses, during this period, occurred in February 1933 when Gehorghiu-Dej of the illegal Communist Party led a strike of oil and railway workers. Subsequently he and other Communists were held for years in Doftana, a humid, pitch-dark, completely unfurnished hell-hole where, a generation earlier, survivors of the 1907 Peasants' Uprising endured confinement and torture.

Also during the 1930s, Rumania's homegrown fascists – Codreanu's Iron Guard – were rapidly gaining strength among a traditionally anti-Semitic population. When these thugs became anti-monarch as well as anti-Jew the king outlawed all political parties in February 1938 – a move which did not go against his grain. Nine months later he ordered Codreanu to be shot 'while trying to escape'.

There are noteworthy resemblances between King Carol II and Ceausescu. After the Depression, which caused most Rumanians to suffer acute deprivation, he deposited at least $40 million in his foreign bank accounts. Much of this loot was acquired through business deals with such men as Max Aushnit, who founded Rumania's steel trust, and Nicolae Malaxa. The latter was an armaments billionaire, a fervent though closet supporter of the

Iron Guard, a well-known Nazi collaborator and – when he fled to the US in 1946 – a protégé of one Richard Nixon, who helped him to get his residency permit.

In 1940 Marshal Antonescu took over as *Conducator* (the Rumanian equivalent of *Führer*), following King Carol's abdication and the ceding by his heir, the present ex-King Michael, of dictatorial powers to the Marshal, backed by the Iron Guard. Antonescu, however, 'wasn't the worst of them' – as we say in Ireland. His personal integrity was beyond question, which made a nice change. Also, he was unusually realistic in his assessment of Rumania's potential for economic progress; and he seems to have been sincere in his wish to see that progress benefiting the entire population. In September 1940 he established the National Legionary State (the Guards' formal title was 'The Legion of Archangel St Michael') and he never pretended to be anything other than a fascist military dictator. But this didn't worry the Rumanians, who gave him genuine majority support from June 1941, when he rashly took Rumania into the war against the USSR, until August 1944 when Soviet troops marched into defeated Rumania – which promptly changed sides, though not promptly enough to secure Anglo-American support and save itself from Communism. One friend of mine pointed out, 'Antonescu fought with Hitler only to get back for us Bukovina and Bessarabia – and that was his duty. The British fought with the Soviets because it was their duty to oppose Nazis. That did not mean they were Communists or approved of Stalin's death-camps in Siberia.'

Part of Rumania's present demoralisation must be rooted in its pre-Communist history, though various 'revised versions' glorify some of Rumania's least savoury leaders as national heroes. However, a people's social history does not have to be learned from books, in each generation, to influence their gut-reactions. And one comparatively recent chapter – foreign profiteering – must surely be contributing to the post-revolution reluctance to see Rumania's economic doors again thrown open to Free Marketeers. Rumanians have never had a democratically elected government with responsible public representatives concerned about their constituents' welfare. Why should they believe that in

99

the 1990s a coalition of fundamentally right-wing parties, however prettily tinted with 'liberalism', will not yet again betray them
for its own profit?

Next morning Gheorghe was waiting for me outside the bloc
at 6.55. He had 'made my programme'; I was to meet Marie, his
ex-aunt-by-marriage who taught English in a large school on the
far side of the city. 'She have a big likening for peoples with
English,' explained Gheorghe. 'Then to work I go and after we
talk more.'

At first Marie's English was rather hesitant; clearly her 'likening' was not often indulged. Yet within half an hour she had
regained fluency and then she said, 'I feel we are on the same
wave-length, yes?' The feeling, I assured her, was mutual. All her
grandparents had come from Ruthenia when it was part of
Czechoslovakia – 'So I don't look Rumanian, and sometimes I
don't feel it . . .' She was small, plump, flaxen-haired and blue-
eyed, with soft blurred features and a lot of sadness behind her
good cheer.

The teachers' Common Room – long, low-ceilinged, mustard-
painted – would have been dismal if not filled with early golden
sunshine. As we sat at an unsteady formica table Marie introduced
me to her colleagues, who were all the time arriving. The majority
showed a predictable tendency to forget their pupils when Marie
announced that I was spending the morning with her. Repeatedly
the door opened and youngsters of both sexes slid shyly in to
present to the women teachers bouquets of primroses, crocuses
and violets, interwoven with fir-top sprigs. This was World
Women's Day, Marie explained – an occasion taken very seriously
in Rumania.

Then a gangling, blushing youth, distressingly acne-afflicted,
arrived with a laden tray – the staff's breakfast, I assumed. But
Marie laid a firm hand on my shoulder and turned me towards
the platters of sausage and salami, the three kinds of cheese, the
hard-boiled eggs and the stack of thickly sliced bread. 'Eat!' she
urged. 'It is your breakfast.'

My claim to have eaten well only an hour before was not an
acceptable excuse. 'You must eat often in Timisoara,' insisted
Marie, 'because in Maramures you may need extra fat!' She then
set about the tedious – and to my eyes perilous – process of

making coffee. The water had to be boiled in a mug containing a minute electric element, the wall socket was so loose that a hand had to be kept on the plug throughout – and the mug took longer to boil than a full kettle back home.

Suddenly an excited young woman rushed in, flung her brief-case on the table and clapped her hands. She was the bearer of such sensational news that momentarily everybody forgot me. An elderly teacher, who had been mysteriously absent for a few days, had fled to his brother in America after discovering that he was about to be exposed as the school's chief Securitate informer. The elated reaction to this news indicated that he had been no one's favourite colleague. Several exclaimed, 'I told you so!' – or words to that effect. There was much laughter at the fugitive's expense; only Marie looked pensive. She beckoned the young woman and asked in English, 'What about his wife?'

The young woman shrugged. 'She stays – he wouldn't waste dollars on *her* fare!'

Marie looked at me and sighed. 'Now too many families are being shocked to find one of them informed. Last week my neighbour collapsed with hysteria – her seven-year-old daughter was terrified and came running to me. The husband had dis-appeared overnight, a kind, gentle husband and father – also a loving, generous son and brother. He left a note to say he would live in Germany because someone wanted to kill him for revenge. He told her to look in a cupboard and then follow him. She found hidden $2,700, for us huge riches. Then she knew what was the problem – in his job he could never find so many dollars. But she cannot follow him, he is not who she thought he was. Now even their two children frighten her because she feels no trust in *his* children. He is another person and she hates him and her whole *self* is broken. What she thought was reality, with their good marriage, is only a dream.'

The responsibility for disrupting that day's schooling was not solely mine; most of the female teachers and some of the males would in any case have relaxed in honour of the World's Women. And now all were eager to 'explain' the revolution to the for-eigner.

One young woman asserted, 'There has been too much foolish talk about our courage – the demonstrators never expected to be

101

fired on, with young women and small children in the front line!'

'But', argued an elderly man, 'when they did see how dangerous it was they stayed on the streets – even some of the women
stayed.'

Marie leant across the table and pretended to hit him. 'Especially *today* you must not talk this way about *women*!'

A gloomy stooped man in his forties remarked sombrely, 'The
foolish talk is calling our tragedy a "revolution". It was prepared
by Iliescu and his comrades. They used us here in Timisoara to
get rid of one dictator to make way for another.'

'In Bucharest', said Marie, 'they think *they* got rid of the
dictator!'

A tall slim young woman, with curly black hair and angry grey
eyes, responded quickly. 'So why did Bucharest wait five days
before joining us?'

There were then about a dozen teachers in the room and one
could sense antagonism to Bucharest uniting them.

'How much did Bucharest *know*?' wondered Marie. 'When my
friends there rang me, to ask about the rumours, I was afraid to
tell them anything. Did anyone here tell their Bucharest friends
exactly what was happening?'

There was a significant silence. I broke it by remarking, 'To us it
seems frightening that modern communications could be so
controlled, that Bucharest really didn't know what was happening
in another Rumanian city, only 563 kilometres away, for two or
three days.'

'They *did* know,' persisted the angry-eyed young woman. 'They
were told by the BBC and Radio Free Europe and Voice of
America.'

'How many people listen to foreign broadcasts?' challenged
Marie. 'Only a few! Most couldn't know!' She turned to me.
'Dictatorships rest secure *only* on this foundation of controlling
information. And Ceausescu had *total* control, more even than
Stalin, because Rumania is quite small. Where else did you have to
get a police permit to own a typewriter!'

A young phoney-blonde with high cheek bones was applying
Gypsy-smuggled Hungarian varnish to very long nails. 'All the
Securitate can't have been bad,' she reflected. 'If most hadn't held

102

back, there would have been many thousands dead! So all should not now be punished.'

'Not *one* will be punished!' the elderly man exclaimed vehemently. 'And they only held back because they had changed sides, from one dictator to the next. Tomorrow if Iliescu told them, "Kill thousands!", they would obey.'

Dorana, a gaunt chain-smoking woman with greying hair, spoke from a corner where she stood cross-legged, leaning against the window ledge. 'I believe last year even some of the Securitate felt pity for the rest of us. And they knew soon we would rebel. It was in the air. I watched faces in the street. Last autumn I saw sad despair becoming desperate defiance. Little children cried with hunger. A cauldron was seething. When the revolution started, no one thought "I am starting a revolution". But the cauldron boiled over. People *had to* express their hatred for the Ceausescus – not really hoping or planning to make a big change.'

'So now,' said the gloomy stooped man, 'they will be satisfied because they have made a *little* change!'

At some stage someone decided that the Irishwoman was to be guest of honour at the school's World Women's Day luncheon party in one of Timisoara's posh restaurants. Soon after 1 p.m. we all squeezed into a fleet of decrepit Dacias and juddered across the city to an exclusive windowless 'banquet-hall' in a Stalinesque hotel. The kitchen staff's timing had gone so agley that we were all pie-eyed on *tuica* before any food appeared. Looking around the long table – while I could still focus – I marvelled at the variety of physiognomies: Italian, Turkish, Irish, German, Jewish, Slav and sheer Anon.

The intense young man on my right – Marie was on my left – wanted to know how much longer it would take Ireland to get rid of the 'British imperialists'. He believed the IRA to have killed thousands in Britain and saw Northern Ireland as another blood-drenched Lebanon. To him the IRA were 'Freedom Fighters' and he physically shrank away from me when I described them otherwise. 'You betray your country!' he barked, staring at me with contempt.

Marie intervened. 'This may be a complicated problem. Dervla could know more about it than we do in Rumania!'

103

The young man gestured dismissively, overturning a *tuica* bottle; but then he so swiftly rescued it that not much was wasted.

I asked Marie, 'From where do you get your information about our Irish problem?'

'In the past from the Soviet Union – but not now. Now they have stopped anti-British propaganda. So we hear about Ireland only when the IRA kill someone else and they are described as "terrorists". For us it is very confusing.'

'And for us,' I assured her. I felt too disheartened to embark on a debate about why the fiercely anti-Soviet Rumanians should have been so influenced, in relation to Ireland, by Moscow's propaganda. On every continent I know (four) the IRA are the propaganda champions, proving how little the British understand about – and thus how inadequately they explain – their own problem in Northern Ireland.

The Headmaster was not amongst those present, nor were several other teachers who had been in and out of the Common Room all morning without ever lingering to talk.

'There is a big gap', said Marie, 'between those who had to be Party members, like most of us at this table, and those who are now *ex*-Communists only because there is no more a Party!'

I asked how much school time had been wasted on indoctrination. 'Not much, for the last decades. It wasn't necessary to have direct brainwashing like I had at school thirty years ago. The whole curriculum had been so twisted by Communism – our own sort of nationalist Communism – that almost every lesson was indirect indoctrination. And that's so much worse! Some children can resist direct indoctrination, but the other sort is like polluted air – you take it in without knowing it's damaging you. This is why many of our best teachers left to take other jobs, even jobs that seemed less suitable. For them, not to be free to teach honestly was impossible. Others, like myself, had not courage to do that. And some of us hoped to be able – very quietly – to pass on a little real education. In the villages and small towns that was easier. City schools all had their informers. And now this is one of our biggest problems – we have few truly educated people. We have been kept in an intellectual prison, given only food without nourishment. So it is important that visitors talk with us and bring us books. This is the sort of aid we need most, even more than medicines and food.'

Marie's parents were retired university lecturers – 'with small pensions and big worries! Since the revolution so many things have *not* changed . . . I have my own small house since I was a baby – of course my mother's, but as a wife she could not keep it because my father also had a small house, so hers would be confiscated. But these places are old, always needing costly repairs. First you go to the office and pay in advance for materials – floor-boards, roof tiles, window frames, door handles. Then you wait a long time. To and fro to the office, queuing – then the office closing when you're half way up the queue. So back next day, and next week – until you're told *nothing* is available. But your money doesn't come back. You go on then to pay the black rate, and to get materials even at that big cost you must always first pay the official rate. We would be richer living in a bloc, but only money-richer. My mother would weep without her cats and my father would die without vines to make wine every year. And I would have no little garden for growing us all flowers and vegetables. So if our houses do not really fall down, we should think we are lucky people!'

Later, when we were on our own, Marie explained that she was Gheorghe's 'ex-aunt' because of infertility. Pre-revolution she had had to pay an annual 'childless' fine of 2,400 lei (her monthly salary was 3,000 lei) and had she remained married her husband would have had to pay the same fine. Soon after their divorce he remarried and now has two children.

Walking into the Centru, on my third day in Timisoara, I saw a heart-wrenching bit of new graffiti (something rare enough in Rumania) on the wall of an *alimentara*. NO FUTURE it foretold in large black letters. The site had been well chosen. Standing on the far pavement, looking through the long window of the customer-less shop, I could see exactly the same choice of dusty bottles and rusty tins as had been on offer in February. Seen in Timisoara, this legend had a peculiar poignancy; and it tersely conveyed the mood of almost everyone I had spoken to since my return.

It suddenly seemed strange – as I walked on, past the Botanical

Gardens – to see ordinary European human life going on all around: young lovers kissing on park benches, children playing with the family dog, parents worrying about examination results, young women seeking new blouses for springtime wear, OAPs discussing their aches and pains, adolescents queuing for the cinema ... Normality, apparently, prevailed. And yet, in conversation with individuals, one realised that after forty-five years of Communist repression few Rumanians are entirely 'together'.

In the Centru I bought – for fifteen pence – a real leather belt from a shop assistant who asked, 'Have you been to our Cathedral? Have you lit candles at the shrine? It is good to believe ... Here in Timisoara, before the revolution, religion was our last refuge. We had nothing else, only hope and trust in God. In October, November things got so bad we wondered had God forgotten us. But still we believed and prayed and then this revolution miracle happened. We don't know why God wanted so big a sacrifice, so many dead young. But we must not argue with God. Then it was right that the Ceausescus were killed on Christmas Day. It was symbolic. The birth of Christ who is all Good and the deaths of the Ceausescus who were all Evil!' This young woman, speaking such excellent English, was not in a more appropriate job because both her parents were semi-invalids – 'So I had to leave school quickly and earn.'

That evening I supped with Dorana in her one-room flat; she was unmarried at thirty-seven, which is unusual in Rumania. 'I'm too much of an individualist to marry,' she self-analysed – it seemed to me accurately. She would have liked to become a single mother – 'I love children very much and they love me'– but that was not possible. Her adored and 'old-fashioned' widowed father would be too devastated. 'He would die of shame, he could never be happy again with a "bad" daughter!' So instead she was planning an adoption from one of Rumania's infamous orphanages – more correctly described as 'Children's Homes'.

Dorana was equally unusual in her attitudes to Gypsies and Jews, sympathising with the former and greatly admiring the latter. Many of Rumania's three million (or so) Gypsies have long since, she told me, been 'settled'. Some cities built special blocs for them, in others the Rumanians tended to move out of an area when they moved in. It took time to overcome their 'readjustment problems' – using furniture and doors as fuel and lighting cooking fires in the middle of floors – but now most live as 'normal people' with steady jobs. However, a significant minority remain reluctant to send their children to school, calculating that they could be more gainfully employed begging, thieving and/or acquiring smuggling skills. Several Gypsies attended Dorana's primary school and one boy was rather backward. A teacher therefore asked Dorana to help him with his homework and for several years they regularly studied together. Then they lost touch – until one day a tram made an unscheduled stop in the Centru and the driver leaped out and rushed to embrace Dorana. But then he drew back – 'Maybe you don't want to remember me? Now you have a diploma and I am only a worker!' He was not long left in doubt and soon Dorana spent an evening in his apartment getting to know his wife – also a Gypsy, working in a *magazin* – and their two children.

As we ate a tender casseroled chicken, skilfully herbed, Dorana looked into the future and was gloomy. 'The system wasn't really shaken by our so-called "revolution". Why? Because in every shop, school, factory, university, hospital, office, state farm there are stupid people in power. They could get no other job if Communism was finished. They got their jobs only for one reason, not to do with talents or training. A real revolution would put them with the garbage. They would need a dole which our government couldn't afford. When a situation is like this, a country needs some moral and intellectual giant to make a revolution. Where is our giant? Maybe he is among the young . . . It is like a miracle, but we do have many strongly thinking young – especially in Timisoara. Only one thing is sure. Another revolution we must have – the real one next time, made with brains instead of blood.'

I didn't doubt Dorana's estimate of the present Party bosses and their henchmen, in all spheres. Yet during the latter half of the 1950s, the fulfilment of some of the Party's industrial ambitions fired many ordinary workers, as well as their enthusiastic and able technocratic leaders, with considerable pride. By 1962 Rumania's industrial growth rate was the fastest in Eastern Europe and her trade with the non-Communist world was also increasing rapidly. It is startling, now, to think back to that era, when Rumanian

107

defiance of the Soviet bloc had led to the country's being regarded, in Stephen Fischer-Galati's words, 'by Rumanians at home and by sympathetic observers abroad as a respectable member of the international community, as a "third force" in the international Communist movement, as the most influential small Communist nation in world affairs'.

8

A Minor Mishap in Maramures

Sitting on a platform bench in Timisoara's *gara*, awaiting my train to Satu Mare, I was shaken – not for the first time – by the violence and cruelty that in Rumania run parallel with so much spontaneous kindness and generosity. A score of teenage army conscripts, boarding the Bucharest train, were being typically giddy and giggly in the most innocent way possible. Then along came their youngish officer who behaved barbarously, punching and kicking them onto the train. They reacted like maltreated puppies, cowering and whimpering. One could easily imagine that officer in the Iron Guard, with his hard pale eyes, tight grim mouth and blatant enjoyment of the sort of debased power that confers the 'right' to bully. This was qualitatively different from our violent crime, which is recognised as such. It was licensed thuggery and, though so obvious, it seemed to attract no re-proving – or even surprised – glances from anyone else on the crowded platform.

Six hours later, Satu Mare's broken pavements would have been treacherous without a bright moon. Just occasionally, during my long walk to Agnes's house near the Centru, dim street lights briefly flickered. As Rumania is not famous for its night-life there was no one around of whom to ask directions – until I met an elderly Magyar priest, outside the Catholic cathedral, who de-clared himself to be a friend of Agnes, invited me to coffee next day and directed me to a long, wide street nearby. All the houses, I saw later, were one-storey century-old stucco villas – unpainted but very bourgeois – some detached, others 'semi' and each with its little shrub-filled yard to one side, entered off the street through six-foot iron gates that were always, significantly, kept locked.

An obese xenophobic dachshund named Isty (short for Istvan) barked shrilly to warn of my arrival and Petru picked him up before admitting me. Petru – Agnes's Rumanian husband – was tall and burly, with thick tousled grey hair and a ruddy complexion. His lack of English took nothing from the warmth of his welcome; while he kissed me Isty tried to have my nose for supper. From the doorway Agnes called, 'You should have told us which train! We could have met you – you've been lost!'

When I explained that I had spent many hours trying to telephone Satu Mare, Agnes chuckled. 'It is your mistake, coming back to this terrible country where nothing works!'

Gabor appeared, towering over his diminutive mother and holding a very small baby under one arm, much as Petru was holding Isty. 'My son,' introduced Agnes. 'He is a new father and not yet expert.' She rescued the infant while showing me into a large over-furnished living room. Lisa, the new mother, was heating a feed in the adjacent kitchen.

'My wife has no milk,' said Gabor sadly. 'For her first six months from conception we lived in Bucharest and she had never enough good food.'

'Except what we sent,' interjected Agnes, 'and though we sent what we could it was not *regular*.'

I denied being hungry, to no purpose. Superior Russian salami, sweet sheep's cheese, potato and egg salad, stale bread, home-made plum jam and a shapely china pot of Russian tea were swiftly spread before me on a white cotton tablecloth edged with heavy lace. As I ate, Lisa fed the baby and Agnes made up my bed near the gigantic stove – twice the usual size and semicircular. Then Gabor – whose English was fluent – proudly showed me a massive leather-bound album of coloured photographs of family holidays, during the 1980s, in France, Germany, Switzerland, Spain. For dessert a two-kilo box of Russian chocolates – wearing a huge nylon bow – was ceremoniously offered. And then there was a choice of finest Russian vodka, genuine Scotch whisky or double-distilled cherry *tuica* – the best *tuica* I have ever drunk.

In addition to teaching Rumanian and Russian, Petru had been for many years employed as a tourist board guide-interpreter who accompanied Soviet groups all over Rumania – a coach tour being their reward for meeting production targets. I felt vaguely uncomfortable (while recognising the reaction as absurd) on realising that these congenial people were my first discernible contact with the Ceausescu 'Establishment'. Agnes had naturally said nothing to betray their status during our long January conversations in my hotel bedroom; but here the evidence lay all around me. And now they were fervently pro-Iliescu – 'An honest, clever man!'

Hungarian was the family language, though Agnes teased Petru for still making mistakes – 'After thirty years of marriage!' (I found this wholly unsurprising.) They had met in Cluj as students. 'There were then more mixed marriages among intellectuals – lately the communities are drawing apart. Of course my parents would have better liked a Roman Catholic Magyar for my husband, or at least a *Magyar*. But Petru was a very nice young man – you can see he is still a very nice old man! So they made only a small fuss. And he has let our two children grow up religious Magyars, while we respect that Pappa is an atheist Rumanian.'

The morrow was Reunion Day, when I delivered eagerly awaited books to the several Magyars who had befriended me in my January hour of need. Eva invited us all – and half a dozen more – to a buffet lunch; she too lived in a comparatively spacious old house, on the same street. Her husband, Tamas, blunted my appetite for an excellent meal by declaiming: 'Here, like in the USSR, liberty means nationalism can talk. We have waited a long time to be able to tell the world how Magyars have suffered. Now the world must listen and force the Rumanians to treat us with justice. Now we must have compensation for our culture being degraded for seventy years.'

The Transylvanian Problem makes Northern Ireland look like a four-year-old's jigsaw puzzle. Almost every English-speaker I met, on both sides, asked my opinion of it and my responses had to be trite – though none the less sensible for that. I could only say it is time human beings stopped looking back into history and keeping ancient – and often irrelevant – grievances on life-support machines. Most of the political 'Past' is bad news for most of us: only negatively useful, as a warning notice. But the future, if constructed along the lines suggested by Mikhail Gorbachev in his book *Perestroika*, could be good news. As no one I met in Rumania had read *Perestroika* (or wanted to), this argument failed to win wild applause.

111

Next morning Gabor (my translator) and I had coffee with Father Banyasz in his roomy book-filled flat in a converted Magyar mansion. The once-splendid courtyard held a collapsed stone fountain and was overlooked by fanciful but disintegrating wrought-iron balconies; the wide outside stairways had finely carved but rotting banisters. I was vividly reminded of North Dublin's Georgian slums.

Father Banyasz was short, thin and bald, with deep-set grey eyes and a long chin. His faded blue jeans and frayed scarlet sweater looked incongruous. We were given instant German coffee and invited to sit on a long, unsteady horse-hair couch – while Father Banyasz, who lived in a state of permanent warfare with his pipe (or maybe it was the tobacco) sat in front of us on a high stool. This odd placement made me feel I was going to be preached at or lectured to – as was indeed the case. It at once became apparent that I was taken to be a zealous Irish Catholic, a misapprehension I did not correct for some time.

'You know', began Father Banyasz, 'we have here more than one million Magyar Catholics?' I confessed that I hadn't known there were so many. 'Yes – we are about one point two million, mostly in Transylvania, in the dioceses of Satu Mare, Oradea, Timisoara and Alba Iulia.' (He used the Magyar placenames but I will spare you that confusion – e.g., Gyulafehervar for Alba Iulia.) 'We have about 650 priests and 800 churches for nearly 520 parishes. And we are very proud because only the Catholics have kept their independence under Communism. Like in Poland, we stayed free, we would not compromise – *ever* – about anything. The Orthodox Rumanians and even the Magyar Reformed Church let the party have total control. The government chose their leaders, so their leaders obeyed the government. For Magyar spiritual freedom, for our liberty of conscience and independent thinking, *only* the Catholic Church has struggled – and won!'

When our host went to the kitchen across the wide hallway, to make more coffee, Gabor said, 'Everywhere it is easier for the Catholics to keep their independence, under dictatorships – with the Vatican behind them. But other Magyars were also good Christians though many of their clergy let them down, like his bishop betrayed Laszlo Tokes. There are nearly a million Calvinists and the rest little groups like Baptists and Adventists. Christianity is more serious for us than for the Rumanians, who don't even understand their own Orthodox cult very well.'

I felt a by now familiar Rumanian fog descending on my brain. Tentatively I mentioned this new source of muddlement. 'How did Magyar support for the left wing between the wars come about? And why was there such strong Magyar support for the Communist take-over when so many are Christians?'

Gabor's expression conveyed that I had committed a major *faux pas*. At that moment Father Banyasz returned and Gabor translated my query. The priest snapped at me, flushing with anger. 'That is not true! It is Rumanian propaganda! Always most Magyars fought Communism!'

Gabor backed him up. 'Yes, you have heard a lie the Rumanians spread to make us more hated – that only we and the Jews supported the Communists.'

Cravenly I said no more, though I knew it was true that there had been considerable Magyar support for Communism; one would need to be a highly qualified psychiatrist to tackle either Rumanian or Magyar historical misperceptions. Later, in Sibiu, a scholarly Saxon cleric explained that between the wars many Magyars saw the then illegal Communist Party as a valuable bulwark against the fascist anti-Magyar governing élite. And for the same reason a significant number backed the Communist take-over. Disillusion came fast and was so humiliating that by now most Magyars have discarded the facts in favour of a soothing myth.

As we walked home (my *faux pas* long since forgotten) Gabor observed, 'Father Banyasz is not a typical Magyar. In Transylvania we have been famous for centuries for our religious tolerance, long before anyone heard of an ecumenical movement! But this Father is a little bit fanatic, not all the time fair to Orthodox priests. Many of them stood out against the Communists and were killed or disappeared – *thousands*! The Government discouraged people from going to church because they knew some Orthodox clergy would always talk against them. Especially in the villages they couldn't depend on clergy support. The top clergy and most city clergy were bought over, that's true – but it is not only Communism that made it bad. Always the Orthodox leaders were ready to support any vaivode or king or general or pasha who would keep them in luxury!'

After a few days among those Satu Mare Magyars I had got a strong whiff of 'ghetto' and that word was used by Agnes on my last evening. She and I had been to visit Eniko, who was so determined to move to Hungary when we met in January, 'because of the children'. Since then she and her husband Tibor – Eva's younger brother, a corpulent man in his mid-thirties with a harsh voice and abrupt manner – had changed their minds.

Tibor said (Eniko translating), 'Why should we allow ourselves to be frightened and driven out? *Transylvania* is our homeland, not any other part of Hungary [*sic*] and like all civilised people we have an attachment to our homeland. We are not Gypsies, content to wander and have no roots.'

Eniko added, 'It is important too that we are educated. So it is bad for the Magyar nation left behind if we go. Since Trianon thousands of Magyar intellectuals have left, to enjoy their cultural freedom in Hungary.'

Later, Agnes commented to Gabor and me, 'I see it that Tibor and Eniko are afraid to leave. Here they have grown up in what is now something like a ghetto and is very comfortable for them in some ways – though difficult and maybe soon dangerous in others. In Satu Mare they are known and respected, like their families for generations. So they have that sort of security. In Hungary they would be just two more refugees from Rumania. They have friends there, people who went earlier and could help. But as more and more went, during the last few years, it became harder and harder to help newcomers and the welcomes get less. The Budapest government, talking about the problem in public, always sounds very welcoming to us. But in the real life there is not always love between us and the Hungarians. Sometimes I think they love the *land* and the *wealth* of Transylvania more than the *people*!'

Lying in bed that night, I reflected that in a totalitarian society not all the collaborators have to be 'baddies', horrible people with whom one wouldn't wish to associate. The West's crude dividing line – nasty Commies on one side, nice dissidents who think like 'us' on the other – is quickly blurred when you are in the middle of it all. Then you begin to wonder: how many 'nice' people in the democratic West don't think too closely about from where (and at whose expense) they achieve prosperity? Is Petru's toeing of the Party line, which gains goodies and privileges for his family, any more reprehensible than the toeing of the Stock Market line by a capitalist also keen to benefit his family? That led me to speculate about the Agnes–Petru marriage. It seemed tension-free, blessed by much mutual affection and consideration. Yet the husband was an irreligious Party man, the wife a devout Roman Catholic. Ethically and ethnically they should have been oil and water, but plainly neither had any inhibitions about 'compromising'. I transposed their relationship to Northern Ireland and there it didn't work. No such flexibility would be possible: emigration to a 'plural society' would be essential. So was Transylvania more civilised – or merely more wily and less genuine in its commitments? At which awkward point I drifted into sleep, thinking as I went '– Maybe it's something to do with the Balkans . . .'

At breakfast next morning Petru looked embarrassed; he had not enough petrol to drive me to Baia Mare – please, would I stay another day? A tankful had been promised by that evening. No one understood my recoiling from the very idea of their squandering precious petrol on my transport. I was their *guest*, their foreign *friend* – I was carrying heavy books – transporting me would be their duty and *pleasure*. To placate them, I agreed that Petru should drive me to the obvious hitching-spot at the edge of the city. On the way, Agnes mentioned the importance of having family cars in action again, even if they couldn't get very far. 'For all of us, it is a symptom of recovered personal freedom. We had earned and saved to buy our cars, then we couldn't use them – which made us feel like serfs. It was *very* enraging!'

There was considerably more traffic than on this same road in January. Soon I was picked up by what would elsewhere be described as a bush-taxi. The small jeep, driven by a Gypsy, had long since lost all its doors and exhaled life-threatening fumes from unlikely apertures. Huddled in the back, among a selection of timid, smelly, dejected-looking peasants, I covered fifty miles for the equivalent of eight pence. No one else was travelling far and we stopped often, usually where narrow tracks met the road. At each stop the trussed sheep on the passenger seat bleated piteously, hoping for release.

115

After another reunion-cum-book-delivery day, I stayed the night with Justinian and his mother and baby son; his wife, a teacher, was doing her compulsory stint in a village near the Bulgarian border.

Mother, from Moldavia, felt personally and obsessionally embittered about 'half *my* country' having been given to the USSR by Churchill. Justinian observed that Rumania has always been treated as though not inhabited by humans – as mere *territory*, the pawn of various empires. Which is terribly true ... Mother could find food for her obsession in *1945: Year Zero* by the Hungarian-American historian John Lukacs: 'Not to bother about Bulgaria or Rumania when, in exchange, one could get a free hand in Greece was Churchill's old way of doing business.'

Throughout supper Justinian waxed very anti-imperialist, while all the time implying that the cultural and economic development of Rumania's various regions had depended on the quality of the conquerors. And, despite being virulently anti-British in relation to Rumania, he saw the British Empire as 'civilising' in relation to 'primitive coloured people'.

Next morning, as I climbed towards the Gutii Pass, crowded cars suddenly began to overtake me at regular intervals; evidently a local petrol station had just received its quota. Sometimes cars had to queue for thirty-six hours or more, relatives and friends taking it in turns to guard the vehicle. The longest queue I ever saw stretched for almost five miles (seven kilometres) on the outskirts of Cluj. But that was in summer, before an extended holiday weekend – a post-revolutionary novelty that tempted everyone to escape into the countryside.

I had walked about twelve miles when, without warning, a blizzard struck. Dolefully I plodded on; where magnificent views should have rewarded my exertions, visibility was down to fifty yards. Eventually I thumbed a beer-truck. The young Moldavian driver offered me a lift to Suceava, many miles away, and looked disappointed on hearing that my destination was the capital of Maramures, Sighetu Marmatiei (Sighet for short), only twenty-five miles ahead. He opened a bottle of beer for me but didn't have one himself; most Rumanians obey the law forbidding drivers to drink *any* alcohol.

On the 3,300-foot Gutii Pass several vehicles were parked outside a grotty chalet-type 'motel'. In the large gloomy café – without tables or chairs – people stood around devouring whole chickens like there was no tomorrow. Otherwise only 'cognac' and real coffee were being served. The availability of coffee was the most dramatic sustenance development since January and Bogdan, the driver, ordered three cups simultaneously but disdained the chicken when I offered him 'lunch'.

We emerged to find the sky blue and the noon world dazzling. To the north sharply peaked hills and long rough ridges overlooked narrow valleys – all brilliantly sparkling and beckoning. But when I eagerly made to take my rucksack from the cab Bogdan registered extreme alarm – it would be dangerous and foolish to walk, more blizzards were on the way. He laid a restraining hand on my arm, looking touchingly worried. I hesitated, then reminded myself that in such situations one should always heed local advice.

The next half-hour was unnerving as we very slowly descended, without chains, on a narrow road two feet deep in new snow. Then came a wide, fertile, densely-populated valley where pale grey tin roofs have replaced the characteristic Maramures shingles on many churches, houses and barns. These however are not the crudely applied corrugated sheets common throughout the Third World. Here tin is used with considerable artistry, in carefully shaped panels, and much work has gone into creating replicas of the traditional carved eaves.

Suddenly, in mid-valley, Bogdan's prophecy was fulfilled by a dramatic meteorological phenomenon. The sun was still shining when a mass of silver-grey cloud poured over a mountain wall to the north-west. At ground level and hurricane speed, it swept towards us across the flat fields like some fabulous gigantic live creature, writhing as it raced. We were still in sunshine when it hit the road some hundred yards ahead, ripping branches off the wayside trees as though they were twigs. Moments later the windscreen was obliterated and it seemed the high truck might keel over, despite its heavy load. Before stopping, we rescued a little girl going home alone from school and sobbing in terror. Within ten minutes the hurricane became a mere gale, driving sleet almost horizontally. When Bogdan got out to clear the windscreen a figure appeared, far away, wavering in the mighty gusts and wailing like a banshee. It was the little girl's mother, certain that she had lost her ewe-lamb. A mile further on we dropped them off at their isolated roadside shack.

On the 'systematised' outskirts of Sighet I descended into ankle-deep yellow mud. All around cranes gangled beside half-built blocs. The rain had just stopped but the wind was icy and water gushed everywhere – including down my neck, off gutter-less roofs, as I walked towards the storm-emptied, branch-strewn Piata Libertatii. Happily Sighet's dignified old Centru has escaped modernisation, apart from a crude concrete fountain (non-functioning) in front of the Tisa Hotel.

That agreeable three-storey Austro-Hungarian legacy offered remnants of gracious living for £3.75 a night. My high-ceilinged room had faded rose-and-silver embossed wallpaper, a tall, arched french window, leading onto a wide wrought-iron balcony, and a dehydrated *en suite* bathroom. Unfortunately the warped window wouldn't quite close, the antique radiator didn't work, and by 8.15 my hands were too numb to write. Then, just as I had thawed in my flea-bag, and was drifting towards sleep, the maze of archaic bathroom pipes began to shudder and growl and hiss. Moments later cold water came gushing in noisy spasms from all four taps, which could not be fully turned off. When I pulled the lavatory chain – its ivory handle was delicately carved – the cistern made a noise like a large animal in pain. Nothing else happened. Grumpily I dressed and went downstairs in search of plumbing advice.

The shadowy foyer was occupied only by a ragged drunk with a week's beard who lay snoring on a leather couch with a pile of vomit beside him. Maria, the young woman at Reception, was having a major row on the telephone. Tall and much too thin, she had long straight black hair drawn tightly back from a pale oval face. While yelling abuse into the receiver, she gestured elo-quently with her free hand as though the enemy were present. Clearly she was in no mood to consider plumbing problems.

The rest of the staff were standing on ladders in the huge restaurant, decorating it with jolly bunting. At 11 p.m. a World Women's Day party – postponed to this Saturday evening – would start and continue until dawn. My foredoomed attempt to complain about defective taps in sign language caused much hilarity; two waitresses fell off their ladders and rolled giggling around the floor – perhaps they had already begun to celebrate World Women's Day. Defeated, I returned to my noisy taps – and found them silent.

Three hours later, Maria roused me from a deep sleep. The party had begun, the Irishwoman was invited – *begged* – to attend. Feeling churlish, I explained 'At night I like only to sleep.'

Maria smiled grimly and moved to the door. 'Tonight you won't sleep,' she foretold threateningly – and she was right.

My room happened to be immediately above the jollifications and for hours I was tantalised by trying to recall in which compositions Dvořák, Kodály or Béla Bartók had used popular local themes. Here too I met my only Rumanian fleas, who for a week kept me shamelessly scratching – a common activity, I noted, in Sighet.

Sighet's end-of-the-road atmosphere caused me at once to fall in love with the place. My journal records:

Sunday   After an all-night party, it would have been callous to demand breakfast. At 8 a.m. the hotel was silent, the restaurant a shambles, the air noisome with stale cigarette smoke. On the foyer couch two waitresses wearing balaclavas lay asleep under a pile of sheepskins.

The Centru was deserted, the sky low and grey, the wind icy. Soon deep-toned church bells began to chime, sounding curiously assertive in the empty Piata. Three churches were visible: Orthodox, Calvinist and Roman Catholic – from whence the bells. Here the Soviet border is only half a mile away, with no crossing-point, and despite modern transport nowhere else *feels* near. Having failed to find an open café, I rambled around the old residential area – long straight nineteenth-century streets of solid one-storey Magyar houses, some newly painted in contrasting pastel shades, some with pairs of gaudy plaster gnomes grinning in porches, or comic wooden masks (locally carved) hanging beside hall doors. This is a pleasingly rural town. Cocks crow far and near, hens wander on pavements, turkeys gobble in little front gardens, invisible pigs grunt in sheds.

Later I joined the Mass-going Magyar bourgeoisie, all
wearing their dull respectable Sunday best with expressions
to match. For late-comers there was standing room only in
the large unremarkable church. A superb children's choir,
accompanied by a teenage boy guitarist, made that a memorable Mass. In contrast, very few (mostly elderly peasants in
village attire) attended the Orthodox service in a new church
– traditional design, modern materials, not quite finished.
Opposite, the enormous bleak Calvinist church is semi-
derelict with broken windows. That joyless service drew only
a few dozen; I slunk out after ten minutes – attracting some
reproachful or angry glances.

Brunch happened at 11.30: two fried eggs, four thick slices
of well-flavoured bacon, a dish of shredded pickled cabbage,
six slices of bread (slightly improved since January) and
strong Russian tea with *lemon* – a staggering innovation!

I spent the afternoon in a cold, dirty, uncomfortable
peasants' café – part of the hotel but crowded with wild-
looking types (male and female) who eschew the rather
elegant and for them expensive restaurant. One can enter
this café only from the street; the connecting door to the
hotel foyer is kept locked. No booze was available, after the
all-night party. Behind me in the long, slow coffee queue
stood a handsome shepherd – tall and courtly, with weather-
beaten but fine features, wavy grey hair, deep blue eyes. His
woollen knee-length jacket and tight pantaloons were homespun, his cowhide boots handmade – by himself. At a nearby
table sat his round-shouldered, anaemic-looking son, on sick
leave from Cluj University. He is suffering from asthma and
a stomach ulcer and arrangements are being made for him
soon to have medical treatment in Vienna. (Shepherds are
among Rumania's richest citizens; they were never collectivised.) As we savoured our Turkish coffee, father condemned the Front for maintaining the embargo on hunting
big game. Ceausescu allowed no one else to hunt bears,
wolves, deer or wild pig *anywhere* in Rumania, a manifesta-
tion of megalomania that appeals to me but was totally
impractical. Immense damage is now being done to crops by
bears, deer and wild pig. And to flocks by wolves, who are

also becoming increasingly dangerous to humans, because small game may be shot or trapped – so while the unmolested wolf population expands, its food supply dwindles. Farmers and shepherds sent several mass petitions to Ceausescu, pleading to be allowed to cull big game, but never got any reply. I asked why, in remote areas, they didn't simply ignore the law – a stupid question. Everywhere the Securitate were feared; nobody could trust *all* their neighbours not to betray them. The black joke is that Ceausescu rarely shot even a rabbit – he just longed to project a macho image of himself as The Great Hunter. His last recorded bear-hunt was with his close friend, the Shah of Iran. How odd that his final days were spent with another close friend – called Rafsanjani! He must have been an adaptable chap. I'm invited to stay in the shepherd's small hamlet, somewhere in the mountains between here and Salva; his son wrote detailed directions on the back of my notebook and warned me to beware of wolves – not sure if he was joking . . .

Monday   Today a cloudless sky, warm sun, cold breeze. Went to explore hamlets on high roadless hills west of Sighet; the steep tracks mucky, as first spring heat melts packed snow and iced mud. Photographed the most attractive of the all-wood houses, and the artistically built hay-ricks under their shingle roofs, and the long line of snowy USSR mountains in the near distance. Then was physically attacked by a youngish farmer who darted out from behind his hay-rick, twisted my left arm and tried to grab the camera. Naturally I was bewildered, the more so because *he* was appalled to discover my foreignness. Looking stricken, he apologised with tears in his eyes and invited me into his cosy wooden house for *tuica*. He and his wife (fair-haired and blue-eyed, with rotting teeth) tried frantically to explain the misunderstanding but left me baffled. We parted the best of friends, wife hugging me and stroking my hair and presenting me with an embroidered tablecloth. Later the mystery was solved by Mircea, my teacher friend. I had been mistaken for a 'spy' from a political party which advocates an immediate division of local collective farmland, giving equal shares to all. Sounds fine – but before collectivisation there were Big Farmers and Little Farmers and the descendants of the former don't accept being put on an equal footing with the descendants of the latter. So they passionately oppose the plan and are suspicious of, and quite often violently antagonistic to, un-announced strangers who come to report on the lie of the land – literally! Since this isn't a tourist area, my camera at once marked me as a 'political spy'. The implications for the future of democracy are grim – if you deal with political opponents by assaulting them on sight . . .

Needed a drink when I got back to Sighet at 3 p.m. Only Murfatlar 'vermut' available; took a bottle to my room where I was due to meet Mircea. Not being used to vermouth (if such it really is) I tossed it back like wine and was quite tiddly when Mircea arrived. Wavered down to restaurant to sober up on tender stewed pork, tinned runner beans, spaghetti, yet another bowl of pickled cabbage and lots of bread. This pickled cabbage, Maria says, will be served to everyone with every meal till hotel's quota used up – to be replaced by pickled cucumber or apples. Only under the influence of Ceausescu would anybody think of pickling small sour whole apples: the result is nauseating beyond any possibility of description.

Alas! my left shoulder has been dislocated again: something easily done since it first happened when I fell off a path in the Andes. That farmer really did have a hate for 'political spies'. Mircea has relocated it – a simple matter – but it will no doubt take a few days to settle down.

Mircea believes the Front is 'very good for Rumania' but says they are making one big mistake, being too soft on the Securitate and leaving most of them free to cause more trouble in the future. He'd like to see them under strict army control, forced to work unpaid 7 a.m. to 7 p.m., then confined to their homes all evening. He reckons they're so rich, having been paid in dollars, they can afford to sit around drinking all day, eavesdropping on everybody's uninhibited political conversations – which they may yet use, if restored to power. I argued that if the Front is genuine about establishing democracy they can't submit all Securitate

122

officers to hard labour and a curfew under army control. Unless formally charged and tried, they cannot be punished. Mircea couldn't see that, though he claimed to be 'a real democrat'!

But for the revolution, Mircea was sure many Rumanians would have died of hunger next winter. He has a son (five) and daughter (two) and one morning last November he could find *no* food for them; children, however hungry, won't eat pickled cabbage, cucumbers, apples etc. As a comparative newcomer to the town, he lacks 'contacts'. Some black market meat, milk, eggs, were always available but not affordable on 2,800 lei a month. That particular November morning, he spent half a month's salary on enough food for *two* days.

Tuesday For breakfast a giant omelette and six slices of yesterday's stewed pork reheated in a frying-pan: potentially lethal but very tasty. Another day of low grey skies but much milder and no rain. Explored three big roadside villages on the left bank of the Tisa, which here is the frontier – an unimpressive river, meandering between straggling alders. To celebrate being in Free Rumania I photographed several watch-towers: most now empty. From the one occupied, two conscripts waved cheerfully – then posed with their rifles pointing towards the USSR. After all, Rumania *has* had a revolution, however partial or unsatisfactory. As elsewhere, most of the local garrison work on collectives; two downy-cheeked conscripts, driving a primitive wagon, obligingly reined in their horses to be photographed. Last evening, in the hotel restaurant, a young career officer shared my table and was fretting because the Front shows no inclination to treat the army seriously, rather than as an endless source of slave labour.

In one village I came upon a land-reform quarrel – enraged men and women shouting abuse, with much stamping of feet and waving of fists. The positioning of the groups – a dozen or so in each, on either side of the wide road – seemed curiously ritualistic, but eventually several women had to restrain their menfolk from taking the matter a stage further. When I addressed a youth in English – deliberately loudly – the quarrelling at once stopped and a beaming neutral woman led me by the hand into her spacious farmhouse. Elaborately carved wooden tankards hung from the ceiling; embroidered cushions brightened every corner; hard-boiled eggs and *tuica* were lavished on me. Quickly the room filled with excited protagonists from both sides, their animosity in abeyance. No one spoke English but some communication was possible with the aid of my mini-dictionaries.

Even by Rumanian standards, Maramures hospitality is extraordinary. In Sighet total strangers (usually an impoverished-looking peasant) often insist on paying for my meals, coffees, drinks – and will never allow me to stand the next round. I must be their guest because Ireland sent so much 'gift meat' to Rumania within days of the revolution.

Wednesday   By noon the sun was warm and the Centru thronged, mostly with peasants each carrying two huge striped woollen sacks over one shoulder – fore and aft, in imitation of pack-animals. Why have they not invented some less masochistic method for transporting heavy loads? Sighet really is a marvellously vivacious town: one wonders what it was like pre-revolution. This light-heartedness can't be all new – perhaps remoteness to some extent insulated it from the Ceausescu depression? Significantly, the locals don't all the time talk politics. Also they look less starved than most of their compatriots. Yet even here too many young faces seem old and most primary school children (I've studied them *en masse*) have black bags under their eyes. Hungry children don't sleep well. The problem of protein-deficiency brain damage is never mentioned in Rumania, though inevitably it will affect some of the generation born around 1984. Probably most parents are mercifully unaware of that risk.

Urban Rumania encourages escapism; at least half of Sighet's 40,000 inhabitants live in new Ceausescu-land but I've confined myself to the quietly imposing, once-prosperous old Sighet. Much of its prosperity was based on smuggling, in a fairly decorous way, to and from Ruthenia –

then Czechoslovakia's eastern province. Always there's an odd feel about places so visibly/architecturally at odds with their present dominant population. Maramures peasants now dominate – they and the Rumanians from elsewhere who've been settled in Ceausescu-land. Very much in the background are the Magyar descendants of the founders and builders of Sighet. No wonder they look – most of them – defensive and dour.

Sighet's Ethnographic Museum has an international reputation – in certain circles – but during most of the year is opened only on request. The town's Culture Officer was rumoured to hold the key and I not unreasonably expected to find him in the House of Culture – a bizarre 1911 hybrid, part Victorian gaol, part Loire château. Originally a Magyar theatre, it has long since been overtaken by silent, sad, damp-smelling dereliction. A white marble stairway, cracked and muddy, sweeps up to a circular gallery where the corpse of a grand piano – legs in the air – lay on a mound of rubble. Off this gallery, down high narrow creaking corridors, little girls were typing in little offices. My arrival caused them to crane incredulously over the tops of cumbersome (1911?) machines and then titter nervously. None made any attempt to communicate in any language.

At last I found two older, sour-faced women; they shared a small desk, surrounded by tall filing cabinets, and were barely discernible through a haze of cigarette smoke. The Culture Officer did not in fact operate from the House of Culture but they – somewhat reluctantly – telephoned him. It took seventeen minutes to get through, though his office was less than a mile away, which could explain their reluctance. A slim, blue-eyed teenage girl, tongue-tied with shyness, was then summoned to guide me to the Museum.

Dumitru – small and dark, with longish hair and a drooping moustache – spoke fluent English. Alas! the keys to the display rooms were at his home, far away in a bloc. But he would be happy to show me round next day – meanwhile would I drink coffee with him?

Over our first cup, Dumitru began to unburden himself. His engineer wife was on sick leave, suffering from a serious sight impairment, and they were saving up to go to either Hungary or Russia in search of 'special spectacles'. But how long would it take to save so much on their joint monthly income of 7,600 lei? *And* with two children to feed . . .

Over our second cup, Dumitru revealed that until 1985 he had taught in Timisoara. But at the age of thirty-two he felt compelled to quit a profession that made him feel 'false'. Given his qualifications, the only alternative job on offer was in Sighet, where his wife was 'all the time lonely and restless'.

Over our third cup, Dumitru observed that Rumanians are now suffering from collective guilt, asking themselves why they didn't get rid of the Ceausescus ten years ago but unable to find any morale-boosting answer. 'It is important for foreigners to understand this because our mental state now is making it harder for us to behave the way the Occident thinks we should. You must be patient while we recover our self-respect. Soon after the revolution, the Front began to expose the true nature of the Ceausescu regime in detail, scandal after scandal being shown and discussed on TV. All these proven scandals traumatised us – this wasn't only rumour. For years we'd known things were going dreadfully wrong but Ceausescu's propaganda made us so confused we couldn't understand how or why the country was becoming like hell. So those programmes made us feel like fools. We hadn't believed the propaganda, but also we hadn't been clever enough to see the truth. We only went on and on, suffering more and more, like people mesmerised, till those brave revolutionaries in Timisoara inspired Bucharest to kill the Ceausescus. And now we're ashamed of having been so weak for so long. Especially my generation, whose children were damaged.'

I was relieved, next morning, to find Dumitru in a more cheerful mood – almost a mood of elation, so dearly did he love his museum and so rarely did he have anyone with whom to share it. The main exhibits are Maramures wood-carvings – every conceivable household object and agricultural implement, from salt spoons to ploughs. Most beautiful of all were the ten-foot-high farmyard roofed gateways, the traditional peasant status symbols: the bigger and more elaborately carved a gateway, the more impressed were the neighbours. As my enthusiasm for wood-carving equals Dumitru's, we had a blissful morning. But it

126

ended on a mournful note. 'Soon,' said Dumitru, 'the status symbols will be tractors.' It would have been unrealistic to dispute that point.

One evening I asked Mircea about the strong metal mesh that defends many Sighet shop windows. He explained it as a relic of pre-war days, when most of the town's richest merchants were Jews, living aloof from the rest of the community and mistrustful of everyone. 'In 1944,' he added, 'the Hungarian police took them all away, to help the Germans. During that war the Hungarians ruled northern Transylvania again, including Maramures. Hitler gave it to them, to make them help Germany. Then we got it back when Germany was beaten.'

Deviously I asked, 'So what happened to Sighet's Jews in 1944?'

'They never came back. Rumanians got their shops, which was good.'

'*Why* didn't they come back?'

'I think the Germans killed them,' said Mircea. 'Hitler didn't like Jews – they had too many in Germany, taking all their money.'

Later I asked Dumitru if Sighet's Jews had had any reason to be mistrustful of their neighbours.

'Of course not,' he replied, 'but they were very nervous people. You see how friendly Rumanians are, you have told me how many good friends you are making. But the Jews were afraid of everybody else.'

To question people about their local Jews is not tactless, Rumania's history of anti-Semitism having long since been 're-vised'. On my next visit to Bucharest a forty-year-old historian gave me the official version: 'During the first half of the nineteenth century, Moldavia and Wallachia were dominated by the Ottomans and then by Czarist Russia, which for a little time was supposed to be protecting the Rumanian Christians from the Turks. Then many Jews moved in, from Poland and Russia, and took over local trade, squeezing out our hucksters and pedlars because Jews always had more capital. And they invested every-thing in commerce – at first they weren't allowed to buy land. Then in 1859 the nation of Rumania was founded and one of the conditions of international recognition was giving Jews equal rights – which was no problem. But soon many Jews became

127

stewards for boyars who preferred city life – people who wanted only profits, not to trouble looking after their land and people. Most stewards were as greedy and cruel as the Phanariots. So the peasants and small merchants resented Jews more and more, because of their behaviour. Quickly they became more numerous and powerful and richer. By 1918 they were between one-third and half the population of Iasi and not popular in the city – or anywhere in Moldavia. In the 1920s many Iasi students marched against Jews and broke Jewish shop windows – but this was nothing serious. Then an important professor founded the League of National Christian Defence and Jewish students were kept out of the university, not by law or by force but only by intimidation. One of the League's student leaders, Corneliu Codreanu, soon after founded the Legion of Archangel St Michael – the Iron Guard – which became very influential and was later used by the Nazis.'

My tutor was misleading me – though not deliberately, I am certain. He was simply passing on the 'revision' which his genera-tion has been unable to check for itself. The ferocity of the Iron Guards' 1920s anti-Semitic campaign – vigorously supported by the Moldavian peasants, in particular, once Codreanu had roused their blood-lust – was not mentioned. Nor was the anti-Semitic legislation passed by the Bucharest government in 1937. The impression was given that only as a result of Nazi pressure did the Iron Guard become Jew-killers – assisted by simple people too easily persuaded to focus all the angry frustration of immemorial-ly oppressed peasants on Europe's traditional scapegoats. History revision is alarmingly easy in 'an intellectual prison'. I was often assured that Marshal Antonescu had done everything possible to protect Rumania's Jews during the war – including putting them on trains which were sent chugging round and round Rumania in circles, to deceive the Nazis into thinking their passengers had been sent to concentration camps. Although my informants were intelligent people, they resented this story's authenticity being questioned.

By the end of that week, it was clear that my Maramures trek must again be postponed. Although the weather had settled, my shoulder had not; it couldn't yet bear a rucksack. On an in-

furiatingly perfect early spring morning, I took the 7.20 train to
Salva, *en route* for Cluj.

Walking to the *gara*, with the rucksack over my right shoulder, I
passed the local offices of various new political parties, including
the Front – buildings to which I had repeatedly failed to gain
access. It seemed characteristic of Sighet that they were always
locked and no one knew how to contact the parties' representatives. Then I noticed an angry-looking young man with long
brown hair photographing the widely scattered contents of three
outsize overturned dustbins. He spoke only Rumanian, but his
message was simple enough to be easily understood. As a member
of the local Front Committee, he objected to Sighet's dustmen
feeling free, post-revolution, to neglect their duty. If they didn't
get off their arses (his tone suggested that sort of phraseology), he
would send his photographs to the Front Headquarters in
Bucharest. So Sighet does have its political activists; I wished we
had met sooner.

The long but almost empty Sighet–Salva train was a marvel.
There seemed to be no technological reason why such a specimen
of nonagenarian machinery should have retained the power to
move, even at ten m.p.h. At frequent intervals it paused for
breath, as nonagenarians will, allowing me ample time to appreciate the landscape.

For an hour or so we dawdled along the frontier; the few Soviet
hamlets of timber shacks on the far bank of the Tisa looked much
less prosperous than their Rumanian neighbours. Then, turning
south, we crossed several awesome gorges. There was no new
growth: the thaw had just begun. Sheep were still crowded in
round or square pens, skilfully constructed of woven strips of
wood, eating hay from carved hollowed-out tree trunks. As we
descended, the first lambs appeared; and two water-buffaloes,
pulling a cart, induced nostalgia for India. Their ancestors
presumably accompanied the original Gypsy migrants.

At Salva Junction I was reunited with my old friend, the
Iasi–Timisoara 'express'. It did now seem express-like; the fifty-
mile journey from Sighet had taken five and a half hours.

9

Klausenburg/Kolozsvar/Cluj-Napoca: Transylvania's Capital

I was lucky to find the Vladeasa, Cluj's oldest hotel, long since demoted to a peasants' and Gypsies' hostelry. Only by chance did I notice an inconspicuous plaque by an old arched entrance two minutes' walk from Liberty Square. Beyond the high wooden double door a vaulted passageway – wide enough for a horse and carriage – led to a quiet shrub-filled courtyard from which a curving stairway gave access to unsteady timber galleries. Off these were many small but comfortable bedrooms, each with a moody washbasin. Every evening savoury smells came from the Gypsies' rooms, as suppers were cooked on home-made charcoal stoves.

It seemed tourists were then unknown in the Vladeasa; the tense young woman at Reception developed a nervous tic on seeing my passport. Anxiously she consulted a bearded ancient with only one visible tooth and a bad limp. He scrutinised my visa as though it were a suspect currency note, then nodded at the young woman and limped away, ignoring me. My last leu went on the hotel bill – £1.10 for bed minus breakfast – so I at once hastened out to change dollars.

Much of old Cluj is 'neo-' but seems none the worse for that. Irrelevant yet attractive flourishes of neo-Gothic and neo-Romanesque enliven many Centru buildings and in Victory Square a neo-Byzantine (1930s) Orthodox cathedral faces a superb neo-Baroque (Helmer and Fellner) opera house. All around Liberty Square skittish spires and jolly cupolas overlook the mellow red-tiled roofs of stately three- or four-storeyed ex-Magyar mansions. The florid-elegant Continental Hotel at one corner is tentatively neo-Renaissance and in the midst of all this neo-ness stands St Michael's genuinely Gothic Roman Catholic church – outwardly unexciting and not enhanced by a nineteenth-century north tower.

Frequently, when the traveller wants to change money, nobody else does – or can. Late in the afternoon I turned reluctantly towards the Transylvania Tourist Hotel, where dollars could certainly be sold. This domineering tumour on Cetatuia Hill can be seen from almost everywhere in Cluj and seems perfectly to symbolise forty-five years of Communist bullying. Hundreds of broken concrete steps ascend the steep slope – partially wooded, densely littered – and noisome fumes from the hotel garbage, slowly smouldering nearby, become increasingly apparent. Half-way up there is a visual assault, the sort of mindless, soulless 'decoration' (always concrete) for which I was fast developing a pathological hatred. Four Soviet coaches were parked outside the entrance. In one of them, Rumanian-made lavatory bowls occupied every seat – each labelled with its new owner's name.

The enormous foyer's violently-hued carpet was strewn with cigarette ends and soiled paper napkins. The staff looked predatory and sullen. The dollar-shop shelves were almost bare – evidence of the extra dollars in circulation post-revolution – and half-empty showcases loomed everywhere, displaying scandalously over-priced folk art. Shallow steps led down to a smoke-hazy coffee-bar the size of a football pitch; it was crowded with raucous Russian coach-tourists, swigging vodka from their own bottles, and with the Securitate-linked layer of local society. The décor was a frenzy of coloured glass, contorted metal, glossy varnished wood. Stalinist architects and interior decorators, intent on being 'posh' for the benefit of hard-currency tourists, attained a degree of ugliness far surpassing even the worst of their utilitarian constructions.

I had to share my low table – two seats on each side – with an unpleasant pair. The wheezy elderly man opposite me wore a fox-fur jacket and sat with his multi-ringed hands clasping a gross pot belly. His younger swarthy companion – sitting beside me – had compressed lips and blood-shot eyes and carried an expensive camera. Both feigned to ignore me and as friendship seemed unlikely to burgeon I applied myself to note-taking – in between trying to catch and hold the waitress's attention. Here was no over-manning and that solitary, sweating young woman had a forgivably anti-human glint in her eye.

Ten minutes later Swarthy turned abruptly and asked, 'What is your purpose in Rumania? For how long do you stay in our country?'

Blandly I replied, 'I'm writing a travel book so I'll stay several months.'

Pot-belly leant forward to peer at my journal (that was an effort) and said accusingly, 'You are writing in shorthand! Do you understand Rumanian?'

'I am not writing in shorthand,' I snapped. 'And I don't understand Rumanian.'

Swarthy demanded, 'What is this kind of book, a *travel* book?'

'It describes experiences in foreign countries.'

Pot-belly scowled. 'Why do you describe Rumania? Why do you have money for this? Who pays you?'

'No one, yet,' I said. 'But when the book is published the people who buy it pay.'

Both looked angrily disbelieving and Pot-belly almost shouted: 'That is *not* possible – you say now, what government gave you money to write about us? Who is wanting to know what you see in Rumania?'

At last my coffee came. I gulped it and said, 'In the Occident writers work alone – never for governments, always for themselves.'

Suddenly Swarthy looked at his watch and bellowed for the waitress who at once came running. His wallet was stuffed: dollars on one side, lei on the other. But, unlike the impoverished Sighet folk, he did not offer to pay for my coffee.

Some ten minutes later the waitress suggested a meeting in the *toalet*. There we did our deal and she confirmed my suspicion. Those nasties were indeed 'retired' Securitate officers, the only ones I am aware of having spoken to – though the waitress herself, like most tourist hotel staff, was almost certainly a professional informer.

On the summit of Cetatuia Hill I sat on a grassy slope, with my back to the hotel, and gazed over Cluj. To the Dacians and Romans it was Napoca, to the Saxons who founded the modern city Klausenburg, to the Magyars Kolozsvar. In 1974 Ceausescu decreed that it be known henceforth as Cluj-Napoca, to remind everyone that the Rumanians' forefathers had been settled here a thousand years before the Magyars' forefathers moved west from who-knows-where.

Frenetic industrialisation has transformed Cluj since 1970 and from Cetatuia Hill its ancient Centru seems a compact oasis of faded beauty, surrounded by mile after monotonous mile of Ceausescu-land. According to rumour, local Magyar and Rumanian Party officials united to defend the Centru from 'systematisation'. I would like to believe that rumour. And perhaps shared loyalty to an historic city did indeed overcome inbred hostilities, despite the very different images of Kolozsvar/Cluj held by the two communities. To the Magyars (still about two-fifths of the population) Kolozsvar is their beloved capital, symbolising a millennia of achievement, in which for the past three humiliating decades they have been made to feel like second-class citizens. Even the present student generation think back compulsively to the days when Kolozsvar was famed for its opera and theatre, its urbane genial café society, its vigorous literary life, its illustrious university. In painful and dangerous contrast, the Rumanians think of Cluj as the city from which their ancestors were for centuries physically excluded as mere serfs, despised 'Vlachs' – a term of contempt equivalent to 'nigger' and still, tragically, in use. Among the Magyars, old attitudes die very hard.

Among the friends I was to make in Cluj were two Magyar university students, both charming young women – intelligent, witty, well-read, outgoing. When we discussed Northern Ireland I mentioned Corrymeela, where groups from both sides, including some 'extremists', regularly meet to consider each other's point of view. Tentatively I suggested that similar meetings might be useful to counteract the fast-rising tension in post-revolution Transylvania. My companions stared at me, in astounded silence. Then together they exclaimed, 'But the Rumanians have *no* point of view!' That was a chilling moment. Even Northern Ireland's Paisleyites do implicitly acknowledge their opponents' point of view, much as they may detest and revile it. Here was a loud echo of Koloman Tisza's retort when it was suggested, in the 1870s, that non-Magyar schoolchildren should be taught their national history. 'Non-Magyars have *no* national history,' declared Tisza.

This leader of Hungary's pseudo-Liberal Party – soon to be premier for fifteen years – was already infamous for having pronounced, 'There is no Slovak nation'. Rumanians were not the only victims of the Magyars' psychopathic arrogance.

Given the city's history, it is not surprising that modern Cluj seems at one level a melancholy place – visibly a *Magyar* creation that has recently been made predominantly Rumanian through the crudest form of social engineering. Inevitably there is an undercurrent of unease, a taste of tears. Ten years after unification, Walter Starkie naïvely wrote: 'Here are Hungarians, Rumanians, Saxons, Szekels, Jews and Gypsies, all of them conscious of their own individual qualities but living at peace with one another. The atmosphere of the city is calm and serene . . . The Rumanians of Cluj are as tolerant in their manner as they are in their laws and it is impossible not to be charmed by them.' He foresaw a happy future for Cluj. But there was too much agonised resentment on the Magyar side, and too much understandable insecurity and regrettable vengefulness on the Rumanian side, for the atmosphere long to remain 'calm and serene'.

At another level, however, I found Cluj more vibrant and enthusiastic than most Rumanian cities. To Walter Starkie it seemed 'the Oxford of the East of Europe, with its students and its traditional buildings'. Now the enormous student population, including many foreigners, gives the Centru a curiously familiar flavour: the flavour found in Salamanca, Berkeley, Oxford, Benares, Galway or wherever else the intellectually effervescent young are numerous enough to dominate.

Back in Liberty Square – crowded now, as the cupolas and spires caught the last of the sunlight – I at once smelt politics. Outside the vast University Bookshop, tense-looking students and intellectuals were eagerly reading or vehemently debating the full text of the 4,000-word Timisoara Proclamation, newly posted on a long display board beside revolution-related press-cuttings and photographs from abroad.

Ioan and Bogdan, two twenty-year-olds, volunteered to translate the Proclamation's most important points. Then we were joined by Toni, one of their philology lecturers, and withdrew to the dreary restaurant of the Central Hotel – diametrically across the Square from the Continental – where all the food had run out and there was nothing to drink but an anonymous 'fruit juice'. Both students were 'high' on the Proclamation, describing it as the first coherent plan for Rumania's future. After ridding the Front of Communists, they saw as the next most crucial need a truly independent television station prepared not only to report events objectively but to undertake the political education of the populace. The Front, they asserted, was now manipulating the media, both nationally and internationally (especially national television), much more subtly and effectively than Ceausescu had ever done. The previous Sunday's formidable 'Proclamation Demo', proving the strength of anti-Front feeling in Timisoara, had been all week cleverly misrepresented on television as a demand for Banat autonomy, led by subversive agitators in the pay of 'foreign fascists'. (Banat autonomy is not of course even a fringe issue.)

Ioan said, 'Foreign reporters are happy because they can see we have a free press, with 200 new newspapers since the revolution – or maybe 300 by now. They write about "no more Communist censorship". But if they could read Rumanian they would laugh at us – most of those papers are nonsense. And what percentage of the population reads any newspaper, compared with nearly one hundred per cent watching television every day? It is more cleverness to give this nice picture of a free press while still the only communication that counts is strongly controlled.'

Toni surprised me and exasperated his pupils by expressing admiration for the brainpower, sincerity and courage of Iliescu, Roman, Brucan and various other Front leaders. But he assured us that he wouldn't vote for them. 'They are too brainwashed to abandon Marxism and no one can blame them for that. Of course we must be on guard against their only half-hidden attitude that Communism is good, that it only failed in Rumania because Ceausescu was mad.' His main worry was the Front's refusal to commit itself to any definite policies – on land reform, the free market, trade union reform, education – before the elections. 'Putting off such decisions contradicts democracy. We are being advised to give control of our country's future to a government that won't tell us its policies until we've elected it! In the Occident you must think Rumanians are a bad joke!'

Although Toni would not vote for the Front, on principle, he felt it might be best for Rumania if they received a clear mandate.

No other party could hope for a majority and an incessantly fractious coalition of mutually antagonistic minor parties would be even less likely to 'save' the country. 'I worry also that those parties won't be able to work together in opposition,' he said gloomily. 'And without a strong opposition there is no democracy.'

'But most of them will not be there after the elections,' Ioan pointed out. 'Only five or six are real – the Front made the rest to split the vote. They offered one million lei to anyone who wanted to start a new party. And some foreign reporters were impressed, thinking this was a real democracy – giving funds to the opposition!'

'Everything in this city' – enthused Walter Starkie – 'predisposes the stranger in its favour.' I would have agreed but for the lack of breakfast. None of the hotel restaurants opened before 11 a.m., when they began to serve early lunches to groups of slightly scruffy men who by then had been sitting for hours around bare tables, drinking a fizzy liquid. This was labelled 'champagne' and corked accordingly; otherwise it bore no resemblance to the wine of that name and the local surplus said it all. Every *alimentara* displayed thousands of dusty bottles and one enormous shop stocked nothing else.

Mercifully, good coffee was available from 7 a.m. in two cafés. One operated a Moscow-type double-queue system. The first long queue was for a blue plastic tiddly-winks counter with a hole in the middle. These were dispensed, in exchange for four lei, by a heavily moustached, treble-chinned woman suffering from splintered cerise nails. Some considerable time later, having reached the top of the second queue, you received a tiny cup of coffee in exchange for your disc which was then slipped onto a wire spoke standing upright on the counter. This lunatic procedure helps to explain the economic collapse of the Communist world. And it was matched in my favourite Liberty Square café, almost opposite a sculpture of Romulus and Remus imbibing from the she-wolf. There I thrice watched mega-queues being slowly served by one girl while her comrade thoroughly washed already clean windows. Every morning, before opening, cafés must be scoured inside and out. So if the staff arrive late, cleaning has to be given precedence over customers, though by 9 a.m. there would be no queue and ample time to scour.

Economic reform cannot happen until the mind-set of Rumania's work-force has been changed. Some of my friends argued that the mere establishment of a free market would itself ensure change by showing the capitalist carrot. But this I doubt. When people have all their lives been trained *not* to use initiative or imagination, in response to varying situations, how can the free market be expected suddenly to revive those qualities? Workers may yearn for that carrot, but they won't be able to reach it.

Every morning, after coffee, I visited St Michael's Church for my shot of Gothic, just as the rising sun came slanting through a glorious stained-glass window – almost Chartres quality. Unfortunately those first rays precisely spotlit a regrettable (in that Gothic context) Baroque pulpit, half-way down the nave. Whoever commissioned this extravaganza in dark carved wood should have been struck dead by St Michael's sword. But perhaps he liked the idea of being represented over the pulpit, dominating a brood of life-sized pirouetting cherubs and a row of seated bishops looking glum, threatening or just plain pious.

Outside the church – with his back to it, supervising the Square – King Matthias Corvinus sits on his charger, clad in full armour. Gathered below his lumpish plinth are warrior henchmen, dramatically offering battle standards or trampling the Ottomans' Crescent banner. This stolid and stereotyped memorial seems unworthy of the man who ruled Hungary from 1458 to 1490 and is described in the *Encyclopaedia Britannica* as 'one of the greatest monarchs who ever reigned'. It belongs in spirit to the decade of its creation – the 1890s – rather than to the fifteenth century. Because King Matthias was born in Cluj, the son of a Hunedoara Rumanian noble family, Rumania now claims him as a national hero, which often baffles outsiders. His father, John Hunyadi, went over to Roman Catholicism – the religion of the Magyars – like many other ambitious Transylvanian nobles of that period. A little later, many Irish nobles abandoned Roman Catholicism and went over to Protestantism – the religion of the English conquerors. Ambition is corrosive, in all climates.

Unless one knew exactly when and where to look for what, the city's shops offered only stale bread and frozen chickens imported

137

from Bulgaria. These then formed the centre-piece of Cluj supper-parties and often tasted half-rotten. However, no one else seemed to notice; years of Ceausescu-fare must have atrophied the Rumanians' tastebuds. When I asked why chickens were being imported, when Rumania pullulates with poultry, I was told the native birds are too thin to be worth killing.

In the desolate city market scores of empty stalls alternated with the usual pathetic piles of onions and a surplus of red chilli powder, just released. But the flower-sellers' stalls at the entrance were a joy, each laden with and surrounded by masses of daffodils, red tulips, lily-of-the-valley, carnations red and white, freesias, primroses. Gazing avidly, I realised that I had been suffering from colour-starvation. The uniform drabness of most Rumanian towns and cities induces an odd form of *visual* depression; this must explain why even impoverished Rumanians are compulsive flower-buyers, gladly spending more on a bouquet than on a meal.

It always pleased me to find parallels between Walter Starkie's Rumania and post-Ceausescu Rumania, and in Cluj our experiences were identical. He wrote: 'Though I had arrived two days before at Cluj an unknown wanderer carrying a rucksack, today I was a member of the small *cenacle* of artists and intellectuals in the city.' Within forty-eight hours I, too, had been 'absorbed' and half-a-dozen friends were urging me to move to their apartments. This avalanche of hospitality of course prevented my moving – how to choose one family without offending the rest? Instead, I lunched and dined all over the place and rarely got to bed before 1 a.m.

My Magyar invitations were to spacious though decaying flats in or near the Centru, or to ramshackle old family homes in tree-rich suburbs. Most of these residential suburbs have suffered grievously from systematisation but enough remain, often in the shadow of remorselessly proliferating blocs, to prove what a crime was the demolition of the rest. Numerous nervous break-downs were provoked, sometimes followed by the suicides of elderly people for whom the razing of a family home, in which several generations had grown up, was the final, unendurable assault of a regime that had already reduced so many other areas of their lives to rubble.

In one Centru flat, alarmingly afflicted by dry rot, an octogenarian writer brought me close to tears. In 1986 his seventy-four-year-old widowed sister was compelled to move to a fifth-floor flat in a bloc from which she could see only other blocs. 'There was no room for her grand piano, or her library, and she was not allowed to keep her small dog and two cats. And her garden – without that she could not live. It was only a little garden, but beautiful at all seasons. After one year she drank poison. No one blamed *her* – we only blamed ourselves. We wanted her to come here and we should have insisted more. But you see how it is – only three rooms and our son an invalid . . .'

My Rumanian invitations normally involved long trolley-bus journeys into Ceausescu-land. I soon learned to give myself an extra hour – having arrived at the bus stop – to pinpoint my friends' apartments. This may sound neurotic but you do have a bone fide problem, especially after dark, when the address is something like this: Strada Tineretului Nr. 47, Blocul 8, Scara B, Etajul V, Apart. 32. To leap blithely off the bus on seeing 'Strada Tineretului' is rank folly; Nr. 47 may be two miles away. Having found it, your heart rises – but twenty minutes later has sunk to a new low because, though you have found Bloculs 2, 3 and 6, Blocul 8 seems not to exist. And you know that when/if it has been located, it will probably take another fifteen minutes to find Scara B, which may or may not be still legibly marked. Then, as likely as not, the lift will be broken, necessitating a long climb to Etajul V. Usually there is nobody around, after dark, of whom to ask the way; and the occasional bod who may appear knows only where his/her own bloc is. A pocket torch sheds little light on numbers a hundred feet up and the municipal lamps shed no light on any relevant area. More than once, in despair, I knocked on an apartment door, asked if I might use the telephone (in itself a time-consuming operation, even from one bloc to the next) and then waited to be collected. The Rumanians being as they are, my frayed nerves were usually *tuica*-repaired while I waited. It consoled me to find that my Rumanian friends have similar problems, even when seeking apartments previously visited. Ceausescu-land is not designed to facilitate human contacts.

After failing one such test, I had to be rescued by Calin, an elderly scientist who had spent his working life in a dead-end job, deprived of all the resources needed to make it worthwhile. In his bloc the lift sank a foot lower than it should have, on reaching 'G', and he had to fiddle with the buttons as though opening a combination lock before it rose to admit us. Wearily he commented, 'You must laugh at us, to see how things are made here. We say, "In the Occident a manager keeps his rump on his chair and his eyes on production, in Rumania he turns his rump on production and keeps his eyes on his chair!" He only wants to hold his job by being a good Party boy – which is not changing, though now they tell us we have no Party!'

Calin believed Rumania would have been slow 'to take the revolutionary path' had Ceausescu not gone mad. 'For most people, life was OK in the late '60s and up to '77 or so. We all had secure jobs – with small wages, but prices were low. Everyone had cheap housing and enough to eat and wear. They had no pressure on them, like Western workers have. Most knew nothing about liberty, democracy, holidays abroad. If they were clever, university degrees were free. The old middle class had mostly been got rid of – killed or imprisoned or fled into exile or terrorised into silence. And what did the rest know about anything better than Communism? Rumania's peasants and workers were always exploited. When they were moved into blocs they had comforts they never saw before – hot water, bathrooms and WCs, gas cookers, central heating. Only when Ceausescu's paranoid economies took those things away they turned against him. Then Iliescu gave them back and now they love him, though he is still a Communist!'

Calin's wife Elena – an English teacher – saw it as the intellectuals' pre-election duty to go forth and preach democracy to the simple people. 'They need us,' she said, 'even if at first they don't want to listen. Why criticise them for knowing nothing about liberty if we're too afraid or lazy to teach them?'

I agreed, while suspecting that Elena would instinctively react undemocratically should the simple people, despite recognising the Front as Communists in disguise, persist in voting for them because they feared the Great Unknown – private enterprise. Even Rumania's intellectuals have only a limited understanding of democracy. It bothers them that in free societies the will of the majority really does count, however ill-equipped that majority may be, in their view, to elect a government.

An embarrassing feature of many Rumanian discussions is the inability of intelligent people to think a problem through – or analyse an event – logically and consistently. Healthy saplings, planted in the wrong place, must adapt to constriction, and many good brains seem to have been alarmingly stunted. Every day I was becoming more aware of the gravity of Rumania's long-term problems. Decades must pass before the country can be expected to recover from an educational system designed to paralyse independent thinking, an artistic and intellectual life warped by censorship, a legal system (if one can call it that) based on terrorism, an economic system based on the ambitions of a megalomaniac, a social life overshadowed by fear of informers, a domestic life dominated by the quest for food and medicines, a sex-life inhibited by bizarre restrictions. A few of my friends defined their country, in 1990, as a lunatic asylum, a land in which no one, including themselves, was quite sane.

At the end of another long evening my hyper-tense host – a middle-aged professor – demanded, 'How could we be normal people, like you in the West? All my life has been spent under a regime dedicated to destroying the human soul, the individuality that is God's gift to every baby born. We were so spiritually weakened *before* the 1980s that our sufferings then unbalanced most of us. Yet we have one of Europe's richest countries – valuable forests, fertile soil, gold, tin, coal, oil. We have no droughts, floods, famines, epidemics. We have beautiful land-scapes and a happy racial temperament. We are not doomed, like some places on other continents. We have all we need for contentment.'

Opposite me sat the professor's cheerful seventy-four-year-old peasant mother, yet another example of the oldest generation having weathered the Communist storm more successfully than their children. She had a strong calm humorous face and the sadness behind her eyes was quite unlike that bitter grief – verging on despair – too often seen in younger faces. Yet Communism had re-moulded her life at the age of thirty.

When I remarked on this generation contrast her son said, 'But my mother grew up free, she has always known another sort of life is possible. She had time to develop her individuality and then it could not be crushed, even by Stalinism. We had no such possibility and it is not true that what you never had you never miss. Freedom is natural for human beings. Even when the conscious mind is not complaining about the lack of it, the soul is in pain. Yet now we are afraid of it – even I am! Next academic year I must live in America with my family, as guest professor. This is a wonderful opportunity, something I have dreamed about all my life. But I worry and worry about the strange new domestic responsibilities in a capitalist country. Until now the state has looked after everything ... If this is *my* reaction, how would our ignorant workers react to a market economy? It makes me sad that even my fourteen-year-old son is afraid of America. Then I think that for his group there is more hope, if they have grandparents to give them the courage to enjoy liberty.'

Mihai, the adored son – very tall, much too thin, incipiently handsome – showed all the signs of life-long protein and calcium deficiency. By early 1987 the food shortage had become so desperate that this family, like many others, sold their car (for an absurdly low price, there being no great demand during the petrol shortage) to enable them to cope with the black market. Black market dealing was against their principles – an unusual scruple in Rumania – but I heartily agreed that principles have to be abandoned when children are starving.

The professor's wife Ana, a primary school teacher, explained that those not lucky enough to have something valuable to sell often chose to leave their children outside churches or police posts, rather than watch them becoming more and more debilitated – and then quickly dying if they picked up some trivial childhood disease. Hence Rumania's over-crowded and now AIDS-stricken Children's Homes, where babies were regularly given blood-transfusions to supplement their inadequate diet.

Two months after the revolution, Ana's pupils – forty-eight nine-year-olds – were asked to make a list of three things they would immediately change 'if they were wizards'. For twenty-eight their number one wish was 'Not to have an empty home after school'. These were the unfortunates without a resident granny (or grandpa), whose parents had to work late. Sixteen put first 'Somewhere to play'. Forty thousand people are squeezed into this area of Ceausescu-land, yet there is not one playground, the schools have no playing fields or sports facilities, and the nearest swimming-pool (Cluj has two) is an hour's bus ride away and too crowded when you get there for anyone actually to *swim*. Moreover, every square metre of the meagre strips of soil between the blocs is cultivated by 'private enterprise' vegetable growers. So the children can play only on the streets, which are put out of bounds by most parents. The remaining four pupils gave priority to 'More food'; Ana reckoned the majority couldn't imagine even a wizard being able to conjure up edibles.

At 1.30 a.m. my taxi arrived, pre-arranged by the Professor. Very soon after the revolution, all over Rumania, independent taxi services had become the flagships of free enterprise.

During that week, water from a leaking pipe near my favourite café froze on the pavement every night. Yet by 9 a.m. the sun was warm and by noon people were sitting around Liberty Square in their shirt-sleeves, exclaiming that it felt like *May*! This was dangerously abnormal weather; no rain in March presaged a poor harvest.

I often joined the Liberty Square sun-worshippers to write up my notes and one afternoon an emaciated Gypsy girl, aged six or seven, came begging. Her face was dreadfully expressionless and her right hand deformed – lacking three fingers and reversed. She wore her alms pouch over that wrist as she walked slowly past us, staring straight ahead, the pouch extended but making no other effort to stimulate generosity. The only reaction to her presence was a twitch of disgust on some faces; she collected not even one coin from the three hundred or so citizens in the Square. I followed her down the Strada Petru Groza to the Orthodox cathedral, where she curled up on the steps and seemed at once to fall asleep like a weary puppy. Beggars do best outside the churches of all denominations, where they gather – both Gypsies and Rumanians – before every service.

Cluj's large Gypsy population is as evident now as in Walter Starkie's day, though not as 'accepted'; the present attitude to Gypsies makes British racialism seem almost benign. Frequently I heard them denounced for a) making a fortune as racketeering smugglers and b) never working. It apparently occurred to no one that large-scale smuggling is a business requiring much harder work than the average Rumanian puts into his/her job. And, in a country where everyone survives by wheeling and dealing, moral objections to Gypsy free marketeering sounded downright hypocritical. I sometimes argued, 'Why shouldn't the Gypsies use this period of quasi-anarchy to amass capital? Why not be grateful to them for providing essential goods not otherwise available?' Reactions to those remarks suggested much unconscious envy of Gypsy vigour, initiative and sheer impudence – two fingers to everyone's rules and regulations. They at least have escaped being terrorised and standardised.

Admittedly, many Gypsies are now insolent and aggressive: a natural response to being despised. Early one morning, when a boy of about twelve entered my café and was hurrying towards the kitchen, an angry man stepped out of the queue and ordered him to leave the premises. The boy continued on his way, shouting defiance over his shoulder, whereupon he was pursued and clouted hard while everyone looked on approvingly. But he refused to be bullied. Eluding his attacker – I glimpsed a narrow brown face distorted with hate – he darted into the kitchen where he evidently had an important appointment. The man, flushed with rage, resumed his place in the queue and was soothed by his neighbours.

Two days later I saw a Gypsy trio who continue, irrationally, to haunt me. A boy of about five – his never-washed face covered in sores, his only garment a torn adult T-shirt – was leading his blind mother by the hand. Her eyes were sealed with scum, her face twisted with pain. She could hardly walk; a clumsy blood-soaked bandage covered her right leg from knee to ankle. Behind her, clinging to her short ragged skirt, a girl toddler – snotty-nosed and shit-defiled – was quietly sobbing: the terrible heaving sobs of toddlers who cannot understand their own misery. The boy was beseeching alms, desperately chanting the same phrase in an oddly adult yet high-pitched voice that could be heard a hundred yards away. His eyes were wild with fear and sorrow. I stood appalled, too shocked to think of taking out my purse. The trio moved along the crowded pavement very, very slowly. People altered course to avoid them; otherwise they were ignored. Then I overtook them and gave the boy all I had in my purse: three 100-lei notes and a jumble of coins. At once two young women and an elderly man surrounded me, protesting angrily – I presumed against this flahulach subsidising of good-for-nothing

Gypsies. They apologised on realising my foreignness but still looked indignant.

In India one rapidly becomes insensitive to both extreme suffering and extreme callousness; in Europe no such adjustment is possible. Does this disparity entail a form of racialism? Or does the extent of Indian misery make numbness an inevitable self-protecting response?

When I described this incident to one of my new friends – a paediatrician – she reproved me for imputing callousness to her fellow citizens. 'There is a reason for it,' she said. 'I will explain. Our beggar problem is very serious and it's important to know about the three categories. First, a minority who like begging more than working. Second, the disabled who could do some job if they had a walking machine or false limb or even crutches. But they can't afford those helps because they have no work so they can never get work . . . If you watch, you will see that we *do* give to such people. The third category is shameful. Children are found abandoned, or are kidnapped, then maimed – a limb cut off, or blinded, or deformed in some horrible way. Many babies and small children are stolen. Some years ago a two-year-old Cluj girl, playing with older children near her bloc, disappeared. Everything was done to find her, with publicity and police searches – then even her parents lost hope. But four years later, near a *magazin* door, the mother noticed a filthy skeleton beggar girl – one arm missing and the stump showing. She looked in the child's eyes and was certain – "That's our daughter!" Her husband thought her stupid but she insisted – "I know it is, I *feel* it!" They hurried to the police who sent plain-clothes men to watch. At sunset a man in a closed van took the girl away and collected seven more maimed children. The police followed to an old house in a big garden and arrested everyone – an elderly doctor had done all the maiming. He and three others got life imprisonment – I'd have shot them! A birth-mark proved the mother was right. Still the parents can't leave that child alone or she gets hysterical – they love her so much it makes you weep to see it . . . But how can she ever recover? The others are unclaimed, in a Children's Home, and if they survive must become adult beggars. So don't blame Rumanians for not supporting this industry!'

On the following Sunday the Timisoara Proclamation was a week old and solidarity rallies were held all over Rumania. At noon the Professor collected me from the Vladeasa, having appointed himself my translator for the occasion; his English was near-perfect. At least one-third of the assembling marchers were elderly or old, respectable middle-class folk dressed in their Sunday best; many had just been to church. Under a cloudless sky scores of colourful banners and placards – roughly made, but verbally and pictorially witty – were converging on Liberty Square, coming mainly from the nearby university area. The collective mood was serious yet happy as we watched the organis- ers clambering around King Matthias's plinth, struggling with an archaic public address system. Soon the huge square had over- flowed, as more and more family groups arrived with babies in push-chairs, toddlers on paternal shoulders and schoolchildren waving homemade Rumanian flags. There wasn't a policeman or a soldier in sight; but the Professor noticed several 'retired' Securitate officers sidling through the crowd.

After a devout recitation of the Lord's Prayer, in which most people joined, came a minute's silence in memory of the revolu- tion's victims. Then we were addressed by Calin Nemes, a frail-looking young actor who works in Cluj's puppet theatre and was the first to defy the armed forces on 21 December, when he is said to have emerged from the crowd, knelt in front of the soldiers (some, it is believed, were disguised Securitate) and shouted, 'Kill me if you will! *Jos* Ceausescu!' A moment later Captain Dando Carp cocked his pistol and Calin was shot in the stomach. The following burst of automatic fire killed eight. Later the army alleged that Calin had just left a nearby bar and was drunk. The shooting was immediately investigated by Colonel Tit Liviu Domsa, who arrested two officers and sent a report to Bucharest – whereupon the officers were released and the Col- onel was posted elsewhere. Subsequently the editor of the army newspaper, Colonel Gheorghe Vaduva, wrote an article alleging that 'The army was provoked into shooting and a terrible tragedy ensued ... They did not shoot at the people. They fired warning shots into the air, but the guns moved around in their hands.' As the Professor remarked, this was yet another example of the impossibility of establishing the truth about any aspect of Ruma- nia's revolution.

The few brief opening speeches included urgent pleas for 'No hooliganism' and 'Magyar–Rumanian unity'. Then we all moved off in an impressively orderly fashion, though without visible stewarding. After all those pleas for unity, the crowd's enthusiastic singing of 'Rumanians Awake!' seemed a trifle tactless. It has not been forgotten that this 'freedom hymn', written by the nineteenth-century Transylvanian poet Muresianu, was banned by the Magyar rulers – as were all other Rumanian songs and all displays of the national colours.

During the two-mile march to Piata Mihai Viteazul my technique for observing marches necessitated a temporary separation from the Professor. I sped back and forth, joining different sections for a time, then standing aside to watch, then to-ing and fro-ing again – rather like a dog on a country walk. The pessimists who had forecast a poor turn-out were right; by current Rumanian standards, 10,000 or so in a city of 300,000 was a small crowd. Many individuals were obvious proles, but organised banner-carrying groups of workers were conspicuously absent. All over Rumania, the workers' support for the Front was then hardening, as was the intellectuals' opposition to it.

The marchers chanted non-stop. '*Jos* Iliescu! *Jos Communismul!*' – but mostly, and most heart-feltedly, 'Timi-*soar*-a! Timi-*soar*-a! Timi-*soar*-a!' This last was the chant that brought tears even to the eyes of tough-looking young men. The atmosphere became strangely exalted. I sensed no ugly undercurrents of violence or hatred, despite the fervour with which thousands were passionately condemning Communism, and Iliescu as its agent. This felt like a pure celebration of freedom, a joyous exercise of the *right* to protest, rather than a demonstration channelling anger and hostility. Crowd-emotion always generates palpable energies and here all the energies were positive. When feeling depressed about Rumania's immediate future, I reflect that throughout the country such minorities exist – a leaven which must surely, given time, transform the inert post-Ceausescu political mass.

Old photographs show Michael's Square surrounded by the agreeably unpretentious town houses of the lesser Magyar nobility. Now it is an expanse of concrete dominated by a nine-storey intrusion from Ceausescu-land. Another new addition is Michael the Brave on his mettlesome charger – he who briefly united Rumania at the end of the sixteenth century and is therefore not a

Magyar hero. Under his undoubtedly approving eye the serious speeches began, explaining the Timisoara Proclamation point by point. For two and a half hours everyone stood motionless and attentive, from schoolchildren to great-grandparents. The speakers included the elderly Mayor of Cluj, a young dissident who had been in exile in West Germany before the revolution (and who soon after was charged with 'fascism' and again had to flee) and Doina Cornea, Cluj's very own special heroine who got the warmest applause of all – though her speech was far from being the most substantial. Meanwhile the babies and toddlers obligingly dozed off in the hot sun, causing me to marvel yet again at the docility and adaptability of the Rumanian (very) young. That climax was no less significant and moving than the march: a vast silent throng concentrating on *real* politics with the intensity of a people starved all their lives of open debate.

The Professor agreed with me that the Timisoara Proclamation had the potential (not since realised) to revive January's spirit of hope, which had already evaporated by my return in early March. A reaction was of course inevitable, after that month of boundless euphoria during which an entire nation felt liberty-intoxicated. But it seemed the Rumanians had, in general, returned to earth with a very hard bump. There was a fast-growing distrust of the Front, among intellectuals; an amorphous but unsettling Iliescu-prompted suspicion, among workers, of 'foreign interference'; a general chagrin because nothing was changing as quickly as had been expected; a bleak conviction that in Rumania democracy was, and would remain for the foreseeable future, a chimera. Also, insidiously demoralising doubts about the genuineness of the revolution were gaining strength. Perhaps it had not been the glorious thing it seemed, which aroused the admiration of the world and helped to restore Rumania's self-esteem? Perhaps it had been a cunning Iliescu *coup d'état*?

On 27 December 1989 even sober newspapers like the *Irish Times* had sensational headlines – 'Estimated 70,000 Killed in Rumania'. At the time I wondered, 'Estimated by whom?' Over-excited media reporters, perhaps. But that didn't then seem important; we were all merrily drinking to the liberated Rumanians and I was on Cloud Nine because at last I could afford to explore Transylvania. Yet even after several drinks nobody who paused to consider that figure could believe it. Rumania hadn't had a civil war between armed factions, cities hadn't been bombed or set ablaze. In a country with a population of twenty-three million it was inconceivable that 70,000 could have been killed in an uprising largely confined to two cities, with minor disturbances elsewhere.

Within days of the revolution, a few Bucharest observers were seeing it as a *coup d'état*. Behind the planned removal of the Ceausescus, staged as a media event to deceive the Rumanians and the world, Iliescu and his friends – it was argued – had slickly taken over under the guise of an interim government willing to organise 'fair elections'. In Bucharest, in January, two of my casual acquaintances told me that on New Year's Day they themselves had counted fifty-five truckloads of Soviet food arriving in the capital – despite formidable midwinter transport problems *en route*. Could the Soviets, they wondered, have achieved this feat without prior knowledge?

Certainly rumours of a plot had been circulating throughout the 1980s – and had been less improbable than most Rumanian rumours. In Cluj, a famously anti-Ceausescu city, the Ceausescus arrived one morning in the mid '80s to attend a series of events – then left hastily after the first event, never again to return. A military assassination attempt, planned for that day, was to have begun with a massive attack on the Securitate bodyguard – or so most people believed. (Why was this solution to the Ceausescu problem not implemented years ago, somewhere in Rumania? The popular explanation is that the army were terrified of the Securitate's incomparably superior weapons.) During the 1980s two 'private enterprise' assassination attempts threatened Ceausescu's self-sculpted image – 'the most beloved son of Rumania' – but were successfully hushed up. These explain all his food and drink having to be pre-tasted, in the best medieval tradition, and various other neurotic security precautions.

In November 1987, after the eruption of ferocious anti-Ceausescu riots in Brasov, Silviu Brucan – then aged seventy-one and an ex-editor of the Communist Party newspaper – told the Western press: 'The cup of privation is now full and our workers no longer accept that they can be treated like obedient servants.' Ten months later he wrote a detailed and devastating critique on

149

Ceausescu's misrule and smuggled it abroad. After its publication, in early 1989, the Securitate kept him under house arrest for some months in a village near Bucharest.

According to a *Romania Libera* report, an anti-Ceausescu conspiracy had existed since 1971. (*Romania Libera* is Rumania's nearest equivalent to the British *Independent*.) Its founder-leaders were four soldiers and two civilians; one of the latter was Mazilu, a senior Securitate officer, another was Iliescu. It may not be a coincidence that 1971 was the year of Iliescu's mortifying demotion from Director of the Communist Youth organisation to Director of Rumania's water resources programme. And in 1984 came a still more drastic demotion, to an insignificant job in a technical publishing house.

During the 1970s the conspiracy gradually expanded and by 1980 had the support of many anti-Ceausescu Securitate officers. But few yet realised how dangerous Ceausescu was becoming and a *coup* then would have been unpopular.

In 1980 General Militaru contacted Moscow and was assured of Soviet moral support (*only*) in the event of a *coup d'état*. He also contacted the Rumanian ambassador to Turkey (a peculiarly unsavoury character) and asked him to provide stun-gas grenades; the conspirators planned a bloodless take-over. The ambassador obliged but when the pro-Ceausescu Securitate detected his 'treachery' both he and his son were assassinated and the rest of the family gaoled. From 1983 onwards, Ceausescu regularly heard rumours of a plot to replace him with Iliescu, but uncertainty about their source remains. Had they been spread by the anti-Ceausescu wing of the Securitate to unnerve him, or by the 'loyalists' to warn him? By then he was so deranged that no one dared tell him the truth, bluntly, about his loss of popularity; that messenger would undoubtedly have been shot.

The *Romania Libera* report claimed that, after Mr Gorbachev's coming to power, Iliescu, Brucan and other conspirators made many unofficial visits to Moscow and also occasionally visited London, when they were supposed to be elsewhere, for significant meetings. Meanwhile Stanislav Petukhov, then *Pravda*'s correspondent in Bucharest, was the link between Brucan and Moscow. The *Romania Libera* journalists were apparently allowed to read a thick file, recording conversations between Brucan and Petukhov, which proved that early in 1989 Moscow informed Rome and Paris that the Bucharest conspirators had Soviet support. Budapest also knew this and so the Hungarians were poised to begin a world-wide campaign, immediately after the revolution, demanding a fairer deal for Transylvania's Magyars.

By then about half the Securitate had joined the conspirators. During the summer Brucan and Iliescu met irregularly in a Bucharest public park to discuss plans and Iliescu was also in touch with Petru Roman. The plans under discussion were probably Bucharest-centred. No one yet knew that a slow-burning revolutionary fuse had already been lit in Timisoara, where a Magyar Calvinist priest, the Cluj-born Laszlo Tokes, had recently moved onto the international stage. In relation to his own Ceausescu-controlled Church he was a maverick who since 1982 had been continuously harassed by the Securitate. The Bishop of Cluj, Gyula Nagy, treated him perfidiously – as did the Bishop of Oradea, Laszlo Papp, and various of his fellow-pastors.

In July 1989 Hungarian television recorded a hard-hitting political video interview with Tokes in his Timisoara manse. When this was broadcast on 24 July 'the Tokes case' immediately became a national cause in Hungary. The interview was given wide publicity by the BBC and Radio Free Europe – much of it emphasised the iniquity of razing Magyar villages – and Securitate harassment increased, directed against Tokes's wife and child as well as himself. On 14 October he was dismissed by the intimidated elders of his Timisoara church and the authorities demanded that he should be appointed (exiled) to a remote village, north-east of Oradea. Bishop Papp, who had jurisdiction over the Banat, obliged; but Tokes refused to leave Timisoara and his congregation continued to support him – hence the revolutionary fuse.

Tokes defied a City Court eviction order for 20 October, despite increasing pressure from the Securitate, and by November the world was noticing him as no other Ceausescu-victim had ever been noticed. In Budapest the Rumanian ambassador was put on the mat; the European Parliament praised his courage, the World Calvinist Federation deplored his ill-treatment; the Hungarian National Assembly jointly nominated Tokes and Doina Cornea for the Nobel Peace Prize; the foreign media regularly reported details of 'Lone Priest's Brave Stand'.

On 28 November the City Court ordered Tokes to leave Timisoara within six days; the order was ignored. On 6 December the interim President of Hungary sent a plea to the Rumanian President; the plea was ignored. All the time Securitate pressure was being ostentatiously increased, yet no attempt was made forcibly to evict Tokes on the Court-appointed day. Then, on Sunday 10 December, Tokes told his congregation that the Court had set another date for eviction – 15 December – and added, 'If anyone would like to see an illegal eviction, I invite him to come and watch.'

On the morning of 15 December about sixty people gathered around Tokes's church; no police appeared, only a few plain-clothes Securitate officers. By that evening, however, several hundred had assembled, the Magyar congregation being backed by Rumanians, Serbs, Swabians and Gypsies. This crowd re-mained 'on guard' throughout the night.

On 16 December – an unseasonably warm sunny Saturday – the crowd rapidly increased to a few thousand and the scene was set for the opening act of the revolution. But why was Tokes not arrested early on the morning of 15 December, in accordance with the Court order, *before* his defenders gathered? And why did he encourage his congregation, on 10 December, to rally around him on the fifteenth? Was this not an imprudent – even irres-ponsible – gesture? Had he been forcibly evicted or arrested on that date, some of the original small group of parishioners would undoubtedly have confronted the Securitate and been dealt with ruthlessly – leaving Rumania's *status quo* unchanged. Was he acting independently, intuiting that, given the public mood of desperation, a major uprising could be provoked by his resolute defiance of the authorities? Or was he acting in collusion with people who had decided to take advantage of the burning fuse? Already he had caused an unprecedented amount of media attention to be focused from outside on Timisoara; thus it was an ideal location for the eruption of what could be made to seem like yet another Eastern European 'People's Power' victory.

The few thousand gathered around Tokes's church on 16 December were not enough to ignite 'a popular revolution'. Vandalism then broke out, all over the city. Shop windows were smashed, though no shop contained anything worth looting, and there was much arbitrary stone throwing by gangs of youths. This utterly non-Rumanian behaviour was at first blamed on the Gypsies (who else!) but is now interpreted by some as part of a plot to create an anarchic atmosphere – an atmosphere in which it would at last seem psychologically possible to oppose the Ceausescu regime.

Tokes's arrest, at dawn on 17 December, brought many more thousands onto the streets in protest. According to the *Romania Libera* report, Soviet *provocateurs* and some Rumanian soldiers killed most of the victims – though everyone, in Rumania and abroad, was misled to believe the Securitate responsible.

In Bucharest, on 17 December, Ceausescu feigned a willingness to resign and asked 'Do you want Iliescu instead?' Everyone reassured him; those thousands of tiresome youngsters who had been rampaging around Timisoara for two days, yelling '*Jos* Ceausescu!' were mere hooligans. It was never hard to persuade Ceausescu that 99.9 per cent of Rumanians adored him and he at once sent a message (the transcript appeared in *Romania Libera* in mid January) to the Timisoara army commanders: 'All who don't submit to the soldiers – I've given the order to shoot. They'll get a warning, and if they don't submit, they'll have to be shot. It was a mistake to turn the other cheek . . . In an hour, order should be re-established in Timisoara.' Then, satisfied that he had coped effectively with a little local difficulty, Ceausescu departed for Iran on a three-day state visit, leaving *Her* in charge. (The Iranian ambassador to Bucharest, who on 17 December had assured Teheran 'There's no problem here', was summoned home nine days later to be given a piece of Rafsanjani's mind. More understandably, the *Guardian Weekly* also commented on 17 December: 'In Rumania the leading role of the Party and of Nicolae Ceausescu does not appear under threat.')

Immediately after the revolution, much was made of this Teheran visit. Many then erroneously believed that Iranians, Libyans, Iraqis and Syrians, chosen from among Rumania's numerous foreign students, formed the élite corps of the Presidential bodyguard. So rumour had it that Ceausescu was trying to recruit more Iranians. *Or* he went to beg for chemical weapons . . . *Or* he had taken billions of dollars to Teheran for safe keeping . . .

(I can think of safer places for my nest-egg.) In fact this was a routine state visit arranged months before, as such visits are, with Ceausescu acting as salesman for oil-drilling equipment – made to a high standard, 'for export only', in Rumania. He had by then been reduced, somewhat belatedly, to visiting Rafsanjani – also excluded from the World Club of Respectable Leaders – if he wished his people to see him on the international stage.

Ceausescu arrived home to a seething Bucharest; the grossly exaggerated Timisoara casualty figures – '4,000 dead!' – were having their intended effect. The major tactical blunder of his last appearance on the Central Committee balcony – an attempt to rally a population that had totally rejected him – remains unexplained. Was this his own arrogance-cum-stupidity-cum-madness, or had he been deliberately ill-advised? Why did the Securitate not warn him of how the situation had been developing in his absence? When the crowd's anger forced the Ceausescus to face reality and they fled by helicopter, the crowd invaded the Central Committee building. Why did none of the hundreds of nearby armed Securitate men try to stop them? Many thousands would indeed have been killed had those officers, highly trained in the use of sophisticated weapons, been united in an effort to put down the revolution.

All afternoon confused fighting seemed to continue around the Central Committee building but much of it may have been fake; firing simulators were certainly used near the television station to heighten the atmosphere of violence and danger.

Meanwhile Tokes had been released, on 22 December. Soon after, he was touring Europe and North America, tendentiously putting the case for the concessions being demanded, post-revolution, by Transylvania's Magyars.

Someone quickly produced a list of ninety names – a 'spontaneous committee' – to govern *pro tem*. The suspicion that Rumania had experienced a coup rather than a revolution was immediately sparked off, in a few minds, by the rapidity with which this interim government was formed. It included at first some genuine idealists and brilliant minds (and spirits) – people like Ana Blandiana, Ion Caramitru and Doina Cornea, who soon quit in disgust as its disinclination to bring about real reforms became apparent.

While the Front was being born at the Central Committee building, Ion Iliescu and Petru Roman arrived by army jeep – after dark, at 5.45 p.m. All fighting ceased as their vehicle appeared and for forty-five minutes no shots were heard as they stood exposed on the balcony, confirming the flight and capture of the Ceausescus. Why, if the Securitate had really been fighting the army all afternoon in that area, did they then stop? How come it was safe for those two 'arch-traitors to Ceausescu' to stand, *spot-lit*, within range of Securitate sharp-shooters? Again, had the Securitate really wished to take control of the television station, they could easily have done so. But it seems they didn't seriously try, though all around simulators gave the impression of fierce fighting and several nearby dwellings were shelled and set alight to increase the illusion of a desperate struggle between the gallant 'People's Army' and the wicked 'tyrant's mercenaries'. So successfully was this illusion created that on 27 December the *Guardian* referred to 'the tens of thousands of people who have died in more than a week of fighting between pro-Ceausescu security forces and the Romanian army'. Now, even the most melodramatically-minded Rumanians concede that there were comparatively few casualties of the revolution. The official figure, given months later – 689 – is incredible because so precise, yet is generally agreed to be 'about right'. Rumanian cynics (or realists) also note that the '70,000' briefly credited by the world's media served the useful secondary purpose of arousing the sort of emotion abroad that fuels emergency aid convoys in vast numbers – aid vulnerable to the depredations of those 'in control'.

I often heard it argued that had the conspirators not used the Timisoara fuse, a revolution would almost certainly have started somewhere quite soon – perhaps as an authentic popular uprising. This would have made it much more difficult, at the dawn of the post-Communist era, for Iliescu's Front to take over. World opinion was certain to sympathise with the new regime if the Ceausescus' overthrow were seen as another example of victorious 'People Power'; a *coup d'état* by a rival group of Communists would have evoked a very different response. My Cluj friend, who translated the *Romania Libera* article, emphasised how confusing and humiliating it was for Rumanians to know that initially they, like the rest of the world, had been deceived – and that hundreds of innocents had been killed because the Front couldn't think how else to get rid of the Ceausescus while retaining power for themselves. But did this, I wondered, give the conspirators more credit than they deserved for forward-planning?

Some of the details in the *Romania Libera* 'Conspiracy Report' are contradicted by apparently equally reliable evidence from other sources. Yet only a conspiracy of some sort can explain the many inconsistencies exposed, especially in relation to the behaviour of the Securitate. It is certain that an ineffectual but steadily growing anti-Ceausescu faction had long lurked in the Bucharest wings – it would be astonishing if this were not so – and the newspaper's sources are significant; General Militaru and Nicolai Radu, old soldiers at the end of their careers, had no discernible motive for misleading the public. Probably they spoke out in an attempt to dissipate the foetid miasma of rumour by then surrounding the revolution; but for that purpose they did not say enough.

In my view, neither 'revolution' nor *'coup d'état'* accurately describes the events of 15 to 25 December. Genuine revolutions have leaders and long-term plans. And a *coup d'état* suggests something more structured – not necessarily neatly planned in detail, but much more dependent on cool calculation than on the supple opportunism shown by the Front both during and after the overthrow of the Ceausescus. What *really* happened, and why it happened, is not merely of academic interest; the aforementioned miasma has further demoralised many Rumanians, if only because nobody likes to look foolish. Now it seems their shining January vision – a free Rumania sanctified by the blood of thousands of heroes – was an hallucination. The glorious new *Romania Libera* was not a phoenix but a stool-pigeon.

The saying 'Truth Will Out' does not apply in certain countries. Rumania's escape from the Ceausescus is so enmeshed in allegation, speculation, accusation and deception that the whole truth seems unlikely ever to emerge. It may not be in the possession of any one individual; and those who possess fragments may not sufficiently trust each other to co-operate in putting the fragments together. Balkan history is littered with question marks; this is just the latest.

10

Wheeling and Dealing

Even immediately post-revolution, a glance at any crowd revealed a minority of comparatively prosperous 'survivors'. These were not necessarily, I soon realised, Securitate or Party activists, but ordinary folk who knew how to operate the system. Typically, university lecturers or school teachers conserved energy during official working hours and later earned their 'supplement' as private tutors. Their pupils desperately needed extra tuition because the schools' standards had fallen so low – and anyway most teachers were conserving energy ... Rural pupils paid in *tuica*, wine, meat, dairy produce. Others paid in goods or cash acquired by parents who, in their own jobs, knew how best to glean personal benefits from the system. A furniture factory official might sell to a teacher whose tuition fees enabled him to afford a chair (For Export Only) that would not fall apart in months. Then that factory official could engage an eminent professor to coach his son or daughter for university entrance examinations. (In practice, a variant of private education had long since evolved.) Again, supplementary income might go to buy foreign luxuries – soap, coffee, chocolate, contraceptives, cigarettes, alcohol – with which to barter for the scarcest everyday goods: razor blades, new tyres, electric light bulbs, a piece for the broken cooker. Workers who stole these essentials from their factories could always sell the luxuries for many lei, often to a wealthy doctor, and thus afford under-the-counter food. To me this merry-go-round seemed inordinately complicated. Why couldn't a worker who had stolen – for instance – a tyre, sell it for lei to a doctor instead of bartering it for whisky with a teacher and then selling the whisky to the doctor? But of course it all depended on who knew what about an individual's needs at a certain time, and who could trust whom, and who had access to what. As a way of life, this keeps certain areas of the brain agile but shreds the nervous system.

The food black market seemed to be reasonably straight-forward. Having acquired extra lei or a few luxury goods, you gave an appropriate present and received a little meat, flour, sugar from an *alimentara* supply inaccessible to the impoverished majority. The same system operated when you coveted a new poetry volume, of which only 300 copies had been printed, or when you needed petrol to stock up on parent-produced (or stolen) food in your distant village.

The more I saw of the foreign aid scene, the less I liked it. Watching a friend unwrap a block of processed cheese, apparently made available to her *alimentara* by the kindly Front, I chanced to notice a scrap of alien tinfoil embedded in one corner. Having carefully extracted and washed it, my suspicion was confirmed by five words of Dutch.

'You should join the Securitate!' laughed my friend.

It seemed to shock no one that aid food was being sold in state shops, though it had been donated for free distribution among Rumania's starving millions. The fact that the comparatively affluent could *buy* donated goodies was simply an extension of those privileges which most intellectuals took for granted.

Notoriously, Communism leaves no scope for the average comrade to think about fellow-comrades' needs. Although individuals feel almost excessively responsible for their extended families, those at the bottom of the pile are usually forgotten. Life in a sick centralised economy fosters a primitive concentration on what *we* can get for *us*. Yet Communism alone cannot be blamed for this mind-set. Rumanian feudalism, which survived until a century ago, discouraged the development of any sense of social responsibility – on both sides of the social divide.

Excluding the Ceausescu mafia, there are now no rich Rumanians – only a poor majority and a modestly well-off minority. When the Communists took over, a minority of the minority contrived to retain some of their 'old money'; the Economic Police, established to reduce such families to the norm, quite often slipped up or could be induced to do so. But recently 'old money' has been dwindling fast and must in many cases be augmented by the sale, to the despised and hated mafia, of valuable inherited possessions.

Here, as in so many areas of Rumanian life, state terrorism was unpredictable – unpredictability being in itself a useful weapon with which to unnerve and demoralise. A few years ago the Economic Police raided the home of the one 'old middle-class' family who befriended me. (I met only two such families; probably most of the survivors live in Bucharest.) Three officers spent two days compiling an inventory, their manner all the time threatening and contemptuous. My friends were steeled to either give a massive bribe or pay heavy extra taxes. Instead, one valuable painting was 'confiscated' – and some months later exhibited in Bucharest as the property of a government minister. The family's teenage daughter soon after developed a stress-related heart defect and is still having nightmares about the rough ransacking of her home. Terrorist state hassles affect different people differently; she could not cope emotionally with the contempt of the Economic Police for one of her breed.

The other bourgeois family made a famous and honourable name for itself in nineteenth-century Rumanian politics, on which scene fame and honour rarely went together. Now three generations live in a bloc like any other – but in a flat utterly unlike any other. Bemused, I stood in the middle of the long drawing-room with tall windows at either end – how could it be so *big*? Tina explained: she and her father had bought adjacent flats and knocked them into one. I stared, feeling dislocated (or relocated), at ceiling-high bookcases of leather-bound volumes, delicate watercolours of King Carol I's Bucharest, Kashan rugs, buhl tables, heavy brocade curtains, an elegant rosewood escritoire, a glossy mahogany dining-table. This much had been salvaged when the rest of the family property was 'requisitioned' in 1952; a recently inherited house in another city had been overlooked. Evidently some money had also been inherited; two walls of the children's room were lined with the eye-catching cartons of expensive Occidental toys. In Rumania (another Third World touch) containers are often preserved for their symbolic value, which in a family such as this seems peculiarly incongruous. Sometimes empty foreign beer cans, cigarette cartons, whisky bottles, chocolate wrappings – even instant coffee tins – are proudly displayed as living-room decorations.

The bright spacious kitchen – again two rooms knocked into one – held a deep-freeze unit packed with mutton, pork and salami. Around the walls hung several gadgets not found in every Occidental kitchen and the washing-machine in the larger bath-room still worked. Most of my friends' washing-machines hadn't worked for years. But the most remarkable thing about this family was their being able to live well without dollars, or any other hard currency. As an endangered species, they were much more frightened of the Securitate than were my ex-Party intellectual friends. When I asked Tina to buy me a bottle of Scotch, with dollars, in the local tourist hotel, she was obviously reluctant to do something that had until recently been illegal.

Both Tina and her father had refused to join the four-million-strong Party, despite the consequent loss of promotion opportuni-ties. Almost all my other friends had joined; otherwise they would have been denied appropriate jobs. Significantly, on the eve of the Communist take-over in 1944 there were fewer than 1,000 Party members, yet by 1970 27 per cent of Romanian Academy mem-bers and holders of doctorates, 46 per cent of engineers and 52 per cent of teachers had joined. And by 1989 25 per cent of the adult population and 35 per cent of the work-force had made Rumania's Communist Party the largest, proportionately, in East-ern Europe – including the USSR. No doubt the uniquely nationalistic flavour of Rumanian Communism promoted this widespread acceptance, as it had been designed to do. That whipped-up nationalism was based on a cynically rewritten history which seems to me the most corrupting of the many forms of Rumanian dishonesty. As my historian friend said, 'The sort of aid we need *first* is for our souls. We need professional historians from outside to tell us the truth about our past. How can we build a solid future on self-deceits?'

The national level of dishonesty seemed to have become an obsession; almost every Rumanian I met referred to it. Many spoke with unfeigned anguish in their voices, others with resigned acceptance, a few boastfully – they were clever enough to have become dishonest enough consistently to defraud the state.

One friend recalled: 'We were never hungry, not even in the last months before December when many starved. I always could find food to put on the table – and for our friends, too. In my department are four workers but only employment for one. So we go home every evening not tired and teach for hours. You see what this means? We have become totally dishonest! No one takes their job seriously – only a few genuine doctors, or academics doing work they enjoy. The government dishonestly employs four for the work of one and we go on from there!'

For some, dishonesty seemed the lesser of two evils. Dinu, like all vets, had to refrain from criticising Bucharest-imposed lunacies; otherwise he would have lost a job that enabled him to help retired farm-workers. Also, when animals starved to death he had to fake their death-certificates. Animals don't die of hunger on well-run farms – state farms are well-run – animals don't die of hunger on state farms . . .

For others, dishonesty was a humanitarian duty. Miron, an elderly lecturer in charge of a university blood-collection unit, explained that his conscience forbade him to force malnourished and already anaemic youngsters to donate blood quarterly, especially as they dreaded the process. One local collection had infected scores of students with hepatitis-B, yet even after that tragedy no preliminary tests were done, nor were needles routinely sterilised. (Rumania's juvenile AIDS epidemic probably had its source in foreign students' blood; the parents of most victims are free of the virus.) However, Miron dreaded being deprived of his minuscule academic pension should he fail to deliver the sanguinary goods. The earning effort needed to keep his quota-inspector Scotched was gruelling, but eventually he received two awards from Bucharest in recognition of his outstanding diligence as a blood-collector.

Like many ex-Communists, Miron ranked among the Front's most outspoken opponents. For years such people had been silently resenting the hours wasted each week on 'Party business', the tedious maintenance of the propaganda machine. Some of course had once been True Believers – like Suzana, aged thirty-three, whose peasant parents both became electrical engineers and were proud of their personal contributions to Rumania's rapid modernisation.

'My parents always trusted Gheorghiu-Dej's plans for the future,' said Suzana. 'And for a long time we all trusted Ceausescu's. When I was growing up we had enough food, talking with tourists was allowed, students could go on courses abroad – I spent two months in a language college in England. The old bourgeoisie were out of sight and the atmosphere was calm – nobody cared about the Securitate. But by '78 we could see the economy collapsing. That was after the big earthquake in '77 and a lot of oil problems – then we had two very bad harvests. Ceausescu felt the collapse like a personal failure, which I suppose it was in one way. He began to pretend *everything* in Rumania was *perfect*. The last time he sounded a little bit sane was in '81 – his speech then surprised the whole country. He admitted it was a big mistake to put all effort into industrialisation and neglect agriculture. An "agricultural revolution" was decreed, but using Stalinist methods that made things much worse. Production has been falling ever since. No one dared advise him, his megalomania got so frightening. We watched him going madder and madder – but we just watched, doing nothing, like a rabbit in front of a snake. It seems wrong to blame him for those years, though most of us do. He was always bad, but you can't blame someone for going mad. Why didn't *She*, and the others around him, try to control the disease?'

As a village teacher in the early 1980s Suzana, like most of her colleagues, ignored the diktat to spend an hour a month (after school hours) on Communist indoctrination and an hour a week on Communist Youth activities. Boldly she told her pupils, 'Be careful, remember you've done your civics lesson, if anyone asks – and now you may go home!' But she doubted if any non-Party member would have had the confidence to be so independent; as one of the four million she felt to some extent 'protected'.

Several of my most fiercely anti-Communist friends had been Party officials – not to be confused with the sinister 'Activists', yet conferring a useful degree of authority.

One young man got a residence permit, after six frustrating months, by revealing his status in the Party to the Police Chief and threatening to complain to the Central Committee in Bucharest. Less than ten minutes later the permit was issued. 'Why did I waste those six months!' lamented Titus. 'I had to get desperate before the idea of bullying a Police Chief came to me – then I was amazed how easy it was!'

Urban residence permits became necessary in the mid '70s when all big cities were declared 'closed', after alarming mass-migrations from recently systematised rural areas. Titus had wanted to move only from one closed city to another, and he condemned such prolonged permit struggles as blatant bureaucratic job-creation.

A university lecturer described a successful confrontation with her Chief of Police, when she was being refused a holiday exit visa though a Greek ex-pupil had paid for her ticket. 'I made that fat militia pig look like an ignorant fool!' she recalled with relish – then admitted she would not have dared to do so unless she had been an *official* of the Party. Not long after, she mocked a Securitate investigation. During an international academic conference foreigners visited her flat every evening and the Securitate later demanded a full account of *all* their conversations. Lucia then gave them a file of scientific papers, presented as social exchanges but retaining their impenetrable – to a layman – jargon. I heard of no one who had been punished for defying the ban on 'foreign contacts'; evidently it was not too rigidly applied in the academic world, at least outside Bucharest.

The few intellectuals I met who might be described as 'dissident material' were scattered (in more senses than one) and had been quite unable to think in terms of organised dissent. In relation to a despised regime they preserved their personal integrity, refusing government-funded trips abroad and perks at home. Now they were steadfastly opposing the Front, though aware that as workers in materially non-productive jobs they would be seriously impoverished by a free market economy. But they had never ventured to form the sort of coherent underground movement that could have evolved, post-revolution, into a credible rival to the Front. Nor had they established a samizdat movement – apart from a small group of (significantly) Magyars, who produced one paper for a brief period. Initially I assumed their passivity to have been Securitate-inspired, then I began to suspect deeper, pre-Communist roots. As one friend remarked, 'We Rumanians are still serfs, in our minds.'

Andrew Amalrik's 1969 essay, 'Will the Soviet Union Survive until 1984?', is in many ways eerily prophetic and several passages indicate that Rumania's handicaps closely resemble the Soviet Union's. On the Christian ethic:

It is worth mentioning that Russia received her Christianity from Byzantium, which was rigid and moribund, and not from the developing and dynamic young Western civilization. This could not but deeply influence subsequent Russian history.

And on the growth of Soviet dissent:

> Even in 1952–6 there were a great number of people who were dissatisfied with the regime and opposed to it. But not only was this discontent of a drawing-room character; it also leaned heavily on a negative ideology: the regime was bad because it did or did not do this or that. The question of what was desirable was generally not asked. It was also assumed either that the regime was not living up to the ideology it professed or that the ideology itself was worthless. The search for a positive ideology forceful enough to oppose the official ideology did not begin until the end of this period.

In Rumania that search has only now begun – thirty years later – and as yet the searchers are few, mainly young, rather incoherent and without leaders.

Viorica, one of my porphyrogenite friends, believed that it will take Rumania a very long time (how often did I hear that phrase!) to recover from the loss of its leader class. 'That's why we have two ancient exiles leading the main opposition parties in the election campaign. Seeing a vacuum, they came home to fill it. But the simple people won't trust them – they know nothing about Rumania *now*.'

Viorica's father, like his father and grandfather, studied in Paris, where he was one of a group of fervent admirers of Marshal Antonescu. (I delicately refrained from enquiring if he had also been, as my antennae indicated, a fervent admirer of Codreanu.) In 1939 he returned to Bucharest to volunteer for the Rumanian army and was soon in action as an ally of the Nazis, with the aim of regaining from the USSR Bessarabia and northern Bucovina – both annexed in June 1940. During a brief compassionate leave he married the daughter of a family as eminent as his own and Viorica was born during the retreat from Leningrad, while Pappa was winning honours 'for outstanding gallantry'. Those honours were not normally awarded to noncareer officers but he was among the comparatively few survivors; during that campaign unreckoned myriads of Rumanians died.

In 1947, after King Michael's abdication, the Communists stripped Pappa of his honours. Then one night he was abducted – as were thousands of anti-Communists, all over Rumania, that same night – and condemned to two years' slave labour on the infamous Danube Canal. Allegedly this was a punishment for his having acted as defence lawyer for a candidate accused of malpractice in the rigged (as usual) election of November 1946.

The Danube–Black Sea Canal – a hero-project otherwise known as the *canalul mortii* – served as an extermination camp for Nazi supporters, nationalist intellectuals, unconvertible bourgeoisie and peasants who had imprudently shown 'bourgeoisie aspirations'. All were labelled 'fascists' and before the project was abandoned in 1953 more than 100,000 had died – their deaths an important part of the plan to obliterate Rumania's religious and cultural institutions and traditions. Stalin was then (1948–52) taking a close personal interest in the conversion of Rumania to Communism. 'Proletarian Internationalism' was the current ideal, to be replaced by 'National Communism' in April 1964, when Rumania became detached from the Soviet Union.

Viorica's mother recalled harrowing visits to her husband; quarterly visits were allowed by way of maintaining the fiction that this was a 'hero-project'. Like many others, Pappa tried to believe that soon the US would intervene to rescue Rumania from Communism; the distant drone of an aeroplane always aroused the pathetic hope, 'Maybe *now* they're coming!' For years, an extraordinary number of Rumanians clung to this naïve expectation. They failed to realise that the US, having no economic interest in Rumania – a country unheard of by most Americans – would never tread on the bear's paw in defence of Rumanian freedom. A curious reverberation from misplaced trust was heard on Election Day 1990 when bewildered American 'Observers' were abused in polling booths by angry old men shouting – 'Go home! You're forty years too late!'

On his release, Pappa worked in a factory; resuming his legal career would have entailed collaborating with the Gheorghiu-Dej regime during its most repressive phase. Happily for Viorica, his file was clean. Because he had been abducted and never tried, it recorded that from 1950 to 1952 he had been 'retained for research'; so his daughter was not branded as the child of a convicted subversive and could attend university. Yet she grew up knowing her father's 'research' must never be mentioned, even to her closest friends – or her husband.

Viorica and her mother felt uneasy about Iliescu's burgeoning personality cult. Some outsiders found the Ceausescus personality cult quite comical, a derisory form of clowning that no intelligent person could take seriously. But for years, as Viorica pointed out, the fakery involved – which was so scandalously reinforced abroad by democratic governments and esteemed universities – had meshed with other forms of dishonesty to imprison the Rumanians in a cage of unreality.

I argued that in Western democracies institutionalised dishonesty is equally rampant and accepted by the majority as 'inevitable'. Whereupon Mother retorted that our dishonesties don't cage us because we *can* – even if too often we don't – recognise them, discuss them, expose them and protest against them.

To Viorica the most troubling dishonesty, for twenty-three years, had been the medical profession's profiteering from the Ceausescus' 'breeding programme'. She said, 'It didn't breed all the children it was meant to, but it bred far too many doctors who wouldn't help a desperate woman for one leu less than 3,000 – a month's wage!'

Although the Socialist Republic of Rumania claimed to provide free health care for all, only bribery gave any patient even half a chance of adequate treatment. Significantly, doctors and the Ceausescu mafia could most easily afford those second-hand Mercedes imported post-revolution from Germany, by Gypsies, and sold for one million lei. Many doctors with normal standards of professional integrity chose to emigrate and are highly thought of abroad; Rumania's medical schools have always had a good reputation. 'You can't blame them for going,' is the general verdict. 'If they'd stayed they couldn't do much for us, given the scarcities.'

Of the Ceausescus' multiple cruelties, none repelled outsiders – and tormented insiders – more than their demographic decrees. In October 1966 abortion and contraception were outlawed, taxes on childless couples increased and a minimum of five children decreed. Hence the now-famous 'decree babies', born in 1967–9 and reputedly the most recklessly brave of the revolutionaries in Timisoara and Bucharest. Their growing-up coincided with the collapse of the economy and there were always far too many of them for the facilities available in state crèches, primary and secondary schools, holiday camps, universities.

In 1966 Rumania's natural increase per thousand was 6.1, in 1967 18.1, in 1968 17.1, in 1969 13.2. Thereafter the rapidly declining birth-rate was as spectacular as the original 'bulge'. Traditional methods of birth-control were revived, illegal abortionists flourished, contraceptive smuggling networks were established, sexual activity was limited among those capable of such self-control and by 1983 the annual increase was down to less than half the 1966 level: 2.9. (Newcomers to Rumania immediately noticed the scarcity of small children.)

When it became apparent that the Ceausescus' ambition – thirty million Rumanians by the year 2000 – was not going to be fulfilled, taxes on recalcitrant non-breeders were raised again, even harsher penalties were imposed for trafficking in contraceptives, or having or performing an abortion – and the Baby Police were established. These officers regularly visited work-places (in some areas monthly, in others quarterly) to do abortion-blocking pregnancy tests and ensure that all miscarriages were reported to them for checking. Also they saw to it that every woman under the age of forty-five had a monthly gynaecological test. As the Party daily newspaper announced in March 1984 (*sic*): 'Nothing that happens in society can be excluded from the preoccupation of the party'. Soon after, Ceausescu ordered Party organisations everywhere 'to understand that fulfilment of their leading role requires increasing the responsibility *vis-à-vis* the accomplishment of demographic policy which constitutes one of the fundamental problems in the activity of our party and state.' (Even by Marxist standards, Ceausescu-speak was notoriously inimical to clarity of thought. Translated, the message here is, 'Inform on demographic-law-breakers'.)

Meanwhile, living conditions were deteriorating fast. Dried milk had been rationed (wet milk was unobtainable) and the monthly allowance could feed a baby for less than a week. Power shortages had prompted a ban, enforced through frequent spot-checks, on the use of all household electrical appliances. Even the most adroit wheelers and dealers found it too dangerous to buy contraceptives and the abortion rate soared despite the risks – medical and legal. (Pre-1966, abortion had been the commonest form of birth-control in Rumania, as thoughout Eastern Europe.) When 'amateur' abortions went wrong, as they frequently did, and haemorrhaging women were rushed to hospital, they could receive no attention until they had told the police the name of their 'accomplice', usually a friend or friend of a friend. Over the years, thousands died because they refused to inform; the penalty was a heavy fine or a long term of imprisonment. In 1989, in Bucharest alone, over 20,000 women were treated in hospital for complications resulting from botched abortions. Also, during the 1980s – as all the world now knows – countless babies were abandoned.

Immediately after the revolution, the Front identified two moves as essential if they were to be sure of public acceptance. Firstly, the Securitate were disbanded (in theory); secondly, abortion was legalised. At once, forty to fifty women sought abortions every day in every city hospital. These operations were performed under conditions described by Dr Tim Rutter, consultant to the Marie Stopes International, in an interview (7 February 1990) with Angela Lambert of the *Independent*:

> The organization of the wards was non-existent. There were three patients to a bed, but only because when they arrived, there were no comfortable chairs or waiting-rooms to sit them in. The staff just didn't know what else to do with them. Women were half in theatre, half out, half waiting, half being prepared. I kept thinking, it would be so simple to change a few things here and make it all run much more smoothly. They were doing D&Cs when termination by suction would have been quicker and safer. But overall, the standards of hygiene weren't too bad and the doctors were excellent operators . . . But any abortion leaves physical and psychological side-effects, particularly an illegal one. In Rumania you had to become a criminal in order to control your own fertility.

At the end of May 1990 it was reported on television that most large hospitals were still doing an average of forty abortions a day. Mathe, who told me this, explained that many couples felt too unsure about the political future to risk having a baby; a free legal abortion seemed more sensible. But why was the government making no attempt to provide adequate supplies of contraceptives?

Liliana added to my anthology of gruesome gynaecological tales. On becoming pregnant in 1980 (aged twenty-one), she was found to have an ovarian tumour but her gynaecologist decided against an operation. A week before B-day he took off for a holiday in Spain, leaving as locum a kindly but ineffectual old man who reckoned the tumour must in fact have been a cyst because it had 'dissipated'.

At 10 p.m., when no gynaecologist could be expected to function, Liliana's time came. The hospital porter refused admission to her mother and boy-husband, the latter a severe case of pre-natal nervous prostration. She and a Gypsy woman had to share a single bed with filthy linen. Finding this intolerable, Liliana spent the night in a corner by the radiator (it was midwinter and far below freezing), crying with pain and fear, believing both herself and her baby to be doomed. It was 'lights out' at 11 p.m., when the eight women sharing four beds (all in labour) were scolded for being so noisy and told to settle down to sleep. Then the door was locked; the ward had a lavatory *en suite*. All night the Gypsy shouted obscene abuse of men in general and her husband in particular, which for Liliana added yet another dimension of horror to the experience. Before the staff reappeared at 7 a.m. three babies had arrived.

Hours later the geriatric gynaecologist bumbled in and during a very difficult labour Liliana was repeatedly threatened with the loss of her baby if she didn't push harder. She marvels at the survival of both; many young women, less well-nourished and with fewer inner resources, left maternity wards in a box – and no doubt still do. On going home that evening she was told not to expect to feel well for a month and to return in six weeks – not before – *if* she had a problem. She did indeed have one, but dread of that hospital prevented her from admitting to it.

Three months later the acute pain in Liliana's lower abdomen was diagnosed as a kidney infection and treated accordingly. It was of course the tumour, by then wrapped around one of her Fallopian tubes and needing emergency surgery. Had her father not confronted the hospital Director (whom few would have dared approach) and demanded immediate attention, she might well have died.

11

Village Contrasts

Early in March Costin, a Cluj friend, invited me for a long weekend to his ancestral village in southern Transylvania – for centuries a mixed village: about half and half, Magyar and Rumanian. Now all but four of the Magyar families have left and their church is a weed-threatened semi-ruin, visited only twice a year by a priest from the nearest city. They left, Costin explained, not because of any local dissension but because they felt unhappy when their land was collectivised in 1962. The Rumanians also felt unhappy but 'their hearts wouldn't let them move'. Instead, the younger generation became urban workers – or, like Costin and his brother, intellectuals – while their elders coped with collectivisation and made what they could of the small family plots left to them when their beloved hectares were 'stolen by the state'. But the Magyar elders couldn't accept this down-grading and accompanied their children to the cities. 'They were too proud to take orders from Rumanians,' said Costin. 'And I think they were afraid – afraid to be old and unprotected without their children. Not afraid of *us*, their neighbours, but of village Party bosses and outside Securitate inspectors.' I understood what he meant; everyone had to break the law to survive, but the blind eye often turned on Rumanian law-breaking might not have been turned on Magyar wheeler-dealers.

On the Saturday afternoon Costin and I walked for hours over the nearby hills. It was a windy, showery day – that precious rain brought delighted grins to crinkled old faces all over the village – but, after weeks of drought, the grass remained winter-drab. Yet the steep, scrubby slopes were bright with primrose patches, and misty blue wood-violets, and miniature dandelions – dainty, strongly coloured blooms. The sun was setting as we descended through a glade where four deer grazed – then gracefully fled, their sinuous, slow-seeming bounds taking them swiftly out of sight. Moments later the whole western sky flared crimson and I paused to stare at the fiery towers of cloud, edged above with gold and dramatically underlined by a long thin black plume. Was this some lighting-effect unique to Transylvania?

'It's not possible anywhere,' said Costin, 'to be free of Ceausescu. *He* is dead. But what he did to my valley is alive – you see it!'

From where we stood a humpy hill hid the factory chimney; only its horizontal plume, driven by a high wind, was visible – and had looked quite beautiful, while unidentified.

Costin's brother Ion, a chemical engineer in that factory, was then an angry man. Front representatives from Bucharest had warned the work-force that only Iliescu & Co. could protect them from outside investors determined to replace them with foreigners trained to use modern machinery – an effective manoeuvre where 'the dole' is unknown and unemployment the ultimate disaster. When the workers were asked to sign a pledge of loyalty to the Front, guaranteeing it their votes, only four out of 2,000 refused. That impressive pledge, Ion said, would be used to persuade other work-forces to guarantee their votes: and so the democratic process was being sabotaged, all over Rumania. The International Election Observers, who almost unanimously pronounced the elections 'valid', should have arrived in the country two months, rather than two days, before 20 May.

On the way home we made a detour because this was *Simbata Mortilor*, 'the Saturday of the Dead', when candles are lit at sunset on the graves of relatives and friends. It was already dusk when we entered the hillside cemetery where, in the distance, a few other late-comers moved silently like shadows between the gravestones. Costin's family were buried on the steepest slope, amidst bushes and saplings. When he went first to his grandfather's grave, and laid a hand caressingly on the simple stone cross above it, I realised that for my atheist companion this was no mere annual duty to placate devout parents. He half-whispered, 'This grandfather was my *most* important person for twenty-three years. He taught me all the valuable things – what you don't learn at school. We loved each other like *friends* and I still love him. Does that sound crazy?'

'Not to me,' I assured him. 'I felt exactly the same about my own grandfather.'

Taking three thin candles from his jacket pocket, Costin began a protracted double struggle, with the gusty wind and with Rumanian matches – those most potent symbols of the failure of Communism. Again and again he tried to coax the three candles at the base of the cross to remain alight. Meanwhile an almost full moon – fitfully bright between speeding shreds of cloud – was giving that secluded, overgrown corner the atmosphere of a sacred grove. Patiently Costin built a little grass wind-shield – then stood with folded hands and bowed head, gazing down at the wavering flames. By this reverent act of ancestor-worship – not allowing death to loosen the bonds of gratitude and affection – he was conferring on his grandfather the only sort of immortality in which I can believe.

A rough seven-mile dirt track leads to Costin's village – where it ends, at the base of the ridge. From here one looks across a wide, unnaturally discoloured river to a broad flat valley, scarred and tainted by gigantic petrochemical and fertiliser factories. Beyond, a mighty mountain range, some forty-five miles long, rises above 7,000 feet – and looks higher. Between this dramatic snow-laden barrier and the cultivated land no hilliness intervenes.

During Costin's childhood, thirty-odd years ago, his village was an energetic community of more than fifteen hundred farmers. Now the population is down to less than 500 – mainly old folk, with a few younger people who are, mentally and/or physically, too below par to survive in a city. Anyone familiar with the natural rhythms of village life must find this a tragic place, lacking the sunrise and sunset bustle of noisy animals to-ing and fro-ing, poultry being released or rounded up, children working and playing and laughing and wailing. Here the children are quiet bloc-bred weekend visitors, too neatly dressed. And though the physical farmyard structures remain – stables, barns, byres, sties, coops – most now are empty. Beyond the village, its animals are crowded together in long standardised collective buildings of dead-grey concrete, all enduring concentration-camp conditions and many dying of starvation or neglect – while Rumania's towns and cities depend on Swedish cheese, German ham, Danish butter, Irish beef, Italian salami, Bulgarian chickens.

In this village's typical cow-byre, 150 animals were being cared for (or not cared for) by five Gypsies. The floor of the long shed was inches deep in stale liquid manure and ammonia fumes made my eyes stream as I walked down the centre, to examine several sick cows and calves. The calves were scour victims, lying in their own ominously pale shit and with not much longer to live. In this reeking shed all the hand-milking is done by Gypsies who never wash their hands, or indeed any other parts of their anatomies – you can smell them coming ten yards away. Elsewhere on that same 'average' collective – centred around a Magyar landlord's centuries-old farmyard – hundreds of sacks of chemical fertiliser had for months been lying out in the rain; half the bags were split, their contents long since hardened into unusable lumps. In another corner a superb antique saw-mill (I longed to salvage it for some industrial museum) had been abandoned because the collective was compelled to obtain its cut timber from a county depot three hours' drive away. The fine old stables had been crudely converted into another repulsive shed, its floor a piss-squelchy mess of straw and droppings where lay five sheep too sick to stand up. Incredibly, their lambs had been left with them though suckling was in vain.

Central to this sordid scene was the mouldering nineteenth-century manor house of the local count who, before his flight in 1940, owned half the village land. The rest had belonged to the peasants since the agricultural reforms of 1921. A faded notice on the half-rotten hall door of this modest little manor described it as the office of the commune's agricultural co-operative. Now the old folk recall the era when they were count-dominated as a Paradise, compared with what followed.

The depopulation of rural areas is a global problem but in Rumania the manner of its happening seems peculiarly distressing. As the guest of villagers, one becomes acutely aware of the violence of the process that has torn so many communities apart. These are the homes of an intelligent, thrifty, creative peasantry, proud of their knowledge of animal husbandry and crop cultivation but now humiliated and impoverished by collectivisation. In far-away city offices, bureaucrats called 'agricultural engineers' made disastrous decisions, then drove into the countryside, ordered villagers to do X, Y and Z, threatened them with dire punishments if they disobeyed – and drove away leaving everyone enraged, yet with no alternative but to do what they knew was

174

wrong, what would debase the land and debilitate the stock while leaving them feeling like traitors to their forefathers. No rotation of crops was allowed and in some regions collectives were ordered to produce 5,000 kilos of grain per hectare – a physical impossibility, but failure to reach this target would have involved the stoppage of all wages for one year. So half the pastureland was devoted to crop production and the local cattle have been on short commons since 1963. Many stories are told – all true, Costin assured me – about the ignorance of those theorists from the Central Planning Committee in Bucharest. One 'fruit engineer' arrived to inspect a collectivised orchard and, having surveyed it, gave detailed instructions about what must be done to double apple-production. When he had finished, the collective's chairman said, 'Thank you, comrade, I'm sure that's very good advice about growing apples – but these are plum trees.'

Some of my academic friends insisted that the younger generation had migrated happily to the cities, eager to experience the joys of running water, central heating and nearby shops and cinemas. Doubtless this is true of many. Many others, however, left their villages only reluctantly, having been disinherited by the state and finding themselves unable to adapt to farming methods that outraged all their instincts. The Gypsies who often replaced them had no knowledge of farming and in exchange for a pittance were content to follow directives from 'agricultural engineers'. Corruption, Costin said, was endemic at every level of the collective farm system; and so many labourers being Gypsies ('our most expert thieves!'), with numerous offspring, meant that a considerable percentage of the grotesquely low output never reached any market, black or white.

Costin's parents, in their early seventies, were tall, dignified and weather-beaten. They graciously received their first ever foreign guest, giving me a warm but unfussy welcome – though my arrival was unexpected. Not being able to talk to Mamma without an interpreter frustrated me dreadfully. A handsome woman still, with a most striking presence, she was very keen that I should appreciate how relevant to modern Rumania is some of Eminescu's poetry, written more than a century ago. She found the worn, leather-bound volumes, and the particular poems, and bade Costin translate. One of them went like this:

175

Fallen among these wolfish fools your glory will be torn to
shreds,
While all that is not understood will be decried by wagging
heads.
Then they will probe your private life, dissecting that,
discounting this,
And searching out with eager eyes each little thing you've
done amiss,
To make you even as themselves. They will not care for all
the light
Your labour poured upon the world, but for the sins and
every slight
And human failing they can find, and every petty thing that
must
Befall the life of hapless days, of every mortal child of dust.
And every little misery that harassed a tormented mind
Will seem more tolerable to them than all the truths that you
did find.

(That is Corneliu Popescu's translation; Costin's was more
approximate but no less moving in the Rumania of 1990.)

The outside world was unknown to Costin's parents; they could
not conceive – except unreally, through television – what it might
be like. They had no notion of bloc life, nor did they want to
experience it, even briefly. Every coaxing invitation – '*Please* come
and stay with us, just for a week!' – was firmly declined. During
the war Pappa, like thousands of other schoolboys, had had to
work in an urban munitions factory; but since 1945 he has
remained in his village, apart from a rare journey – once a year or
less – to the nearest market town twelve miles away. Mamma was
born in the village and has never once left it. This degree of
voluntary immobilisation is apparently quite usual among their
generation and Michaela – Costin's wife – wondered if they feel
unable to cope with Communist Rumania beyond the comparative safety of their home ground. Everyone was astounded to hear
that in my corner of rural Ireland some elderly countryfolk have
never been to a city, not because they couldn't afford to go but
because they see no point in going. (We don't use the word
'peasant', which for some curious reason has derogatory connota-

176

tions in Ireland.) Countryfolk are not travellers, unless outside forces propel them; their world is where they are. And from within the calm security of their own territory they often utter words of wisdom that make the judgements of 'the travelled ones' seem trite. Staying with village families, I realised that Rumania's new generation of graduates has been bred not by bucolic thickies but by strong-minded thinkers. Circumstances may have limited the older generation's intellectual development, but their capacity for it has borne fruit among those of their children who have replaced the banished – or at least suppressed – bourgeoisie.

Costin's post-revolutionary wish was to set up as an independent dairy-farmer in his village, making cheese and butter for the nearest city market, and to see Ilie, his weedy, city-pale ten-year-old son, growing sturdy and ruddy-cheeked and one day taking over the farm. Ilie shared that ambition; whenever I stayed with the family in their bloc, 180 miles away, he talked incessantly of grandpa and grandma in the village where he would like to live *always*. Costin's brother Ion – the factory engineer – had similar ambitions; but Pappa and Mamma found this regression deeply upsetting. For thirty years their diminished lives had been made tolerable only by their sons' 'success'. At least Communism had allowed both boys to become 'intellectuals', with jobs good enough to enable them to run motor-cars – when petrol was available. This was their parents' only and greatly valued compensation for the miseries of collectivisation. Having made that adjustment to an alien regime, they were finding it impossible, in old age, to adjust again. *Why* did Costin and Ion wish to reject their prestigious status and revert to being peasants? Their own ignorance of the outside world left them unable to comprehend their sons' longing to escape from it. A return to the village would mean disgrace. Everyone would think the boys had somehow failed . . .

Within days of crossing the border, I had diagnosed Rumania as a far from classless society. Communism made possible the emergence of a new middle class, rather as the Welfare State did in Britain, by providing a free university education for the children of peasants and workers. And these self-labelled 'intellectuals' usually sound either condescending towards or contemptuous of the 'simple people' *en masse*. Yet they remain devoted to their own unacademic relatives – cherishing them in old age, visiting 'our village' as often as possible and teaching their children to love and respect those peasant grandparents whose way of life is so unlike their own. Given a certain unhealthy political climate, this new middle class could easily swing to the extreme right, just as many of Britain's first-generation graduates are among the most fervent Thatcherites. But that analogy with Britain needs qualifying: no Rumanian intellectual is ashamed of lowly origins, as their equivalents so often are in Western Europe. Instead, they are proud of having started out from simple homes and primitive village schools and ended up as graduates. Is this a benign effect of Communism?

A genuinely egalitarian flavour certainly co-exists with Rumania's blatant 'graduate/non-graduate' class-consciousness. This is something impossible to imagine in Britain but quite strong, though not all-pervasive, in modern Ireland – also essentially a peasant-dominated society, though its evolution to that stage took a longer and more tortuous path than Rumania's. It fascinated me to watch the everyday interaction between 'intellectuals' and 'simple people'. They don't often mix socially, unless – pre-revolution – under the aegis of some Party occasion; but in general they do unselfconsciously treat one another as equals. At a military dinner party to which I was invited in Tirgu Mures, I noticed much friendly banter between the restaurant staff and the guests – all senior officers in gorgeous uniforms and government ministers from Bucharest. If an imitation of this took place in the average Western European democracy, it wouldn't seem 'natural'. In Rumania it does and I think 'unselfconscious' is the key word. The intellectuals are not merely being nice to the simple people, as civilised members of a superior class are everywhere 'nice' to their social inferiors. There is a strong and very attractive sense of individuals spontaneously responding to individuals *as* individuals. Since the basis of Rumania's new snobbery is intellectual arrogance, workers as such are looked down on – while simultaneously the individual worker is usually treated as an equal human being. Commenting on the shocking brutality of the miners' invasion of Bucharest in June 1990, a few days after my departure from Rumania, a friend wrote: 'It's terrifying to see how usually non-violent people can be driven into such a mess'. She might have written: 'What else would you expect, when the *hoi polloi* are let off the leash?' But she looked deeper; the miners were normally decent individuals who had been incited to violence by Iliescu – deliberately manipulating ancient resentments – and who then lost the restraints that normally curb individuals and became a savage mindless mob, no better or worse than enraged mobs anywhere.

None of Rumania's Communist dictators – least of all Ceausescu – encouraged genuine egalitarianism; and the tensions that were building up for the new middle class, before the revolution, show no sign of being reduced. One afternoon, as we sat sunning ourselves in the yard, under the leafless vines, Michaela commented on a wireless news item about the election campaign. 'If Iliescu goes on like this, Ilie will be discriminated against as an intellectual. We don't want to go back to the social élite having privileges and respect *only* because of their pedigrees – but Communism making an élite of the workers isn't much better ... Now we're being discriminated against because we think, which makes us dangerous. Ilie's four grandparents are still in our villages, simple people working on the land – but now the workers are being trained to despise every child able to *think*.'

'The Rumanians are still serfs, in their minds,' said Costin. 'Why have we nothing like Solidarity in Poland, no samizdat tradition, no leader like Havel, no clergymen like those who inspired the East Germans to struggle free? We can't take control for ourselves, we must be told what to do – the way serfs always are.'

We were sitting outside a five-room extension that fifteen years ago had been added to the original primitive cottage in which Costin and Ion grew up. It puzzled me that even moribund villages contained several large, well-maintained, newish houses, or elaborate extensions. Admittedly, the spacious bathroom in the Costin extension, fully equipped and pink-tiled everywhere, had to be serviced from the family well and was rarely used; piped water, promised in 1962, had not yet arrived. (Relief showed all round when I intimated my preference for the century-old earth-closet in a far corner of the yard, beside the buffalo byre.) Costin saw house-building as an important 'statement'; in the past of defiance, now of celebration. 'Systematisation' was first announced as part of the Rumanian Communist Party's programme in 1968. During the 1955–65 decade, over a million village

179

homes had been owner-built. After 1968, material shortages and new regulations restricted private building; yet some peasants, in collusion with anti-systematisation local Party officials, continued to defy this most detested of all Ceausescu's diktats. As Michaela pointed out, peasants liked to spend *only* on their homes: not on food, drink, clothes, entertainments, cars, holidays, consumer goods. However, the houses going up in so many villages in 1990 didn't accord with everyone's low wages. Some of these grand-looking suburban villas were visible evidence of Party officials' nefarious deeds and deals. Others proved how well the more enterprising farmers had done on the black market before 1984.

By 1980 the peasants' official income was 40 per cent lower than the workers' and their pensions and social security benefits were only half (occasionally two-thirds) that of the rest of the population. In the mid 1980s fierce new laws threatened them with starvation; until then, they had been free to dispose of the produce of their family plots and of any sheep they might be running on uncollectivised hillsides. When a drastic reduction in plot size was combined with a compulsory production structure, surpluses – in the unlikely event of there being any – could only be sold at fixed low prices. Black marketeering penalties were increased and Securitate officers swarmed through the villages demanding from each household its bureaucratically determined and often wildly unrealistic quota. As always, the poorest suffered most. One elderly widow, living alone and too rheumaticky to cultivate her plot, instead kept a cow on it. In February 1989, when no milk came for lack of fodder, she felt such terror that the wretched animal was sacrificed – tethered one night on the railway track. Costin noted a connection between the effectiveness of state terrorism and the potential victim's relative wealth. 'By '89,' he said, 'even fairly high-up Party and Securitate officials were very hungry and as the laws became more hard they were often enforced more softly – if you knew how to deal with officials and had something to sell. Because that old widow had nothing to sell, she would have been punished – very cruelly, as an example to others. And as proof that the Securitate locally were doing their duty, supervising quotas – though often they weren't! She was not a stupid woman to be so frightened.'

That was a deplorably alcoholic weekend. I suffered (gladly)

180

from an ancient Rumanian custom, the imbibing of neat *tuica* before breakfast – a custom that hits particularly hard when breakfast doesn't happen until 11 a.m. Every night the family sat talking into the wee hours, making the most of their reunion, while I slept soundly in the new parlour-cum-guest-room, with the usual tall tiled stove in one corner, a fine cabinet of old cut glass and 'best china' in another and a handsome new dining-table – unmistakably For Export Only – in the centre. At about 9 a.m., when I got back from my long early walks – already starving – everyone was assembling around the twelve-foot-long white-clothed table in the living-room. Of breakfast there was never a sign but an enormous decanter of pale gold eleven-year-old apricot *tuica* stood surrounded by delicate liqueur glasses. This was Pappa's moment of glory; no one else in the village made apricot *tuica* or knew how to treble-distill it to such a point of pixillating perfection. Of course it was not served habitually: only for special guests, like stray Irishwomen, or on festive occasions. And it had to be drunk on the premises because Pappa believed that even a brief journey would irreparably damage it.

From the old kitchen – cramped, ill-lit, cosy – breakfast was at last carried across the yard by Mamma (a superb cook) and her three small grandsons. We began with two fried eggs each, followed by as much as one could eat of rissoles of veal, thinly sliced *slanina*, three sorts of homemade sausage and salami, buffalo-milk butter and cheese, fresh radishes and scallions, not-too-stale bread, herbal tea and real coffee. This brunch banquet continued in a leisurely way until the early afternoon. Then, between 5 and 6 p.m., another banquet appeared: mutton soup dense with meat, potatoes, onion, garlic; braised veal cutlets, crisp golden-brown chips, floury boiled potatoes, spicy steamed beef sausages, pickled fungus. Luckily puddings never follow such marathons; the prolonged sugar shortage has caused every-one to forget such things once existed. Rumania is the most carnivorous country I have ever been in; when meat is available it is eaten by the kilo in a wide variety of forms, all equally delicious. Our evening meal was of course preceded by more (a lot more) *tuica* and accompanied by an excellent *rosé* which proved Pappa to be as skilled at vinification as at distilling. He and his sons expressed infinite contempt for those uncouth enough to use sugar when wine-making. And they assured me, correctly, that even the most reckless over-indulgence in Rumanian villages goes unpunished next morning.

In Central Transylvania I stayed with friends of a friend – Dinu – in a village very unlike Costin's. When the aid convoys first arrived, foreigners were confused by the many prosperous-looking villages lining Transylvania's main roads. With their brightly painted exteriors – including jolly or sentimental murals on some gables – and their neat gnomed gardens and luxurious vines, and quite often a shrouded Dacia in the barn, they spoiled the 'Rumania-on-its-knees' image. As my daughter Rachel remarked, when she came from Skopje to rescue me after my ultimate Rumanian disaster, 'Yugoslavia *looks* much poorer.'

These main road villages, within bus reach of cities or big towns, look so prosperous because many of the younger inhabitants commute to factory jobs and save on household expenses by living at home. The older generation, often state farm pensioners, tend the small children (if any) and the poultry and livestock: possibly a sow and bonhams – perhaps a few sheep, depending on the nature of the local terrain. In the evenings and on Sundays the gardens are productively tilled and this rural–urban compromise makes these commuters seem the least misfortunate of Rumanians. It also made them the least favourite of Ceausescu's victims. He felt a special impotent hatred for such villagers, who showed open contempt for his December 1987 directive: 'Those workers who live in a commune should move to a work-place settlement.'

Systematisation was not among Ceausescu's unqualified successes. The explanation lies in his concluding statement to the National Conference of the Rumanian Communist Party in 1972:

Despite what we have already stated several times – that new buildings could only be erected in the inner regions of townships – people continue to build houses where they wish, and the People's Councils fail to properly control this and to hold those responsible who violate the laws of the nation in this respect.

182

The People's Councils naturally failed to control this situation because they *were* the people's councils – stubborn peasants who abhorred systematisation. For years Ceausescu tacitly accepted that even he dared not replace some 7,000 villages with 250 new towns (or 'agro-industrial centres'). In 1972–3, forty new towns were hastily jerry-built; since then, only one has appeared. Not until 1987, when his megalomania was in full spate, did he revert to his all-out systematisation obsession. Soon, however, he was thwarted again, by a sustained international protest campaign threatening Rumania's commercial interests.

Dinu's friends, Con and Maria, were a retired couple whose son and daughter commuted to the bakery where Con had worked for twenty-five years. Maria had laboured for thirty years on the nearby state farm, once the property of a Magyar nobleman. On 1 March 1990 her pension had risen from 150 lei a month to 500 lei. An individual could just survive on this, living in misery, but the 150 lei pension was deliberately homicidal. Ceausescu liked people to die very soon after they had ceased to be productive and doctors were instructed not to attend patients over the age of seventy. Presumably the *Conducator* disapproved of his mother-in-law, who died a few days after the revolution at the age of 103. A television camera showed a death-bed face frighteningly like her daughter's.

From my seat by the small window of an over-furnished parlour three storks' nests were visible, cleverly balanced on top of electricity posts (jarring concrete monsters – the only ugly things in most villages, towering over the little houses). According to Dinu, the same pair return to the same nest year after year and storks bring good luck; so this was a particularly fortunate village, with more than twenty nests up and down the long street. The migrants had arrived only recently and, having put their nests in order, were now standing on those unwieldy-looking piles of twigs gazing soulfully at one another for hours on end. Everyone was amused by my interest in the colony; Ireland being storkless confirmed their suspicion that it suffers from permafrost.

Dinu had prematurely white hair, deep-set dark eyes, a wide smile and a long lean face that seemed always aglow with enthusiasm and kindness. Being unmarried at forty-five made him seem freakish in Rumania. When we first met, in his work-place village elsewhere in central Transylvania, he had told me, 'If the Securitate were not so stupid, I wouldn't be here now. I'd be an ordinary married man with some secure academic job in a city.'

As a sixteen-year-old, Dinu was arrested by the Securitate who had mistaken an innocent schoolboy prank for 'subversive activity'. He spent the next five years in a prison work-camp, among many criminals and a few dissidents. From the latter he learned to look at his Communist-throttled country in a new way – having started life in an apathetically apolitical family. Inflamed by the injustice of his own fate, he resolved to become a closet social worker: the only sort that could survive in Rumania. Although city-bred – his father a doctor, his mother a physiotherapist – he developed an almost mystical commitment to helping collectivised peasants to preserve both their traditional skills and their self-respect. He believed Communism to be so evil that it must soon – within his own lifetime – be overthrown. His release coincided with Ceausescu's coming to power and during the 'moderate' years that followed, most of his contemporaries were content to count their blessings while he pursued his mission. Normally it would have been impossible for a convicted subversive to get into a university. However, Dinu's innocence was recognised by 'certain people' who, being afraid to confront the Securitate, made no effort to have him freed but did give him a 'clean file' on his release. He then completed his schooling, qualified as a vet at the age of twenty-eight and has since been working on various state farms, combining his official job with the subtle boosting of peasant morale – including vigorous encouragement to continue practising the traditional handicrafts of Transylvania. Marriage was postponed because he couldn't expect 'a nice civilised wife' to share his spartan accommodation and way of life.

Dinu escorted me around the state farm; its animals were kept in conditions marginally less dire than on the collectives I visited – they might be described as 'Victorian gaol' conditions, rather than 'concentration camp'. This was a mainly arable farm (mile after mile after mile of wheat and onions) but some state farms run three thousand dairy cattle and Dinu has seen more than five hundred dying on one farm at the end of a hard winter. The next county then had a fodder surplus (edible straw) but the transfer of resources from one state farm to another was forbidden. There are of course no milking machines; the villagers to whom I described them simply didn't believe such unnatural devices could exist. Nor did they believe that Irish cows yield a daily average of nine litres. The state cows' average daily yield, in both winter and summer, is two litres – little more than is given by India's scavenging cattle. State farms employ scores of Gypsies to milk their thousands of cows and 'those people make trouble'. A favourite trick is to colour watered milk by adding bicarbonate of soda, and one such contaminated collection ruins a whole tanker-load, which then has to be given to the pigs. To stimulate production, post-revolution, the state was paying six lei a litre to the collectives, though the *alimentara* price was being held at four and a half. 'The Front,' chuckled Dinu, 'won't raise any food prices *before* the elections!'

The élite corps who drove and maintained a state farm's tractors – before these folded up for lack of spare parts, tyres and fuel – earned a comparatively decent 3,000 lei a month. But much of the land was cultivated by slave labour, starvation-driven people who received only one hundred kilos of grain *annually* as their free food ration, and therefore continued to steal food despite being caught regularly. As the penalty for stealing even a pocketful of corncobs was no pay for six months, the poorest workers – those without a family plot – were in fact never paid any wages. Each six months penalty merged with the next, which perfectly suited a bureaucracy predisposed towards slave labour.

Back in the village, we found the commuters (two defiantly childless couples) using the last of the daylight to plant vegetables. Both wives were pregnant – not for the first time, but now they were willing to give birth.

'They have faith in the Front,' said Dinu gloomily. 'All this family will vote for Iliescu. I tell them to support the Christian Democratic Party but they feel too grateful to Iliescu. They think he saved us from Ceausescu and Communism. It's hard for simple people to understand politics.'

The Christian Democrats were among the countless mini-parties with no hope of winning even one seat in the Assembly. Yet according to Dinu only they had a clear policy on agricultural reform and peasants' rights – issues being dodged by everyone else, including the revived National Peasant Party which, in 1990, seemed as ineffectual as it had been when governing Rumania in 1928–30. Dinu was not surprised to hear of my recent meeting with a Front government minister, touring Transylvania on 'election business', who told me he knew nothing about the Front's agricultural policy or Rumania's farming problems. He did look briefly abashed on being informed, by a foreigner, that thousands of elderly state farm workers were terrified of losing their pensions should the Front 'give the land to the people'. But Bucharest Fat-Cats find 'primitive peasants' and their concerns frightfully tedious and he made no effort to conceal his boredom.

Before I left that village, Dinu took me to a pensioners' meeting in the primary school, called by him in his capacity as a Christian Democrat leader. A local Front official (an ex-Party 'agricultural engineer') was spreading that pernicious rumour which I had mentioned to the minister. The objective was to arouse or sustain opposition to land redistribution. The effect was to reduce these already destitute pensioners to a most pitiable state of anxiety. There had never been any basis for this rumour, yet it was being injected into many villages by Front thugs. Happily the under-dogs of that county loved and trusted – almost worshipped – Dinu and his reassurances brought about a palpable relaxation of tension; in the eyes of those sitting near me I saw tears of relief. Rumania could use many more Dinus; I only met one.

12

Footless in Moldavia

Throughout the first half of 1990 there was an extraordinary *intensity* about Rumania, then a country in what can only be described as psychic turmoil. Outsiders were at once affected by this and, after a time, felt mangled by it. An Irishman who has been visiting Bucharest for many years, and is deeply attached to his friends there, responded negatively to my suggestion that he should now explore Transylvania. He said, 'I don't think I can handle any more Rumanian contacts, it's all so *wearing!*' – which of course is a compliment to the Rumanians. Theirs is not a country you can visit as a detached traveller; their own talent for friendship immediately engages the stranger's sympathy and interest and soon one feels irrationally committed, not imagining that one can do anything specific to help, yet wanting to rally round. In practice this means listening, commenting when asked to comment and, above all, giving reassurance – without flattery – to a people who are deeply self-doubting.

By early April 1990 I knew that I was going to have a long-term problem with Rumania, akin to my Northern Ireland problem. Repeatedly I would be drawn back, both to visit friends and because I had become so personally concerned about the country's future. I also knew that I must now have an interlude of solitude, silence and space. (My mental exhaustion was partly attributable to continuously surmounting the language barrier; most of my conversations, especially those involving translation, demanded maximum concentration all round.) I decided on a fortnight's trek through northern Moldavia, an uncollectivised region where the attractive little villages look normally bustling, with individuals tending their own healthy stock and family-sized conical hay-ricks in the sloping fields.

Soon after midday on the 10th, beyond an isolated hamlet of half a dozen wooden shacks, I arrived at the base of the Rarau massif's southern flank. A 3,000-foot climb would take me to the top before dark. Looking up, I could see only the first stage, a grassy mountain that blocked what lay beyond. On either side were even steeper slopes, all forested. A faint path led off the rough motorable track from the hamlet. As I began to climb, the sky was cloudless, the sun warm, the breeze cool, Ceausescu's Rumania forgotten.

Half-way up that first mountain the path faded, but if I kept climbing I couldn't get seriously lost. And it wouldn't matter if I did; my rucksack was packed with camping-gear and food. The first grassy mountain led to another and by now it was cold. Ahead rose a densely forested slope – the steepest of all – and, just visible above it, sharp obelisks of limestone marked the summit.

Approaching the forest, I was astonished to see a strip of ploughland some hundred yards by twenty. Who cultivated what here? The shepherds had not yet moved up and since leaving the hamlet hours before I had seen no one – and no arable land, or livestock, or dwellings. Then, on reaching that thoroughly dug oblong, I recognised it as the oddly symmetrical work of wild pigs. So my farmer friend in Sighet had not exaggerated; rooting on this scale, in a maize or potato field, would cause economic catastrophe. These northern Carpathians support Rumania's greatest concentration of wildlife: wolves, foxes, lynx, bears, roebuck, pigs, squirrels, pine-marten.

In that forest of ancient, mighty spruce firs, still snow-laden, there was no trace of logging and therefore no path. (It is, I learned next day, a nature reservation.) The Bukovina spruce fir has been famous all over Europe for centuries and many of these trees were too stout for my embrace. The numbers which had fallen puzzled me, until I noticed how shallow are their roots – spreading very wide, but with only a feeble purchase on the poor, thin soil. And here the winter gales are ferocious.

That was a difficult climb; the broken ground necessitated much zig-zagging, as did numerous fallen branches and prone tree-trunks. Underfoot was a slippery sludge – snow and ice over a deep accumulation of black mould. Beneath those towering trees there was virtually no undergrowth and within half an hour I saw two bears – one in the near distance, digging under a tree. The other appeared scarcely fifteen yards away, a shaggy lightish brown creature ambling along with the worried expression some teddy-bears have. When he glanced at me I have to admit I felt scared enough to look away, feeling – perhaps quite wrongly – that eye-contact might be best avoided. He was very much bigger than I had expected a Rumanian bear to be: at least five feet long and sturdily built. It would be an uneven contest were he to fancy some protein. But he evidently considered me of no importance, compared to his personal worries, and continued to plod along parallel to me for about fifty yards. I slowed to keep pace with him, the half of me that wasn't scared relishing the companionship of a bear – which somehow seemed appropriate, in that magic forest. Then he turned and disappeared into a gully. This was one of those encounters more enjoyable in retrospect than at the time and it prompted me cravenly to revise my plans. I had had thoughts of camping near the summit, but two bears in thirty minutes indicated a considerable local ursine population and it would be unfortunate should one of them happen to suffer from night-starvation. I had been quite successfully brainwashed by numerous folk-tales – which *might* be true stories – about the Carpathian bear's carnivorous tastes.

Beyond the forest, I was on the edge of a mile-long grassy oval valley containing three enormous sheep-folds. To the west this deep hollow was bounded by a silver limestone wall, 300 feet high and topped by a frieze of frosted dwarf pines glittering against the deep blue sky – and ridiculously reminding me of a punk hair-do. Slim spruce saplings covered the steep slope on my right, each supple young branch bent under its sparkling snow burden. I stopped to drink from an ice-fringed stream; urban life had so deconditioned me that I was sweat-soaked, despite a steely cold wind. Then I paused to examine an old shingle-roofed shepherd's hut – built generations ago but still sound, the thick spruce beams preserved by their own resin. The only nails used were of yew-wood; the yew, known in Moldavia as 'the iron-tree', is now a protected species because of its slow growth-rate. On the last precipitous climb to the massif's long summit, slight breathlessness reminded me that I was now at 5,000 feet.

Rarau is at the very heart of the Bistrita Mountains and as I took off my rucksack, to unpack a bottle of *tuica*, I felt intoxicated even before opening it. To the north and quite close lay the

Obcine range of Bukovina, a curiously neat-looking line of low, rounded, same-size mountains, all spruce-clad and separated by long valleys. To the east was the Stinisoara range: similar, but more close-packed. Behind me, beyond the narrow gorge of the Bistrita river which I had left that morning, rose a chain of rougher, barer peaks, filling the sky-line. And from the west, only a few miles away, beckoned Mount Giumalau, some 500 feet higher than Rarau and with a deceptive 'volcanic cone' which is really a twin summit. That, I then thought, was my destination for the morrow.

At my feet lay another sort of beauty, something never seen before and never to be forgotten. On this exposed crest, where only spear grass grew, the wind and frost had interacted to create a fairyland of fragile pennants of ice, streaming from every hoar-whitened blade. All over the slightly curving saddle this wondrous display caught the rays of the declining sun and trembled brilliantly in the wind, each formation flawless.

Three level miles, on the crest's clear east-west path, ended with a short, sharp drop to Rarau's *cabana* through the thick snow that still lay on this northern slope. Here I could see, below the track on my left, the renowned *Pietrele Doamnei* (the Princess's Rocks). These three isolated limestone towers, hundreds of feet high, look from a distance like the battlements of some legendary vaivode's fortress. Then the blue-black, orange-streaked sunset clouds suddenly became a sheet of greyness and it was snowing – face-stinging dry little particles, driven by a gale. Near the *cabana* I passed close to the *Pietrele Doamnei* but postponed paying my respects to them; it was not a time for lingering.

Mercifully, the lie of the land, aided by surrounding spruces, prevents Rarau's *cabana* from being too conspicuous. In this nine-storey monstrosity (by Swiss chalet out of Stalin) the post-Ceausescu habit of heating buildings had not yet caught on though icicles hung from everything in sight, including the non-functioning lavatory cisterns. In the restaurant a merry party of eight foresters wore mittens, and sheepskin jackets with the collars rolled up, and fox-fur hats with the ear-flaps pulled down. They were celebrating their team leader's winning of 10,000 lei in the National Lottery by mixing cognac, white wine, *tuica* and beer, which seemed to me unwise. I little realised how soon I was to be

190

the victim of their unwisdom. The walls of the vast restaurant were 90 per cent glass, something perhaps appreciated by summer visitors though the view was restricted to a cliff-face covered in dwarf pine. Astonishingly, supper was served hot: a heavy-duty soup of potatoes, tinned peas and tender (non-Bulgarian) chicken, followed by a massif of crisp chips, thick slices of flavoursome fried pork, the inevitable bowl of pickled cabbage and a bottle of excellent Iasi dry white wine – all for seventy pence.

Even after eating, my hands were too numb to write. On the way to bed I passed a dozen wanly exhausted teenagers who had just walked through the blizzard from Cimpulung Moldovenesc, 3,000 feet down. They seemed to be a school party, in the charge of two young men. Doubtless their exhaustion was owing to unsuitable gear: battered suitcases in lieu of 'not available' rucksacks.

In my sixth-floor eyrie the north-facing wall was all window – and ill-fitting window at that, through which came draughts like swords of ice. But once in my flea-bag I slept well, only waking briefly around midnight as the foresters sang and hiccupped their way to bed.

The dawn showed a world all white and still. Although the grey sky remained low the wind had dropped and it was freezing hard. *Cabanas* don't provide breakfast so I fuelled up on bread and *slanina* while still in my flea-bag.

Descending the mock-marble staircase in semi-darkness, I slipped on a pile of vomit and landed five steps down with my right ankle twisted under me. It had taken all my body weight, plus a heavy rucksack, and I at once knew it was broken. Apart from the pain, there is an odd audible thing: the brain, if not the ears, 'hears' bones crunching. Picking myself up – some moments later, after the first pain-wave had ebbed – I accepted that now was the time to do some involuntary research into Rumania's medical service. But alas! now was *not* the time . . .

I could find only the *cabana* manager's disagreeable wife, who informed me in French that the nearest town, Cimpulung, was currently inaccessible to motor vehicles. The prospect of languishing for days in a *cabana* bedroom, awaiting the thaw, with an injury in need of immediate attention, did nothing to cheer me. Being then unknowledgeable about broken ankles, I resolved to try to totter down to Cimpulung, but tottering proved impracticable; at my rate of progress it would have taken days to reach the town. And the pain was all the time increasing, naturally enough; as the doctor later pointed out, broken feet are not for use. I gave in when my leg began visibly to swell, even above boot-level.

An hour later I was back in the *cabana* where – *mirabile dictu!* – an English-speaking final-year medical student approached me as I very slowly crossed the foyer, with no thought in my mind but to *sit down*. 'You have a problem!' exclaimed Virgil. Being by then speechless with pain I merely nodded and was helped up steps to a 'café area', with metal tables and chairs, where I gingerly took off my boot (not to be replaced until 22 June) and displayed the damage. Firmly Virgil diagnosed 'Nothing broken!' – because I could wiggle my toes. I didn't argue but inwardly pitied his patients-to-be. He and his friend, Teodor, a German-speaker, then half-carried me to a first-floor bedroom and swung into action.

The Ceausescu era wonderfully revived folk medicine – perhaps its only beneficial side-effect – and while Teodor soaked my foot in icy water, Virgil requisitioned onions from the kitchen, applied layers of raw sliced onion under a very tight bandage and presented me with a bottle of 'cognac'.

Two very large cognacs later I was able to hold converse. Virgil and Teodor were in charge of the teenagers, whose academic achievements had earned them an Easter holiday on Mount Rarau; when the weather improved they would do a geological project with Teodor. Virgil was of the party because, 'In dangerous mountains it is necessary to have a medical person. So I can give you many bandages but no medicines!' He added, 'For hundreds of years this Mount Rarau is unlucky, the simple people know that. Every year strange things happen – people die from silly accidents, or have misfortunes like you. They tell about a curse on Rarau. A Prince of Moldavia did something very, *very* bad and the person he did bad to, cursed the mountain. *I* am scientific, not liking to believe such things. But sometimes, about Rarau, I feel *not* scientific!' Later, I heard of this tradition from many local people, who plainly regarded me as just the latest victim of an ancient curse.

All day Virgil and Teodor cherished me, regularly changing

the poultice and re-soaking the foot – not as simple a process as it may sound, water being very scarce. I suggested keeping the full basin in my room; but it was the *cabana*'s only basin and Maria, the strikingly beautiful twenty-one-year-old waitress, needed it for washing floors – her main task. It then occurred to me that a basin of snow would prove a more powerful analgesic than cold water: which it did, for a little time. But despite all this loving care the pain worsened rapidly and the boys had to carry me to the *toilet* – unfortunately at the far end of a long corridor.

At sunset my door was slowly pushed open and Bogdan timidly entered – a gnarled little gnome of a man, with tears in his bloodshot brown eyes. He it was who had vomited on the stairs and now, guilt-ravaged, he had come to crave my forgiveness, bearing a large bottle of *tuica*. I was quite overwhelmed; where else in the world, in similar circumstances, would the culprit have confessed and been so genuinely upset? By the end of the bottle (we were assisted by my nurse-attendants) Bogdan looked much more cheerful, having been assured that I quite understood his aberration – that occasionally I, too, had over-indulged to the point of throwing up. This admission on 'granny's' part severely shocked Virgil and Teodor: another example of Rumanian primness.

In February, a London friend had loaded me with pain-killers, lest I might absentmindedly return to Rumania without any, but even a triple dose left my ravelled sleeve of care unknitted that night. And sleeplessness did nothing for morale, which by mid-night had sunk to a new low. Not only was my Easter holiday kiboshed, but a few months of immobility loomed; having cracked my spine in 1984, I knew it would be months rather than weeks. By about 3 a.m. I had convinced myself that my trekking days were over, because old bones never heal properly. Soon after, I desperately needed to pee – which was a good thing, since that conundrum diverted my mind from endless vistas of gloom. After some thought, I cautiously lowered myself to the floor and proceeded, on my hands and bottom, to the balcony . . .

Next morning my foot was, if viewed objectively, quite beautiful – the size and shape of a rugger ball and marbled blue, green, brown and red, like high-quality nineteenth-century endpapers. Virgil, applying more sliced onion, said, 'I think you have sprained this ankle in a very bad way.' Teodor, the geology student, said in German, 'I think it is a broken foot.'

During that second sleepless night my demoralisation was accentuated by the 'If only . . .' factor – always a dangerous one and by now becoming an obsession. *If only* I had noticed the vomit! Then I wondered, 'Why has Rumania been, physically, my jinx country?' Somewhere in my pain-addled brain lay an answer to that, but it didn't surface until very much later.

Towards dawn the temperature rose abruptly; it became less cold than it had been the previous noon. When Virgil and Teodor appeared, bearing snow and onions, they announced that by mid-afternoon the track should be motorable.

At 3.30 I was man-handled downstairs and carefully packed into the front seat of a Dacia. Its tyres, I noticed neurotically, were bald. A weeping Maria followed with my rucksack. She longed to talk to her mother, who lived in Cimpulung, and I had tried to persaude the *cabana* manager that I needed her help. But he curtly refused to allow her even half a day off.

Had I been able to imagine the nature and state of that track, nothing would have induced me to be driven on it – especially in a bald-tyred car. Twenty years ago slave labourers ('hero-workers') from Cimpulung carved it out of the mountainside and its hairpin bends are more suited to roebuck than to wheeled vehicles. The thaw was at that early stage when the new snow has melted, only to reveal sheets of corrugated black ice and a five-months' accumulation of packed old snow. The driver – redolent of 'cognac' – was having an angry argument with his nasty wife and frequently turned to glare at her. I realised then how permanent-ly unnerved I had been by January's car accident. The cold sweat of fear – by some erroneously supposed to be the prerogative of Mills & Boon characters – broke out on my forehead. Our downward journey seemed to last for hours although within twenty minutes we were on the level, in Cimpulung's wide ice-free valley. This is a famously beautiful region, though not without some 'anthropogenic modification of the natural background' – Ceausescu-speak for pollution. Self-pity threatened again: I should have crossed this valley on foot, forty-eight hours earlier on my way to Putna Monastery . . .

At 4.30 I was abandoned at one of the several entrances to

Cimpulung's 500-bed hospital which is staffed by twenty-five doctors – none of whom happened to be around. Nor, it seemed, was anybody else around. With my rucksack dumped beside me, I stood on one leg at the bottom of eight steep steps, hanging on to the railing. As the manager returned to the car I could hear his wife shrilly abusing him for having accepted 500 lei instead of demanding *valuta* (dollars).

Some minutes later – by which time I had sat on a step – a nurse appeared in the doorway above: a thin pale little woman, wearing a tattered butcher's-type coat that may once have been white. She stared at my rucksack, then at me. I jabbed my chest and said *'Irlanda!'*, then pointed to my foot and said, *'Ruptura!'* Her face crumpled with sympathy; she leaped down the steps and embraced me. Cimpulung hospital, I was to discover, is short of everything except loving care. I gathered that a strong man would be summoned: the local substitute for wheelchairs, stretchers, lifts. He arrived quite soon, a powerful, gentle, elderly fellow with kind eyes and a worried expression that reminded me of my bear companion. He indicated that I was to hang onto him with one arm and *hop*. Unfortunately there was a long way to hop (more than a hundred yards) to the X-ray department – also approached by eight steps. It seemed downright sadistic that a hospital devoid of all conveyances for the maimed should have steps at each entrance. Here I was left – I thought – with another patient, a frayed-looking sunken-cheeked woman wearing a shabby brown dressing gown over muddy black slacks. She was however the radiographer, who must have been frayed by her years of struggle with the X-ray equipment. It had been defective since 1976 and worked only after being struck hard with a clenched fist three times in rapid succession.

I lay, the machine was beaten, the foot was X-rayed. Our next hop, to the *ghips* room – down two long corridors, up three flights of stairs – inspired the strong man to remark on my *'curaj'*. The plaster of Paris (*ghips*) expert explained that he could do nothing until a doctor – who would come on duty at 7 p.m. – had seen the X-rays. Then two sturdy beaming nurses hopped me into a ward where only crab-wise movement was possible between the four narrow beds. Two patients shared one small locker; there was no other furniture. Each bed had a rock-hard mattress, a meagre lumpy pillow, stained and torn sheets and one threadbare blanket; during winter, families provided extra bedding. This hospital was half-empty because it could only cope with fracture cases.

At 6 p.m. a nurse wheeled in a rattling squealing trolley bearing four platefuls of something indefinable that smelt nauseating. Solemnly she announced, 'President Ceausescu invites you to eat!' Everyone smiled sourly and the trolley was wheeled out. This ritualistic black joke well conveyed the despair of those for whom nothing had improved since the revolution. Most hospital meals went in vast cauldrons to the local pigs – reputedly an extraordinarily undiscriminating tribe, even by porcine standards.

Soon after, relatives brought soups, stews, sausages, bread and herbal tea. The foreigner's welfare became everyone's first concern; being family-less, I must have something of everything. This was awkward, there being little to spare. I extricated myself by indicating that pain had robbed me of my appetite, which was true.

When the doctor arrived my remoralisation began, not because of what he had to say ('three bones broken') but because of what he was. In the *ghips* room he interpreted while my leg was being encased, from mid-thigh to toes, in a weighty substance unseen by Occidentals for decades past; henceforth hopping would be less painful but much more strenuous. I didn't protest when he ordered my transfer to a tiny private room; by then I was some way beyond having ideological scruples about preferential treatment. The nurses' staff-room was next door; if I needed anything during the night I was to bang hard on their wall. (The bell system has not yet reached Moldavia.) Rumanian nurses – uneducated, untrained, ill-paid – have the status of maid-servants and in Cimpulung the same women were on duty day and night: 'an irregularity', I was told.

Next morning the immobility imposed by an unbendable leg and a mighty load of *ghips* induced slight panic; never before had I experienced such physical dependence on others. Vladimir, the doctor, suggested my staying in the hospital, free of charge, until the *ghips* came off in June; but that was not a real option. I decided to move to Cimpulung's Zimbru Tourist Hotel (the more congenial alternative lacked a lift) and there consider long-term plans.

The region's 'ambulance' fleet, visible from my window, looked like a good start for a scrap-yard. Three of the vans hadn't been used for years; the fourth, unused for months, was now being reactivated on my behalf though I had wanted to take a taxi. At noon the strong man hopped me to an exit, then hastened away to give a piggy-back to a pitiable youth with a mangled leg who had just been delivered by horse-cart. No one could explain why crutches were not available in this region of supremely skilled woodworkers. When I asked Vladimir to order a pair from a local carpenter he said that that would not be possible but promised to try to find a pair himself – somehow, somewhere.

As I balanced on one leg, clutching the railings and trembling with pain, the lean, scowling ambulance-driver – clad in filthy dungarees – emerged from the cab with a tangle of wire and disappeared under the engine. Ten dreadfully long minutes later a sudden stuttering roar fell as music on my ears. Then the driver, having roughly hopped me to the van's three-foot-high side door, left me to sit on the floor and drag myself in backwards, just as we jerked off. The walls and floor were streaked with old vomit, phlegm and blood-stains; but probably time had disinfected everything.

When Vladimir and his wife visited me that afternoon I arranged for an SOS to be sent to Rachel, asking her to bring crutches and escort me to Cluj. There my base could be a ground-floor room in the friendly Vladeasa Hotel, within reach of the university's English Language Library.

That telegram took four days to meander to Skopje. It was 7 p.m. on 19 April before an exhausted Rachel arrived, after a forty-six-hour train journey, bearing a stout pair of wooden crutches borrowed from a Yugoslav neighbour. Apart from the moment of her emergence from the womb, I have never been so glad to see my daughter.

A week later we were in Cluj, where my friends rejected the Vladeasa Hotel plan with shudders of distaste and found me a comfortable ground-floor flat elsewhere – of course rent-free. The Rumanians take their responsibilities to foreign guests very seriously indeed and within twenty-four hours a strong team of Dervla-minders had been formed. For seven weeks these genuine 'hero-workers' saw to all my needs – books, food, drink, postage, entertainment, transport – without ever making me feel a nuisance. As Walter Starkie wrote of Transylvania sixty years ago: 'It would be difficult for me to repay in words of gratitude the treatment I received'.

A broken foot in Darkest Moldavia may seem a wholly negative event but I now discovered an apparent paradox: for travellers, physical immobility can have certain advantages. People who had been amiable acquaintances became trusting friends – trusting enough to give me valuable insights into the foulest corners of Ceausescu's Rumania, these being not necessarily the most dramatic. A few academics needed help with their translations into English of Rumanian plays and short stories – a fascinating exercise, during which they and I learned quite a lot about the very different workings of Rumanian and Irish minds, as revealed through the use of language. My supply of translated Rumanian history, folklore, poetry, essays and fiction was ample and illuminating. And my dependence on others, initially so hard to bear, became much more tolerable when several friends pointed out that ours were give-and-take relationships, that it helped them to have a foreigner around with whom to discuss Rumania's (and their own) problems.

This static period coincided with the run-up to Rumania's (allegedly) 'first free elections' and with the tense three weeks that followed. This was a peculiarly stressful time for the pro-democracy intellectuals, as day by day the ominous design of the election campaign became clearer. In friends' flats I saw for myself the manipulation of public opinion through the Front's complete control of the national television service. By 20 May I was sufficiently expert with my crutches to tour six polling-stations, in and near Cluj. Voting was indeed 'fair', as elsewhere in Rumania – apart from minor incidents. During the previous two months a campaign of systematic intimidation – ranging from subtle threats to lethal physical violence – had ensured that an outwardly honest ballot would give the Front a two-thirds majority in the National Assembly and make Iliescu President with 86 per cent of the votes. There was no need for ballot-rigging, so effective had been the mind-rigging of the electorate.

I was harrowed by my friends' post-election fear, anger and despair. Five months previously, they had seen a mirage of liberty – vivid and inspiring. Now it had vanished and I left Rumania full of sadness, knowing the country to be still in the grip of Communists, thinly disguised as the Front for National Salvation. That was on 9 June, less than a week before my friends' most pessimistic forebodings were justified by the Iliescu-organised miners' attack on Bucharest's anti-Communist demonstrators.

At Cluj *gara* my team of hero-workers helped me onto the train for Budapest–Vienna–Munich–London (I was still on crutches) and urged me to return soon. I promised that I would – early in 1991, on a bicycle. By then experience had taught me that in Rumania trekking is impractical because so much of the country has been despoiled by industrialisation. On a bicycle one could speed through those dreary and often health-endangering areas; on foot it can take half a day to escape into beauty. That so much beauty has survived the Communist era is of course owing to the terrain. I was looking forward most keenly to cycling around – or rather, up and down – Harghita, and to getting onto little motor-free roads or tracks in the heart of the Carpathians.

13

Two Wheels in the Carpathians

No one had warned me that it takes ten days, at least, to buy a Russian bicycle in Budapest: though this may be reduced to five days should you happen to have a celebrated Hungarian friend who can put in a passionate plea on your behalf.

First you find your bicycle, which is easy. Soon I saw what I wanted, hanging high in the window of a vast city-centre state store called Szivarvany. Model 153–421 was conspicuously marked 4,800 forints, then approximately $60. All the non-Soviet models cost at least 20,000 forints, an out-of-the-question investment since this machine was to be left with a Rumanian friend. Inside, hundreds of 153–421s were stacked along one wall in an alarmingly unassembled state; one would need an honours degree in engineering to get them on the road. In sign language I pleaded with a grumpy, undersized young man to sell me the assembled display model. He responded, naturally enough, in Hungarian, which language isolates its users to a unique extent from their fellow-Europeans. Yet his expression and tone conveyed a clear message: in this unreformed state store no rule could possibly be bent for the sake of a mere customer. Despairingly I sought an English-speaker, or even a German- or French-speaker. In any Rumanian city multi-linguists would at once have swarmed, excitedly eager to help the foreigner. In Budapest it is otherwise.

Next I tried to coax the young man into himself assembling a bicycle for me. He looked scandalised and dismissed the notion with a series of graphic gestures. Then he handed me a large twenty-four-page booklet in Russian, amply illustrated with twenty-six diagrams; the first showed a naked man standing beside my bicycle-to-be, measuring his legs against the wheels. Now came *my* graphic gestures, conveying horror and despair. The young man shrugged impatiently and produced a formidable document –

five foolscap pages, hideously resembling an income tax return form. Presenting me with this sheaf, his manner suggested that now my problem was solved.

Page one was headed, in capitals: ELVESZETT JOTALLASI JEGYET CSAK AZ ELADAS NAPJANAK HITELT ERDEMLO IGAZOLASA (pl. DATUMMAL ES BELYEGZOVEL ELLATOTT SZAMLA, ELADASI JEGYZEK) ESETEN POTOLUNK! I wondered if the exclamation mark indicated that this was vital information needing at once to be absorbed by potential buyers of model 153–421.

Briskly the young man turned to another page, borrowed a pen and underlined VALLALAT BELYEGZOJE and ADOIGAZGATASI AZO-NOSITOSZAMA. I looked at him reproachfully, then took out my Angol–Magyar, Magyar–Angol *utiszotar*. It listed none of those words; the nearest was *azonos* ('identical') which shed no light on anything. At last the young man smiled; Hungarians appreciate, as well they might, even the feeblest of efforts to cope with their language. He then noticed a street plan in my shirt pocket. Spreading it on the counter, he indicated Egressy ut., wrote '17–21' in the margin, then turned to another page of the sheaf and there underlined *XIV Egressy ut, 17–21*. Semi-hysterically I giggled as the filler dropped. Of course! My purchase must be taken, with the sheaf, booklet and my receipt, to an establishment on the far side of Pest where some genius would assemble it. Mine not to reason why, mine but to do or die (almost) while wheeling model 153–421 through Budapest's traffic.

That however, was tomorrow's challenge; it was then too late to seek Egressy ut. So model 153–421 spent the night on the first-floor balcony of my friends' flat; he was light enough, I noted with relief, to be easily carried upstairs – an important attribute, since many Rumanian blocs are liftless.

My three-mile walk to Egressy ut. was memorable. Hungarians tend to use Budapest's long wide straight streets as racing-tracks; seventy miles per hour is acceptable, which in a city indicates some sort of mass death-wish. Even the trams and trolley-buses compete at lethal speeds, swaying along as though drunk, while the metro elevators whizz up and down like something in a cartoon film. To the unnerved visitor, it seems that Budapest's drivers display all the most unpleasant Hungarian qualities: aggression, ruthlessness, self-centredness. On my first day in the city, a young woman carrying a toddler was knocked down beside me when using a zebra crossing while the green light was on; a car swooped round the corner, ignoring the lights as too many Hungarian drivers do, and the victim had to be taken to hospital with a broken leg and a concussed child. The driver fled the scene but I was assured he would almost certainly be caught, through co-operation between public and police. My own leg might have been broken *en route* to Egressy ut. when a car parked by the pavement abruptly reversed with never a backward glance; I leaped to safety just in time.

No. 17–21 Egressy ut. was a strange left-over from the Communist era – at least I hope it was strange, not the sort of establishment Hungarians still have to combat on a daily basis. In a dreary barn-sized office men and women sat at metal desks, surrounded by tightly-packed filing cabinets, behind a bisecting counter. They looked pallid and embittered – as would we all, given such a work-place. On the public's side of the counter the queue occupied sagging plastic-covered settees. Their problems were, it seemed, car-related, and for fifty minutes I watched men (only men) with furrowed brows laboriously filling in multi-paged documents which were then – often after much argument – lavishly rubber-stamped and filed away. How, I wondered, was I going to negotiate those bureaucratic shoals *sans* interpreter? But in fact the sheaf from Szivarvany, plus model 153–421, needed no verbal input from me. An elderly woman clerk, with glinting purple-copper hair such as one used to see on celluloid dolls, simply indicated where I was to sign another document guaranteeing that I could collect my property ten days hence.

I stared, appalled, at this rubber-stamped date – then smiled ingratiatingly at the woman and boldly wrote in another, three days hence. The woman ground her teeth and struck out my date. Ten days or nothing, her expression said. And there was no charge; assembly was free and she wasn't interested in (or didn't understand?) my clumsy wordless hinting at a bribe. A dungaree-clad man then materialised at my elbow and wheeled model 153–421 away, beckoning me to follow. Scepticism took over when I saw my purchase joining hundreds – yes, *hundreds* – of unassembled clones. *Ten days?* More likely a month! I filled in the label presented by Dungarees, tied it to the handlebars as requested, was given yet another document – to be shown prior to collection – and went on my way, sorrowfully.

My host, however, was not so easily cowed by the esoteric bicycle-buying rituals of his native city. Next morning he accompanied me to Egressy ut., where I was promoted to being a famous Irish writer who *had* to leave Budapest three days hence and could *not* leave without her bicycle.

Three days later, at the appointed hour – 11 a.m. precisely – a meticulously assembled model 153–421 was secured to the roof of my friend's car and eventually we were dropped off at Nyiregyhaza, some forty miles from the Rumanian border. Naming model 153–421 was easy; he had to be 'Luke', in honour of my celebrated Hungarian friend, John Lukacs.

Cyclists bring out the worst in status-conscious Rumanians. If in middle age you can afford only a bicycle, and are tanned Gypsy brown and shabbily dressed, you must be a total failure and are likely to be treated as such – not of course in the villages, but in tourist hotels or even shoddy urban cafés and restaurants. (Methods of transport are graded thus on the status scale: motor cars, motor vans, horse-carts, ox-carts, bicycles, donkey-carts.) As most tourist hotels excluded Luke, I sometimes had to sit shivering outside in the wind and rain while waiting for the local with whom I had an appointment. I could have left Luke locked, but that would not have deterred fiddling small boys from possibly doing irreparable damage to his delicate gears.

Apart from this easily endured loss of status, Rumania provides excellent cycling territory. There are only a few snags: broken glass; worn-out concrete roads; new concrete roads; Austro-Hungarian pavé roads; main roads (so described on the map) that prove to be uncycleable tracks; hot liquid tar; temporarily (I hope) debilitating agricultural sprays; anti-cyclist truck drivers in urban areas and – the only serious problem – sheepdogs trained to kill intruders in rural areas.

The broken glass sets up a conflict between self-preservation and tyre-preservation; oddly enough, the latter instinct dominates in a country where tyres cannot be replaced. For some reason, perhaps understood by psychologists, the breaking of glass obviously relieves the inner tensions of millions of Rumanians.

How else explain the shimmering proliferation of broken bottles by the wayside on every main road? To avoid this hazard cyclists must suddenly veer out from the verge and only good fortune protects one from the traffic coming up behind.

Worn-out concrete roads may sound like a mere triviality but then don't *feel* so as one judders over miles of large uneven stones that have outlasted the concrete. Even new concrete roads have blocks so ill-aligned that every five yards there is a violent bump, and the regularity of this unpleasant sensation becomes peculiarly irritating. The pavé roads are something else again; where these have emerged from under the post-Trianon Rumanian roads they remain as good as new, a memorial to the efficiency of the Magyar administration but a literal pain in the arse for cyclists. A few such roads, designed for horse-traffic only, are now being used by heavy trucks but show no sign of disintegrating. These are hand-built works of art, rather than engineering feats.

The long-since-defunct main roads are no threat to cyclists, but some bridges have so drastically wasted away that a motor car would inevitably end up in the river for lack of warning signs.

Hot liquid tar is a common hazard in springtime, when main roads are being 'repaired' by work-forces of astounding laziness and incompetence. An excess of boiling, too-thin tar is slopped into pot-holes, topped with a shovelful of chips and left to stream over the rest of the surface – a tyre-endangering menace. One has no choice but to get off that road, not always easy or safe on a mountainside. An alternative form of incompetence is to pile mounds of chips into mega-pot-holes, thus unwittingly creating the sort of traffic-slowing obstacles known in other countries as 'ramps'.

My most memorable encounter with poisonous spray happened near Tirgu Neamt, where the occupants of three stationary Gypsy wagons frantically signalled me to stop; they had the air of people waiting at a level-crossing barrier. Foolishly I pedalled on, having been so often warned against Gypsy hold-ups, and soon I had reason to regret my mistrust. A biplane was spraying the whole area and after a few miles I could scarcely breathe and had to dismount – dizzy and nauseated, with a pounding heart. Slowly I continued, wheeling Luke, and on at last emerging from that zone saw another queue of carts – both Gypsies' and villagers'. This was my only experience of aerial spraying; usually giant tanks lumber over the fields, discharging their lethal load to the detriment of the local wildlife. Near Gheorgheni, where intensive spraying had a dire effect on my eyes and throat, several swallows collided with me, then dropped to the ground. I stopped to examine them; they were not yet dead, but stunned and gasping oddly.

Rumania's truck-drivers relieve their boredom by gambling with cyclists' lives. Habitually their juggernauts roared past within inches of me and a grinning passenger always stared back to observe whether or not I had survived.

And then there are the sheepdogs, a major threat to cyclists between the Balkans and the Khyber Pass; but more of them anon.

At 6.30 on a cloudless spring morning I left Cluj and for an hour was struggling through the noxious fumes of Ceausescu-land. Then I turned onto a rough non-motor road and by 8.15 the tranquil green slopes of central Transylvania surrounded me. Outside a tall ancient flour-mill, on a loud little river, many horses and donkeys stood breakfasting from nose-bags while their loads of wheat or maize were being ground, and old men and women in peasant dress sat against the mill wall chatting animatedly – until I appeared, when they all fell silent and stared, uncertain about responding to my greeting. Soon after, I overtook a wide ox-wagon with the family cow tied to the back and her calf and three pigs standing behind the elderly driver and a small boy. Doubtless his parents were employed in Ceausescu-land. All over the countryside, many couples working in the fields were accompanied by a pre-school grandchild.

There are few state farms in this area and not too many collectives. I noticed throughout the country that within the past year state farm buildings had been repaired and repainted, presumably to foster the illusion that the government is capable of running them efficiently. But machinery continued to rust in overcrowded repair depots and peasants continued to plough and harrow – man and wife working a pair of oxen – as the Dacians were doing when the Romans arrived.

In the little market town of Mociu an animal fair had just ended and the road was thronged with carts and wagons drawn by horses, donkeys, buffaloes or oxen and often carrying calves, sheep, foals, pigs. One minute furry donkey was having difficulty pulling a tiny cart with pram-like wheels from which an immense piebald sow, reclining on a pile of golden straw, regally surveyed the world – looking uncannily like Queen Victoria in middle age. Hereabouts both horses and buffaloes were in excellent condition, but the bony filthy cattle grazing the long acre reminded me of Irish cattle at winter's end in our pre-EEC era.

In Transylvania the size of the village schools – all handsome pre-Trianon two-storey buildings – proves how much denser was the pre-Communist rural population. Some schools are quite magnificent, with attractive decorative plasterwork under the eaves and handsome pillars supporting long wrought-iron balconies. Other public buildings are to match: finely proportioned town halls, hospitals, local government offices, army barracks. Their like is never seen in Moldavia or Wallachia.

It often seems that pigs far outnumber humans in modern Transylvania. Beyond Mociu I stopped for lunch before beginning a very long, gradual climb – typical of this region – and sat opposite a yard where thirteen piebald bonhams, only a few days old, were romping like puppies while Mamma rooted. When I crossed the road to converse with them, as is my dotty wont, a muscular hound – hitherto unobserved – leaped to the end of his chain with such vigour that he almost strangled himself. Pignapping would not have been a good idea.

High above Mociu, on sweeping-to-the-sky grassy hillsides, grazed thousands of sheep, the faint music of their bells a perfect accompaniment to the visual beauty all around. The topography reminded me of the Andean *puna* in miniature. One can cycle along the ridge crests for several level miles, with wide shallow depressions stretching away on either side and, in the middle distance, fold after fold of mountains encircling the horizon – some forested, some sadly eroded with gashes of bare earth on their green flanks. And then comes the long descent, usually to a fertile valley scattered with red-roofed villages, each overlooked by two or three ochre-painted churches – certainly Orthodox and Calvinist and possibly Roman Catholic as well.

Passing through the once-beautiful but now hideously industrialised town of Turda, *en route* for Tirgu Mures, I observed the essence of contemporary Rumania neatly concentrated in one incident. On a long narrow bridge over the Mures, a few hundred brown and white sheep, with half as many lambs again – the majority new-born – were causing a traffic jam of interesting proportions and attitudes. This flock was in direct confrontation with one of those colossal truck-trailers that carry cranes from one high-rise site to another. The truck, having been brought to a standstill half-way across the bridge, was almost completely blocking it: but the sheep had to pass over on their way to the path to the river bank. From my roadside vantage-point, in front of the truck, I could see behind it a queue of seven long Gypsy wagons and a dozen vans and cars. On my side, too, the traffic was building up. And we were all accumulating unwholesome deposits as nine very tall nearby chimneys, belonging to three factories, poured clouds of stifling smoke (grey-black: orange-brown: purplish) over everything.

The three shepherds wearing ankle-length fleece cloaks, carried intricately carved six-foot crooks. The two white sheepdogs wore spiked anti-wolf collars and their terror of motor traffic rendered them useless. The drivers' reactions interested me; all engines were switched off and, instead of showing their breed's usual ill-temper when there is a hold-up, they peered out anxiously and sympathetically as the shepherds coped with the chaos – which was considerable, as panicky lambs tottered off in all the wrong directions, looking like bits of fluff beside the ginormous wheels of the trailer.

Finally one shepherd caught the flock leader, who was unhelpfully trying to retreat up the mountainside whence they had come, and dragged him through the narrow space between trailer and bridge: whereupon the rest began hesitantly to follow, apart from the numerous frantic mums of missing and vociferous lambs, who pursued them under various trucks, carts and vans. This blockage lasted more than twenty minutes; only when the shepherds signalled that every last lamb was safely down on the river bank did any vehicle move. Most Rumanians remain close to their rural background and shepherds hold an honoured place in traditional society. They are also among the richest people in modern Rumania; as Communism never impinged on them, for obvious reasons, capitalism flourished in the mountains while elsewhere falling into ruin.

Beyond Tirgu Mures I was soon in the Szekelyfold, where even now Rumanians are few (and unwelcome). I knew I had arrived when everything became bilingual – e.g., the first village on my route was 'Murgesti' in Rumanian and 'Nyaradszentbenedek' in Hungarian. On principle I support the Magyars' right to use their own place-names, not only in the Szekely counties of Harghita and Covasna but all over Transylvania. However, the Rumanians do have more than one reason for insisting on the use of the Rumanian version, too. Budapest propagandists – and their allies in Rumania – still claim that the Hungarian language remains totally forbidden in Transylvania. Yet the age of many Szekelyfold signposts, and street-name plaques in Harghita's towns, proves that even before 1989 this was not so in practice, whatever the law may have said.

Over the county border a few changes are immediately discernible though the villages' general layout remains recognisably Transylvanian. Some ancient barns-cum-stables are as big as three-storey houses, with twelve-foot-high double doors and three different-sized wicket gates to fit horses, cattle and sheep. (Pigs always have separate accommodation.) The dwellings are more varied in design and the carved and painted homestead gates (many new) are spectacular examples of folk art triumphant. There are conspicuously more very old wooden houses, with splendidly carved pillars supporting narrow balconies under wide eaves. Some are in a state of disrepair rarely seen elsewhere in Transylvania, apart from those tragic, abandoned Saxon villages which have been taken over by Gypsies. Harghita's delapidated dwellings also tend to be Gypsy-occupied; the Gypsies moved in when the owners fled to Hungary during the 1980s – illegally, which meant they couldn't sell their homes. (Now, I was told, they cannot reclaim them; this, if true, is cruelly unjust.) Most houses are dated on the gable end facing the road and the numerous sturdy homes built during the 1930s and early 1940s are evidence that the Szekelys were not then being successfully discriminated against, *pace* present-day propaganda.

A minor but perhaps not trivial difference is that most Szekely geese and hens are confined in wicker coops on the broad grass verges, cloths being spread over the top when the sun gets hot. However, the goslings and chicks can leave the coops to forage; they will always return when summoned. This seemed to me a

sign of greater efficiency among the Szekelys, but some Rumanians deduce from it greater suspiciousness and tight-fistedness.
Rumanian villagers don't bother too much about straying feath-
ered livestock, assuming it will all even out in the end. But the
Szekelys – assert the Rumanians – fiercely protect their property
and have been known to kill a neighbour in a quarrel over a
missing gosling or chick. Conversely, the Magyars and Szekelys
infer that the Rumanians are too lazy and improvident to tend
their livestock responsibly. (And talking of responsibility, why do
ganders, like cobs, continue to take an interest in their offspring
until adulthood, whereas cocks are devoid of any family feeling?)

The Szekelyfold is quite densely populated but one afternoon,
near Praid, I turned into uninhabited – because too steep –
mountains. Gradually the little road climbed, twisting through
narrow valleys between beech-scarved mountains, their lower
slopes pastureland. Only sheep bells, and the rushing of a
boulderous young river, broke the silence. Then a sign officiously
told me that for eleven kilometres (some seven miles) the road
would climb *very* steeply to the Borzont Pass. I dislike such signs;
it's much more fun to round hairpin bend after hairpin bend,
never knowing when the pass will appear and using one's orog-
raphical lore as the basis for guessing games. Moreover, late in the
day, information about severe gradients can be disheartening, if
one has already cycled seventy-odd miles.

Dismounting, I plodded upwards. Soon the beech woods were
mixed with spruce firs, then replaced by them – and long
snow-drifts gleamed in the shadows between those mighty trunks.
Towards sunset I began to worry; this was impossible camping
terrain. Probably I would have to walk on in darkness to the pass,
which presumably would offer a levelish site. But soon a derelict
concrete cowshed appeared, covering a flat ledge by the river, and
I half-carried Luke down the rough slope. The shed was uninvit-
ing, its floor strewn with broken glass and malodorous discarded
garments; gloomily I cleared a space and spread my flea-bag on
the damp mildewed straw.

I was sitting outside, supping off bread and Budapest salami,
when a vehicle approached – the first on that road – and stopped
nearby. Prudently I retreated into the shed, ever conscious of
Luke's being worth four months' wages. Through the river's

209

rushing came the sound of tools being vigorously deployed and twenty minutes later three oil-smeared young men made their way down to wash on the bank. As they returned they noticed me – the shed was too small for total concealment – and hesitated, but didn't greet me before continuing upwards. Listening hopefully for the sound of their engine, I heard instead escalating merriment; it seemed much *tuica* was flowing with a picnic supper. Reluctantly I decided to push on in search of solitude. My Rumanian friends often exclaimed, 'But aren't you afraid to sleep out alone?' To which the reply is, 'There's nothing to be afraid of if you *are* alone, if no one knows you're there.' If however three hard-drinking men know you're there, a move is indicated.

That apparent inconvenience proved a boon; within half an hour I had come to a cosy wooden foresters' stable perched on another ledge on the far side of the fordable (with some difficulty) river. Clearly this had not been used since the previous summer; the six-inch-deep carpet of horse-dung was bone dry and provided a warm, sweet-smelling, resilient mattress. After dark the river sounded much louder, as I lay gazing through the doorless entrance at two towering spruce firs, symmetrically framed against a brilliantly starry sky. That was a perfect ending to a cyclist's day.

At 5.30 the blue-grey dawn light showed a frost-bound world. An unfamiliar bird observed my cursory washing in the icy river – thrush-sized, with a golden back, red wings and a strident call of short, sharp whistles. After more bread and salami I climbed on, up and up, through dense forest, the snow becoming thicker with every bend of the road. I had been lucky; between that stable and the pass there was no other shelter and no level ground.

To mark my crossing of the pass, soon after 8 a.m., the wind rose and the sky quickly clouded over. Like too many Carpathian passes, this one has been ruined by an extensive 'Leisure Development'. *Why*? At almost 4,000 feet the Borzont Pass permits 'leisure activities' during only three or four months each year. So why obliterate its natural beauty, which could be enjoyed by travellers all the year round? Last season's litter had survived in inordinate quantities – enough to give the whole area the flavour of a municipal dump. (Incidentally, Szekely villages are litter-free, well-swept and even *weeded* along the verges; the Magyars and

Szekelys have not allowed their self-respect to be undermined by Rumania's general *malaise*.)

Over the pass, the drops on my right were melodramatic. On such precipitous slopes, how can the mighty spruce firs get a grip? These slopes plunge down and down to invisible, inviolate ravines – among the few remaining refuges for many European mammals. Some people find such densely forested mountains too eerie – or oppressive, or monotonous. But for me there is an enjoyable, mysterious melancholy about them, recalling the delicious childhood *frisson* associated with scarey fairy-tales. I rejoice that their permanently twilit depths are protected by gradients that make logging impossible, or too costly.

Just below the pass I met five elk-sized browny-grey deer, led by one of the famous superbly antlered Carpathian stags. On noticing me, they stopped to stare hard – but didn't much like what they saw and bounded away, white scuts flickering.

The weather now cheated me of my 'reward' for the climb, a six-mile freewheel to the village of Borzont. A vicious wind and drenching rain induced misery and when my hands became too numb safely to operate the brakes I had to walk. In any event the appalling surface would have cancelled out the reward factor; freewheeling between pot-holes too deep to be ignored is not much fun. In Rumania each county is responsible for its own road maintenance and on entering Harghita it is at once apparent – since the county is not exceptionally poor – that the authorities have chosen to deprive it of its rights.

A fortnight later, going from Gheorgheni to Odorheiul Secuiesc, I crossed this same range by a slightly lower and even more beautiful road – under a cloudless sky, with a cool cross-breeze. Again there was no traffic – not even horse-traffic – for hours on end. Here the dark forest alternated with miles of bright hilly pastures, yellowed by cowslips and dotted with lone spruce saplings or pale young larch groves. The numerous shepherds' summer huts, as yet unoccupied, were mostly new-built but in the traditional style. During a pause to relish this sunny solitude I saw, approaching me up a grassy slope, what I at first mistook for a small deer. The enormous hare either didn't notice me or disdained humans. Slowly he walked up the slope, passing so close that I could have touched him. His fur was a white–russet mix – a glorious colour, from which I deduced that Carpathian hares turn white during winter. Crossing the road, he leaped up a steep bank into the forest just as a slightly smaller version (his wife?) appeared below me and followed him, also passing within touching distance. Usually one sees hares gracefully racing, and their awkwardness when walking is unexpected. Later I saw several others, though none so close.

Having descended, I refuelled. (Bread and salami; that yard-long Budapest sausage had by then dwindled to a few inches.) From my seat under an aromatic pine I was overlooking the widening valley's first dwelling, a solitary old two-storey farm-house, stoutly built of tree trunks and stone. It stood – semi-encircled by an apple orchard in full bloom, a mass of soft pinkness – beyond a dandelion-glowing meadow through which flowed a stream, in three wide loops, reflecting the blue of the sky. In the near distance new snow dazzled from a range of gently curving mountains. Behind the shingle-roofed barn – consider-ably bigger than the house – grazed four brown and white cows and a black mare wearing a deep-toned bell. The nearby half-acre sheep-fold had eight-foot-high anti-wolf pine fencing, bound with bark. A dozen adolescent lambs grazed in the orchard, tended by two smallish cross-bred sheepdogs. Faulty their pedigrees may have been, but when an alien lamb strayed in, from another fold far down the road, both pursued it conscientiously, silently guiding it back to the break in its fence. At intervals a woman emerged from the house – headscarved, wearing a voluminous peasant skirt and wellies. She drew water from the stream, brought logs from the barn, searched for eggs, carried pails to the pigs, hung out washing. Long after my picnic was finished I loitered, reluctant to break the spell put on me by this most lovely place.

By mid afternoon I was in Zetea, one of the Szekelyfold's most attractive little towns – all hilly laneways, and flower-filled nooks and crannies, and magnificently decorated gateways. But alas! I could buy no bread; it was a Saturday afternoon and in both Hungary and Rumania – to celebrate the death of Communism – everything closes at noon on Saturday until Monday morning, including cafés and petrol stations. Only the bars remain open, and on Sundays the churches. The effect is a curious Christmas

Day-like stillness, plus frustration for motorists who may urgently need petrol or cyclists who may crave a loaf or a cup of coffee. When/if the free market takes off, this of course will change. Now many Rumanians regard their weekly opportunity to drink non-stop for thirty-six hours as the greatest if not the only benefit of the revolution/coup. (If that's an exaggeration, it's a slight one.)

In 1990 I had noticed the national predilection for excessive drinking, but then it was curbed by an acute shortage of booze. In 1991 alcohol in various – when state-manufactured – artificial forms was more plentiful than food. Moreover, beer cost only twelve lei a litre and state-produced '*tuica*' (made from who knows what) only seventy lei a bottle. The drunkenness seen every day everywhere is both alarming and depressing, a measure of the emptiness of life for people whose inner resources have long since been atrophied by Marxist brainwashing. Youths of sixteen or seventeen are already settling into the boozing pattern of relaxation, for lack of anything else to do, and too often are egged on by their seniors. Luckily alcohol rarely makes the Rumanians aggressive; they waver quietly home to bed, frequently vomiting *en route*, or fall by the wayside and sleep it off, ignored by passers-by. (Their vomiting is probably a safety-mechanism: Nature rejecting chemicals unsuitable for human ingestion.) The occasional drunken brawls tend to be more verbal than physical, which interestingly reinforces the theory that Rumanians, unlike Hungarians, are temperamentally 'a gentle people' – though capable, as history records, of the most savage violence when provoked to it by cynical leaders.

In the space of one typical day I saw: a) two workers in a collective potato field at 10.45 a.m., sprawling senseless with an empty *tuica* bottle on its side between them; b) an elderly man struggling beneath his bicycle, entangled amidst shrubs, on one of Tirgu Neamt's main streets; c) a state farm tractor ahead of me behaving erratically, then stopping in the middle of the road and the driver getting out, crouching in the ditch and, as I passed, sticking his fingers down his throat and vomiting – hoping to be able to drive straight afterwards.

Near the village of Kukullokemenyfalva I became involved in a mini-drama on a level road between fields of state farm winter wheat. What I saw ahead of me there could be described comically but was a potential tragedy for the victim, a hefty boar so insecurely carted by two elderly men (both stocious) that he had half-fallen from the cart and was about to be strangled by his halter. The two horses, doubtless used to such crises, were standing steady. As I rode to the rescue the two old buffers were ineffectually heaving at their squealing pig, who sounded as though he knew his last hour had almost come. The men then collapsed onto the road and each began to abuse the other, while simultaneously they were attempting to help one another to regain the perpendicular. Had the boar not been in such danger I would have left them to it. But something had to be done about him and his rescue was simple enough; he wanted nothing more than to be given a leg-up onto the cart. Helping the humans – firstly to stand, secondly to get aboard – was less simple. They were not *blind* drunk; now they noticed Luke's ostentatious Cyrillic lettering and, instead of receiving polite words of gratitude, I was exposed to an anti-Russian diatribe. But at last I won, despite their persistent swigging from an earthenware *tuica* flask while I was struggling to hoist them onto the cart. As soon as they were aboard – lying on the straw, both clutching the flask – the horses moved on, without direction. Rumanian horses are – and need to be – very clever. One often sees them drawing apparently empty wagons and unilaterally negotiating complicated motor traffic junctions while their owners slumber on the wagon floor. In 1991 a sound, well-bred three-year-old cost about 80,000 lei, almost as much as a Dacia.

Most drunken scenes lacked any comic element. One Sunday morning, in Gheorgheni's only (and non-tourist) restaurant, I noticed a strange pair of boozers. One was a blue-eyed Gypsy, aged fortyish, with a jolly ruddy face, drooping black moustaches and short tangled beard. He wore the Gypsies' distinctive wide-brimmed black hat and greasy sheepskin jacket; his gross beer-belly wouldn't allow his blue jeans to come much above his crutch. The other was a little bald man, his skull ghoulishly obvious beneath tight brown Gypsy skin; a small bunch of woolly grey hair behind each ear gave him the look of a debauched elf. He was a deaf mute, who made pathetic shrill croaking noises, like a bullfrog – some of which his companion seemed to understand. At 9 a.m. both were drinking beer and cognac.

Ten hours later, when I returned for supper, they were at the same table – its cloth murky with cigarette ash and sloshed drinks – now on wine and *tuica*. One of the waitresses, in whose flat I was staying, told me they were weekend 'regulars'. They had just finished a meal – 'To try to get sober,' explained my friend, 'before Josef's wife comes for him.' Then the elfin one stood up, swaying, and tried to cross the almost empty restaurant to the *toalet*, clinging to chairs as he went. But midway he crashed, gashing his cheek-bone on the sharp corner of a tin table. As he lay sobbing hoarsely Josef stumbled to help and with the edge of his jacket mopped up the blood. But unfortunately the crashing sound brought to the scene the restaurant Director, reputedly a loyal Ceausescu man planted in the town to spy on Szekelys. He certainly behaved as such, ordering the elfin one to be dumped on the street, though the evening was cold and very wet. Meekly Josef staggered back to his table and ordered another bottle of wine, making no protest as two kitchen lackeys threw out his friend – still sobbing and bleeding.

'He will be safe,' the waitress reassured me, 'Josef's wife will find him.'

As I reached the street the elfin one, who seemed to have passed out, was being lifted into a covered wagon by two Gypsy youths.

Back in the restaurant, fat tears were silently sliding down Josef's cheeks. Then his wife arrived – a woman once beautiful – wearing a raincoat made of fertilizer sacks. She was followed by three small filthy tattered children; the other six were old enough to fend for themselves. After a low-key argument Josef stuffed the wine bottle into his pocket and allowed himself to be led to the door. On the street, voices were raised and soon he returned, accompanied by his wife but not by the children. This time he sat at the table next to mine and ordered a beer and two glasses of *tuica*. His wife at first refused hers but then, having again failed to persuade him to leave, tossed it down and looked as if she could do with another. As I supped, she continued to admonish him gently, inexplicable remnants of love showing on her worn face. But they were still there when I left.

Sometimes I stopped for a drink where Luke could be wheeled into a state-run beer-hall, in which places one pays as much for the deposit on a half-litre glass mug as for the beer itself. (Is this a measure of the all-pervasiveness of dishonesty? Or of the scarcity of drinking vessels in the average home? Or of the habit of sustaining the ego by cheating the state?) These sordid institutions are patronised by people who only want to get drunk a.s.a.p. and an overwhelming stench of urine comes from the pee-hole in the middle of the floor, designed to prevent drunken men from exposing themselves outside the door and thus shocking the local womenfolk. Once upon a time women shunned these places, but no longer; I often had female company, of a not very edifying sort. Even in the forenoon there were usually a few men eager to grope at me, while hiccupping in my face; already they were too far gone to see that I was old enough to be their mother. (Or, in some cases, grandmother.) What Rumania needs is a Father Matthew, he who rescued Ireland from a similar situation in the mid-nineteenth century.

Rumanian motor vehicles shed a prodigious number of 'pieces'; every main road has its complement. This propensity may seem irrelevant to cyclists, but not so. On my way down from the Toaca Pass I was travelling fast, on the outskirts of the little town of Pluton, when the cab roof of an approaching truck fell off and missed me by a few feet. (I can't believe that roofs fly off cabs anywhere else in the world, though I've seen more than my share of unstable vehicles.) I braked so hard that I too fell off, as the sheet of metal landed a yard away; yet the driver and his mate ignored me when they stopped to replace the roof, which they did with a speed suggesting much practice.

Good fortune often attended me (compensation for 1990?) in the Carpathians, most notably on the Rotunda Pass where occurred a truly preternatural coincidence. I had been warned that there is no road, though the map claims there is, but I reckoned the centuries-old track would allow a cyclist across, albeit on foot.

Not far beyond the village of Sant, where I had become enmeshed in a riotous Moldavian wedding the day before, my walk started on a benign spring morning of warm sunshine, loud bird-song and dazzling wild flowers. At first however I was in shadow; for miles the track followed the young Somes river, here just another turbulently flooded stream between steep forested mountains. In this narrow valley all was as it has been forever, *sans* dwellings, pastures, logging scars. And the Somes, never more than a few yards away, became ever whiter and louder as we ascended.

Then, rounding a sharp bend under an overhang, I saw a major snag immediately ahead. The terrain required a crossing of the Somes, but if this was a fording point it didn't look like one to me. Yet it was; beyond the seething waters the track continued, now at last leaving the river to climb high around the shoulder of the opposite mountain. Obviously people did cross here, though perhaps not often with bicycles.

The torrent was no more than ten yards wide. I removed the panniers, found a stout staff nearby, stripped naked and took the panniers over one at a time. The power of the waist-deep, icy water was formidable and the river-bed unstable, as is the way of mountain streams. I dreaded taking Luke across without the staff, but both hands would be needed to retain him. Then, as I stood holding him, summoning my courage, a wagon appeared around the nearby corner – its passengers three elderly men. They jerked their horse to a stop and for a surreal moment the naked Irishwoman and the Moldavian peasants were paralysed by shock of different kinds. Theirs was shock/horror, mine shock/relief. Mercifully, I had planned to transport my clothes on my head when fording with Luke. Swiftly I bent and pulled on my long shirt. Then, cautiously, the wagon advanced. Not much sign language was needed. Averting their eyes from my lower limbs and adjacent areas, the men hauled Luke aboard while I hauled on my trousers before joining him. The horse shared my reservations about the fractious infant Somes and plunged in only after considerable coaxing. On the far side my rescuers tentatively intimated that I might continue upwards with them but looked hugely relieved when I declined their invitation.

Before continuing, I stoked up on bread and *slanina* and wondered as I munched – *could* I have got Luke across? Or would the Somes have stolen him? We'll never know . . . I still think of the appearance of that wagon at that moment as *magical*, part of a Carpathian fairy-tale. Until I reached the motor road, four hours later, there was no other trace of humanity.

Hereabouts conifers are mingled with birch, poplar, sycamore maple, an occasional yew. Beyond deep invisible valleys white swathes of wild pear blossom draped some slopes and new-leaved beeches glowed in the noon sun – pale green fires amidst the dark surrounding pines. Buzzards glided in wide circles, jays and woodpeckers were noisy and busy. The remains of a few ancient wayside stone fountains – still providing sweet spring water – indicated that in former times this was a commonly-used route. Now the roughness of the track necessitated my walking down as well as up.

An army barracks stands at the junction with the main road and two young conscripts, who had watched the last stage of my descent, asked incredulously, 'You came from *Sant*?' And then, 'What do Irish people *eat*? How has Ireland old women so *strong*?' I replied that at present I was doing nicely on bread and *slanina*.

That was a record-breaking day, when I crossed two of the Carpathians' highest passes – the second the 4,200-foot Prislop Pass between Bukovina and Maramures. This was the route taken by the Transylvanian boyar, Bogdan, in the mid-fourteenth century, when he migrated east with his followers to found the principality of Moldavia. Here we were on one of Rumania's best-kept roads and it was possible to pedal most of the way up. However, despite surprisingly little traffic, and awesome views of mighty snowy massifs, a slight sense of anticlimax was inevitable after the blessed solitude of the Rotunda.

On my return to Harghita, across the legendary Bicaz Pass, I did *not* pedal up; for much of the way the gradient is sixteen per cent.

Finding the village of Ivo took time. (It really is called just that; I haven't forgotten the other twenty letters.) I was seeking Ivo because there lives a remarkable peasant, one Miklos Arpad, to whom I had an introduction from a Magyar friend. Miklos is remarkable on two scores; he has spent years collecting personal memories of the Second World War from the older generation all over Harghita and he has sired twelve children. The latter achievement, I gathered, made him a figure of fun among his neighbours. In traditional Harghita, families of five or six are usual enough; but a round dozen – and Miklos is rumoured to be aiming for a score – is generally seen as reckless. (Other, more earthy adjectives are also applied; and comparisons with the Gypsies are inevitably drawn.)

Charcoal-dark clouds were massing to the west as I turned off the main road where a small faded signpost said 'Ivo'. A rough, steep, muddy track took me onto a long ridge-top – then forked. The sun was still shining as I looked both ways, over a serene landscape of pasture and ploughed fields backed by low forested mountains. Choosing the left fork – it looked more used – I jolted past a few comely farmhouses but had covered scarcely a mile when the rain came, driven by a gusty gale that made cycling in a cape on a deeply-rutted track seem unduly hazardous. So I walked the next five miles as the track continued to climb, gradually, towards the distant dark blue bulk of Mount Harghita. This was a densely populated, non-collectivised ridge.

By the time I reached Ivo at 1 p.m. the track was ankle-deep in racing brown water. Northern Rumania's rain storms are – or were in the spring of 1991 – monsoon-like deluges which a few months later brought tragedy to much of Moldavia. All Ivo's inhabitants were, naturally, indoors. So I sought a young Arpad in the village school – a newish, bungalowish building. The plump middle-aged teacher looked scarcely less alarmed than her pupils when a weird figure in a hooded cape appeared suddenly out of the storm. Uneasily she accepted and read my note, in Hungarian, explaining that I was a writer from *Irorszag* eager to meet Miklos Arpad. Then she summoned a sullen-looking twelve-year-old – Miklos's first-born – who hesitantly emerged from the mass of cowering pupils and was ordered to lead me to his home. His evident hostility was a trifle disconcerting but doubtless based on fear.

My illusion that soon I could get dry and warm was quickly dispelled. For half a mile Gyorgy led me through the deluge on a continuation of the track – now level but a morass – past a line of neat houses, each in a spacious garden. My gloom deepened as we left the last house behind and began a steep climb up a wooded mountain. Keeping my balance on the skiddy mud, while pushing a heavily laden Luke, was difficult. (Unfortunately I had that morning been presented with several stout volumes of Transylvanian history by a Szekelyvarhely friend.) Gyorgy didn't offer to help, but at last I requested him to push from behind. Twenty horrible minutes later he stopped and pointed left, to an almost perpendicular side track. Getting Luke up that was a truly desperate struggle. When the next stage proved to be a pathlet up a cliff face – the way blocked by trees and undergrowth – I almost gave up. Gyorgy somewhat sulkily transported the panniers one at a time, clutching at saplings as he went. But this was not an option for me, carrying Luke, and twice I was nearly there when I helplessly slid down again. Then at last I made it to a grassy field and through sheets of rain could dimly see the Arpad compound, high above, surrounded by a wooden fence. Replacing the panniers, I tacked up, skidding often and by now shivering – sweat-sodden beneath my cape and rain-drenched from the waist down. The muddy slope from the gate to the house was impossibly steep; I left Luke under wide stable eaves.

And after all that, Miklos was not at home. A few hours previously he had left for Harghita's capital, Csikszereda, to try to establish his legal claim to those ten hectares of forest which had been owned by his forefathers for generations. (The legal sharks then were – and probably still are – having profitable fun with land distribution. As peasants don't have deeds, they must depend on aged witnesses who can remember who owned what before 1948.)

Anna had accepted my arrival calmly; Miklos's hobby brings the occasional researcher to this outpost of agriculture – the last house before Mount Harghita, across which there isn't even a pathlet. When I entered the hot, steamy kitchen she was standing over a huge wooden tub of laundry balanced on two stools in front of an iron range, using a chunk of home-made soap on the staggering quantity of dirty garments produced by a well-kept family of fourteen. A small, sturdy, fresh-faced woman, she had thick chestnut hair, wide-set dark brown eyes, high cheekbones, good teeth. As she scrubbed and rinsed and wrung, I noticed her powerful arms. She looked not a day older than her twenty-nine years (she married at sixteen) and radiated a sort of contentment rare among urban mothers of one.

Having done her hostessly duty by fetching slippers, and a blanket as dressing-gown, and hanging my clothes above the range, and fixing me a seat on the log-box, Anna didn't pause to entertain me but got back to her tub. There was no time not to work, yet there was always time for any child who needed attention.

Rumanian primary schools close early and as all the scholars arrived home, at intervals of a few minutes, the situation began to seem unreal – the door opening again and again and again to admit yet another small boy with a convict haircut, big dark eyes in a little pale face and a happy smile. (The two daughters were among those not yet at school.) As each entered mother and son exchanged greetings lovingly and politely while the juniors welcomed the seniors with joyous shouts and squeals and were briefly cuddled and kissed. (There was no changing into dry clothes, a logistical feat beyond any mother of twelve.) When all had assembled, controlled chaos ensued; each knew his chore and set about it efficiently without any direction from Anna. In the large porch stood nine empty buckets; water had to be fetched from a stream fifteen minutes' walk away, down a steep hill – the two older boys' task. Meanwhile another filled the log-box and another changed the baby – at thirteen months she was almost but not quite day-dry – and two others carefully carried in from the porch a heavy cauldron which Anna lifted onto the range. This contained a delicious meal: large cabbage leaves enfolding herb-flavoured rice and strips of tender mutton, served with thick creamy yoghurt. Such a dish takes time to prepare and had been cooked during the forenoon; now it only needed heating up. While awaiting it, the ravenous boys helped themselves, between chores, to chunks torn from a mountain of cartwheel loaves in the dresser cupboard. Another corner cupboard held a meagre but cherished display of 'best' china and glass from which an attractive old pottery plate was taken for my benefit and carefully washed. Everyone else ate off chipped enamel, being fed in shifts at the small table.

A vast four-poster bed occupied one corner of the square, high-ceilinged kitchen and slept the four older boys; the baby and toddler shared their parents' room over the kitchen; the other six slept in a downstairs room, also leading off the porch, and I slept in the hay-loft above them. Anna's unfussy reception put me at ease; she took it for granted that I would be happy to wait for refreshment until the family meal was ready and equally happy to sleep in a loft. Only the pottery plate, and a delicate china cup instead of a mug, set me apart. A peculiarly stimulating and fragrant herbal tea, unfamiliar to me, was served in the cup; the older boys were allowed it, the rest drank water. As dusk fell Gyorgy lit the lantern hanging low over the table, then lit another to illuminate washing-up, done by Anna and two boys in the porch.

Throughout that afternoon and evening I was repeatedly impressed, in all sorts of little ways, by this family's good manners – not only between mother and children but among the children. Miklos must be as remarkable as Anna, to have helped her foster such a harmonious domestic atmosphere. The alternative, of course, would be unendurable; egos have to be restrained when there are fourteen of them around. But to achieve this, while treating each child as an individual, is an unusual feat in any society.

Early next morning the octet were dispatched to school, all neat and clean, and Anna set about preparing that day's mega-meal. As Miklos was not due home for a week I left soon after, feeling grateful, in a way I could not express, for what had been an extraordinarily moving – and enlightening – interlude. This was, emotionally, the best balanced family I visited in Rumania, though among the most materially deprived. Certainly the Arpads would benefit from the conveniences of an urban bloc: running water, electricity, central heating, a gas cooker, a bathroom. Yet Anna was emphatic that she would not wish to exchange her quiverful for mod. cons. And this affection-ruled though spartan home seemed to me to offer a better start in life than the standard bloc family. Filling one's quiver so amply at the end of the twentieth century is not commendable. But – current social responsibilities apart – large families do provide some advantages. Not least are the cultivation of good manners (i.e., consideration for others) and an easy acceptance of a share of responsibility for running the communal show. Is it a coincidence that both those qualities have dwindled where family sizes have dwindled?

By the end of May many flocks were moving up to their summer pastures and in Harghita I noticed more goats than elsewhere, mingled with the sheep. Shepherds rarely returned my greetings; usually they stared blankly for a moment, then strode on. They and their flocks and their dogs seem to form a social unit that has nothing to do with the motor-road world. Often I paused to enjoy the assured professionalism of men and dogs as flocks of 1,000 or more were guided by one or two shepherds, and three or four dogs, across broken, complicated terrain where they must not graze until the appointed hours – noon and sunset. It pleased me to see so many young shepherds. They are far from being a dying breed though should Rumania ever join the EEC, and be forced to 'rationalise' sheep-raising, they will certainly become an endangered species.

The dogs' professionalism came too close for comfort as I crossed a nameless (on all my three maps) pass between the small town of Darmanesti and the large village of Sinmartin. This is surely one of Europe's most beautiful roads, partly because it hasn't been repaired since 1918 and is no longer usable by wheeled traffic – even two-wheeled, so again I had to push Luke uphill for over twenty miles. Carpathian slopes go on and on; a few days previously I had freewheeled non-stop for twenty-eight miles from the Frumoasa Pass.

That morning a truck-bedevilled main road took me from Comanesti – its charms long since stifled by Ceausescu-land – to the oil-spoiled town of Darmanesti in a once-lovely valley where many tall thin chimneys belch black smoke visible ten miles away. So much stinking oil leaks across the streets that I skidded and came off while rounding one corner. However, that desecration was soon out of sight and it seemed the gates of Paradise were nigh: but not yet. I winced when a hairpin bend brought into view one of those would-be-posh tourist developments known as 'hans'. This brash construction overlooks the monumental concrete barrier of a hydro-electric dam holding back the waters of a five-mile-long artificial lake. The notion of using such a concrete monstrosity as tourist bait is peculiarly Communist. Averting my eyes I pedalled faster – and soon could pedal no more. The motorable road had abruptly ended and Paradise begun.

For a few hours the gradient was easy and several antique traffic signs confirmed that this highway, unlike the Rotunda track, had once been a paid-up motor road. At the base of dripping cliffs, festooned with creepers, orchids flourished – the commonest an indefinable colour, neither blue nor purple. A swift wide unpolluted river, coming from places Ceausescu couldn't reach, sparkled and was companionably noisy. All day the sun shone warm though a strong wind blew. At one point, as I approached a semicircle of high mountains, all beech-covered, the sinuous, rhythmic movement of those myriad trees was like a slow-motion dance, directed by the wind – a mesmerisingly beautiful sight. Mostly however the forest was mixed and bird-thronged. Then the valley became a chill, permanently shadowed gorge where a series of waterfalls leaped whitely down the rock-walls with a roaring rush.

Beyond that gorge the forest thinned, the valley widened and on strips of scrubby riverside grassland a few small herds of cattle, unattended and having no visible base, grazed and made music with their bells – which have varying sizes and sounds for the different age-groups. Then the serious climb began, up a range of grass mountains where only scattered stands of conifers remain. On mile after mile of open, sloping pasture I could see distant shepherds' huts and the moving dots of their flocks.

By 5 o'clock it was cold and I donned my padded jacket. Soon after, to my astonishment, the surface improved enough for slow cycling across a wide level saddle. Happily bumping along, I wondered if this reprieve would last beyond the saddle. Then ferocious barking alerted me. I tried to speed up but the four powerful converging dogs – two coming from each side – were racing like greyhounds. They attacked without hesitation, tearing my jacket sleeve, wrenching two spokes from Luke's back wheel and causing me to fall into the ditch on my right elbow – which still occasionally reminds me of the episode. An agitated young shepherd called them off just in time. Apart from the very real risk of being savaged to death, rabies is quite common in Rumania and had I not been wearing a jacket – had one of them even slightly broken my skin – I would have felt obliged to go home at once.

Somewhat shaken, I resumed pushing the disabled Luke after a swig from my emergency supply of *tuica*. On the next steep mountain the road became even rougher – and more beautiful, as snowy crests glimmered above the blue evening shadows filling the deep valley on my left.

An hour later I camped on the pass, another broad grassy saddle strewn with gentians. It was not yet dog-infested, I suppose because it was so cold. Even at the beginning of June, in the freak weather of '91, it was too frosty at that height to sleep out. But I left the tent open, to enjoy the glittering stars.

The descent next morning provided a much tougher challenge than the climb. That gradient was bizarre – it's anybody's guess what 'percentage' – and the surface rivalled the worst of Madagascar's roads. An hour of hauling Luke over chasms, and braking him hard while trying to avoid another fractured foot on the round loose stones, left me trembling with exhaustion in the wondrously lovely valley that gently descends to Sinmartin. Too soon we were out of the mountains, on the main road to Sepsiszentgyorgy, where giant pylons stride aggressively across wheat or onion fields five miles long.

It is not unsuitable that Sepsiszentgyorgy sounds like a disease. I found it a depressed and depressing little city where I lingered only long enough to have Luke's spokes repaired, a job efficiently done by an elderly mechanic whose ingenuity had been finely honed by long years of austerity. His daughter spoke some English and advised me never to try to escape from sheepdogs; one should always, she said, stand quite still.

I took this advice when dealing with the next threat, which came after I had said '*Viszontlatasna!*' (farewell) to Harghita and was returning to Moldavia, now crossing the Bicaz Pass from the west. Half-way up, when it had been deluging coldly for an hour, I came on hundreds of sheep huddling in the thin forest, being semi-sheltered from the sleet. (Already many had died all over Moldavia and Transylvania, having been shorn at the normal time in an abnormal season.) Here I was ready when five great white woolly dogs leaped from the embankment to the road and encircled me, barking and snarling. I froze while they stood poised to attack, some five yards away; their terrifying noise must surely bring the shepherd quickly to my rescue. Not so, however. They then began to advance, in little jerky movements, their snarling becoming almost hysterical. At that moment I was as

225

scared as I have ever been on my travels. I thought very fast. Should I try to remove the panniers and deter them by swinging Luke in a circle? I felt weak with relief when a dishevelled woman (the shepherd's wife?) appeared on the embankment, a cigarette hanging from one corner of her mouth and wearing a peevish expression. As usual, the pack at once obeyed her screamed orders. But their withdrawal was reluctant and they continued to growl loudly and walk along the top of the embankment, parallel with me, until I was off their territory – which is of course wherever the flock happens to be. As I passed a nearby hut I observed the shepherd lying on a fleece by the doorway in – undoubtedly – a drunken stupor.

After the previous encounter I had been told that many of these dogs are trained to kill; hence, in populated areas, one often sees them being led, or tied to a wagon, or securely chained in a yard. Such attack forces are essential to defend the remote high pastures where shepherds would be helpless against a gang of rustlers – and motorised gangs from Soviet Moldavia are reputed to be common, now that the border is open. However, Man's Best Friend seems like something else when multiplied by five and closely surrounding one in a meaningful frenzy.

14

The Flavour of '91

I wish this book could have a happy ending, but that would involve writing fiction. While alone with Luke in the mountains, or staying in remote villages, I rejoiced to be back in Rumania. Elsewhere, this return was often saddening and my journal for 18 April records:

A month after crossing the border, I can see no light at the end of Rumania's tunnel. Several impediments to progress, only discernible in outline this time last year, are now clearly defined. Most serious is a common reluctance to face reality when that means a personal shouldering of responsibility for the future, rather than an abstract analysis of What's Wrong With Rumania. Many are very good at *diagnosing*, objectively and accurately, but if you suggest that they might themselves do something about a cure, in their own sphere of operations, they shy away from the idea. A favourite excuse is that 'the Soviets are now running the country, through Iliescu'. It's grim that people who in any other ex-Satellite country would be the natural new leaders feel so powerless. Is this largely because they've a totally distorted view of the 1991 outside world? But it seems to me many don't want to be deprived of this view, which lets them off the hook. If the USSR is still controlling Rumania, how can anyone be expected to do anything to drag his/her country off the garbage-heap it's now on? Like the Irish, the Rumanians enjoy distilling political moods in ballads, and a popular new song begins 'Ceausescu, forgive us! We were drunk when we killed you!' The ballad goes on to praise Ceausescu for his *nationalistic* defiance of the Soviets and contrasts this with Iliescu's alleged subservience to a Gorby who is widely believed to be a devil very scantily disguised – though his disguise serves to mislead a credulous West. This alarming swing of the pendulum indicates that Rumanians in general don't truly value the freedom of speech and access to outside information which are among the few tangible benefits of the revolution/coup. As for the intellectuals – I've asked several of my friends (old and new), 'What's been *happening* during my nine months' absence? What developments have there been, political or economic or psychological?' They looked at me uneasily, then said defensively, 'There's not much change. We're just getting on with our lives as best we can. What else is there to do, when we're still under Communism?'

Communism does still control many who in theory despise everything Marxist-tainted. But this is unsurprising; none of us is free of conditioning, we've all come off a production-line. The central problem seems to be that Communism maims emotionally, even when intellects have survived brain-washing. Hence intelligent people *fear* to use their sound thinking to initiate reforms they clearly recognise are needed. They came off a production-line that threateningly imprinted the message 'Don't assert your *self*!' And it remains true that if they did assert themselves now, as reformers, the immediate personal consequences could be catastrophic: at best implacable hostility from more timid colleagues, at worst job loss. One friend said: 'This country can't get sorted out without a Havel-type leader, not just a politician but a creative person who can make the rest of us feel it's not only right but *safe* to act free, as individuals!' Too simple a summing-up, but I saw what she meant.

Another problem is that odd low-key anarchy which I (and the Rumanians) regarded as fun a year ago. It's unfunny now – not a symbol of new-won freedom but a symptom of no consistent government control of anything, from currency exchange to building permits to car insurance to the railway system. The sort of dictatorship that meant everyone knew the crazy rules, and how to bend them in a formalised way, has not been replaced by a regime that imposes sensible rules generally accepted. Many complain that now the only rules are those invented on the spur of the moment by some enterprising local bureaucrat who is no longer afraid of his Party Boss higher up – and, ultimately, of the Conducator. Thus every shrimp in the vast bureaucratic ocean can pretend to be a shark and get away with it at the expense of his helpless victims. Helpless but infuriated; the simple people well know what's going on and who's benefiting most from the 'Liberty' they all were celebrating when I first arrived.

With Luke I'm finding the Rumanian compulsion to *organise* me hard to take, much as I appreciated it when invalided last year. This urge to pre-plan my movements doesn't depend on temperament, on whether or not someone is bossy. People are baffled and worried by my sort of happy-go-lucky journey. They feel I'm exposing myself to the dangerous unknown – dangerous merely because unknown. So they strive to arrange my route in a way comprehensible to them – i.e., staying with their relatives or friends, on a definite date, so that they can check that all is well with me. This is both touching and irritating – how to escape from the network without giving offence? I've argued that such obsessional pre-planning is a Communist handicap which must be overcome, a.s.a.p., for a variety of obvious reasons. But they cannot imagine spontaneous decision-making in response to chance events and changing circumstances. Where there is no institutionalised framework, they must create one.

Overall, a cynical weariness seemed to be the flavour of '91. Of course some things had improved for the better-off. Petrol was more plentiful. Everyone was free to go abroad if they could get academic sponsorship or otherwise raise the *valuta*. Few any longer feared the Securitate, though there were constant mutterings about their resurgence under another name – the Rumanian Information Service, established by Iliescu on 28 March 1990. I sometimes suspected that some Rumanians wanted them around again, that they perversely missed the adrenalin stimulus of that particular threat.

There were also countless small private enterprise shops, known as 'boutiques', offering imported goods (usually shoddy) that were undreamed of – some even unheard of – in January 1990. The limited selection of tawdry garments came, usually, from Turkey; a Bucharest–Istanbul return bus ticket then cost US$10 and swarms of traders, both Gypsy and Turkish, filled scores of buses every week. 'Luxury' goods – soap, toothpaste, chocolate, orange juice (very ersatz), sewing needles, washing powder, tins of salted peanuts, Coca Cola (of dubious authenticity), powdered milk – all sold at astronomical prices. State shop windows and shelves displayed 1990's range of goods, the bottles and tins now dustier and rustier.

However, some 'luxuries' were sporadically trickling through the state system and in Cluj I observed a tense 200-yard queue outside a Centru *alimentara*. Each person was receiving four 400-gramme tins of bright pink Chinese luncheon meat, a repulsive substance costing 300 lei a tin. (The average monthly wage was then about 6,000 lei.) Most shoppers were pensioners, queuing on behalf of their working children. There was much ill-tempered jostling and shouting, in contrast to the previous year's docile, disciplined queues. Next day, outside the same *alimentara*, hundreds were queuing for oranges and when the door suddenly closed a mini-riot broke out, anger streaking through the air like invisible lightning. Somehow the crowd knew that six crates were being retained for the benefit of the staff. (Since the state *alimentaras* had become self-regulating, each tried to favour its own employees.) The police immediately arrived and insisted on those crates being sold; they then searched the premises and assured the crowd that not an orange remained within.

Private enterprise was most obvious in Timisoara. But who, I wondered, could afford to patronise so many new shops and restaurants where prices were grotesquely high? On a hot Sunday forenoon I wandered all over the Centru, joining in the novel Sabbath pastime of window-shopping. To the Rumanians these displays afforded glimpses of a world hitherto only contacted through illicit pop music or smuggled Western magazines. Yet most goods were tacky, especially the Italian toys and 'fancy goods'. Crowds thronged around every window, ooo-ing and aaa-ing, the children evidently not thinking of acquiring any toy but satisfied to be able to stare at them, wonderingly. Only around the very long Benetton windows – a recently opened store on a corner – was the atmosphere different. One wouldn't of course expect Rumanians to be impressed by advertisements showing a tall handsome black man kissing a blonde, a slim slinky black girl caressing a blue-eyed Nordic giant and the usual row of elegantly-clad multi-racial children oozing mutual affection. I wished then I had a camera to record some of the expressions of indignation, horror, disgust, scorn or rage on all sorts of faces – the disgust more marked on women's faces, the rage on men's. In one of Europe's most racist countries, how many garments will this gimmick sell? Yet it may do some good, young Rumanians being so prone to ape the West, by conveying the subliminal message that there racial equality is a respected ideal.

Rumanian reactions to the then recent Gulf War were predict-able. Everyone backed Bush, though many women deplored 'the need for violence' while considering it completely justified against Saddam Hussein and 'the brave thing to do'. In Moldavia residual anti-Islamic feeling, after 500 years of Ottoman exploitation, erupted into overt rejoicing because a Muslim country had been reduced to rubble by good Christians. Hatred of the Russians meant the war was also felt, with deep satisfaction, to have been a surrogate defeat of the USSR because all Iraqi equipment was naïvely assumed to be Soviet-made. Television images of Amer-ican hi-tech superiority in battle sent viewers wild with joy. In their opinion, Soviet diplomatic efforts to avert war were made solely to prevent this exposure of their own military weakness. To try to explain the many facets and complexities of the Gulf crisis – including the extent to which the West had armed Saddam – was futile. American propaganda is one hundred per cent efficient when directed towards a people as ill-informed as the Rumanians: which is hardly surprising, given its success-rate among the Free World educated classes.

The most besotted Bush-worshippers are often members of an American-funded Baptist congregation. In Timisoara I attended a Sunday evening service in a church paid for with US Baptists' dollars and opened on 10 December 1989. (Coincidentally, a significant date in the history of the revolution/coup.) This building is quite beautiful, simple and dignified, and the construc-tion materials and fittings are of a quality never seen elsewhere in

Rumania – in fact, of American quality. Built by voluntary labour, it proves how good Rumanian workmanship still is, given competent supervision.

On that sunny Sunday evening the church was, as always, packed. Looking around at the fifteen-hundred-strong congregation, I was reminded of Paisley's lot – in dress and demeanour. Later I was reminded of their bigotry when, in conversation outside the church, one fervent Christian remarked that it was a pity Hitler hadn't completed the job – this was with reference to the Front's three Jewish leaders. Another Christian said he wouldn't mind finishing the job himself, while a third observed that Antonescu had shown foresight in 1940, when he tried to expel all Gypsies into the USSR where they would have died working on the notorious killer-projects. All over the country, I found Rumania's racialism being expressed more openly and frequently in 1991; perhaps it was being used as a safety-valve for post-coup frustrations.

The numerous small children remained unnaturally subdued during that two and three-quarter hour service. There was no communal praying but much hymning by a first-rate choir of 100, plus a full orchestra whose instruments had been donated from America. The pastor regularly tours North America, collecting funds for the starving (?) Rumanians. He claimed to have sat at the President's right hand during the Gulf crisis, when Bush invited Christian leaders to breakfast at the White House, and to have been told by the President himself (so it *must* be true!) that 'The USA is a special nation under God, appointed by the Lord to defend democracy everywhere!' In the course of one sermon, this sentence was quoted in English four times. Other preachers – there were four in all – included repeated references to 'our American friends' and 'the great hero President Bush, who asked specially for the prayers of Rumania's Baptists to get him guidance from the Holy Spirit during the Gulf War'. (By this stage, it will astonish no one to hear, I was almost throwing up.) Each preacher brought in the refrain, 'God Bless America!', the congregation fervently responding 'Amen!' Very obviously all four preachers had been trained in some television evangelism school and their oratory went down a treat, reducing many to tears and shaking sobs and inspiring quite a few to stand up and babble semi-hysterically.

Outside, I remarked to my companion that this was the first Rumanian church I had seen without beggars squatting in the porch. Proudly he replied, 'No beggar would dare come near *our* church!' Parked by the main gate was the pastor's long sleek limousine, an Audi Sport; my companion boasted that it was the only one in Rumania. His expecting this to impress me was worrying. As was the congregation's general enjoyment of the reflected glory cast on them by association with this rich pastor, based in a 'First World' building. Undoubtedly large segments of Rumanian society will be eager to enlist in our 'Go Grab It!' battalions, for which this Baptist 'mission' seems to be a recruiting sergeant. I also came upon its active agents in several remote villages and was made uneasy by the taped Bush-eulogies they distribute for free among a bemused peasantry.

In 1990 I had detected little royalist feeling, but a year later strengthening pro-monarchy currents were perceptible throughout Transylvania and Moldavia. In part this seemed to be a reaction to ex-King Michael's having been rudely refused permission to visit his family tomb near Bucharest at Christmas 1990. (Which refusal suggests that Iliescu then saw royalism as a not inconceivable future threat.) In both Cluj and Timisoara several prominently displayed wall posters called for the restoration of the monarchy, showing photographs in which the ex-King looked remarkably like his distant cousin, King George VI. Yet no one with any political nous allowed themselves to give in to this regressive yearning for a Hohenzollern. Ex-King Michael has no heir and it is impossible to imagine how a not-very-bright septuagenarian, on a dusted-down throne, could possibly solve any of Rumania's problems. However, Communist denigration makes him seem 'good' and increasingly desirable as the polar opposite to Communism. To quote several of my friends, 'He is the only person who could get rid of the Front'. Of course no one can suggest *how* he might achieve that. He couldn't organise either a fair election or a civil war, even if he wanted to, and a royal edict would be unlikely to dislodge Iliescu & Co.

On first arriving in Transylvania, I went along with the Rumanian tide and blamed *Him* and *Her* for everything. But soon the more complicated reality emerged, as it did for many foreigners. Aid workers who rushed to the rescue, moved almost to tears by what had just been revealed, expected the Rumanians to be as concerned as they were about abandoned babies and juvenile AIDS victims. The professionals were not entirely unprepared for what they found; some of the amateurs' eventual bitter disillusionment was in proportion to their original emotional investment. (Perhaps it is an advantage to have had all one's possessions stolen on the border, by Rumanian officials, so that one first sets foot in the country without illusions.)

When it became obvious that the spontaneous generosity of Western Europe was being systematically abused, certain aid-workers began angrily to ask, 'Does Rumania deserve so much help?' Superficially the answer seemed to be 'No'. Yet this rapid curdling of the milk of human kindness was partly owing to the naïvety-cum-sentimentality-cum-impetuosity of uninformed and disorganised helpers. Rumania was a country newly released (or apparently released) from Communism and everyone knows that corruption is endemic in Communist societies. Why were the Rumanians expected to be different? Only by the exercise of superhuman virtue could they have co-operated honestly in distributing luxuries, unseen for decades, among the most deprived – when the average Rumanian considered him/herself sufficiently deprived to be entitled to whatever was going.

Moreover, in relation to the Children's Homes, officialdom had literally degraded their inmates to non-human status, so categorising them that they were seen as not belonging to society. Foreigners noted, with horrified incredulity, the withholding from them of all affection or normal concern. This was the savagely logical consequence of the nature of those institutions, with their shortages of staff, food, medicines, heating, clothing, equipment. The children could only have been treated differently had the staff done the unthinkable and staged their own revolutions, refusing to collaborate in running such hell-holes. It is too easy to forget that our own 'caring society' is a recent development, based on the sort of national affluence Rumania has never known. The profound changes undergone by Western Europe during the past century – changes in perceptions, expectations, sensibilities – make it hard for us to understand Rumania's comparative indifference to those at the bottom of the pile.

It saddens me now to hear and read a growing volume of criticism from which all the 'positives' are deleted: the Rumanians' courage, resilience, unstoppable humour, disinterested kindness. I have never, anywhere, encountered so much of the last – total strangers going to extremes to help me with no vestige of an ulterior motive. True, some of those same individuals remain unmoved by the tragedy of 'Ceausescu's Children'. But is that very different from my – or any other European's – acceptance of children dying at our feet on India's urban pavements? If unable to do anything to help, one must either turn off the compassion tap or develop a neurosis. And the kind Rumanian who busts him/herself to help me *cannot* think in terms of being *able* to help tens of thousands of children. That's a big permanent problem, beyond reach. I'm a little temporary problem, the sort an individual can somehow cope with, even if at considerable inconvenience. Ordinary citizens having a collective responsibility for conditions within a state-run institution is part of our democratic way of thinking. In a state that has never been democratic, the individual feels powerless to change anything organised by the Authorities, be they boyars or Phanariots or Party bosses.

Yet Rumania does have an extraordinary inner strength. How else could the peasantry have survived centuries of tyranny and hardship with their culture intact? They may now have a national inferiority complex but, unlike us Irish, they have no identity problem. And their vividly defined *Rumanian-ness* – which has nothing to do with politically encouraged nationalism – gives an enduring integrity to the spirit of the place, despite all that day-to-day corruption.

Scientists are optimistic about Rumania's topsoil, though it has been so degraded and impoverished by agricultural abuse and industrial pollution; they foretell that time and education will ensure its recovery. The same may prove true of Rumanian society.

Historical Chronology

101–6 AD	Romans conquer Dacia, then the area roughly covered by modern Rumania. Present-day Rumanians believe cross-breeding produced Daco-Romans, their ancestors.
271	Emperor Aurelian withdraws legions from Dacia; too costly to defend against nomadic tribes.
271–896	A historical blank; only known that migrating hordes (Goths, Gepids, Huns, Avars, Bulgars, Petchenegs, Cumins) cross Dacia on the way south.
***c.* 896**	Magyars from Hungary begin gradual settlement and development of Transylvania.
***c.* 1000**	Szekelys posted by King Stephen of Hungary to Harghita Mountains to defend Transylvania's border.
1141–61	Saxons arrive in southern Transylvania from Flanders and Lower Rhine; invited by King Geza of Hungary to colonise strategic areas and given many privileges.
***c.* 1290**	Principality of Wallachia, south of Carpathians, founded.
***c.* 1360**	Bogdan Voda, a Rumanian boyar, refuses to submit to Magyar expansion into Maramures and leads followers over Carpathians to found Principality of Moldavia.
1374	Othodox Church's first Rumanian episcopate established; previously, imported Slav priesthood was ruled from Ochrid.
1437	Prolonged peasant uprising in Transylvania prompts Magyar, Szekely, Saxon nobles to unite to protect their privileges. Throughout 15th century Ottoman armies successfully opposed by Hunyadi in Transylvania, Stephen the Great in Moldavia, Vlad Tepis in Wallachia.
16th century	Hungary partitioned by Habsburgs and Ottomans. Transylvania retains independence. Moldavia and Wallachia acknowledge Ottoman suzerainty but never occupied by Turkish troops or administered by Turkish officials.
1571	Transylvanian Diet gives equal status to 'the Four

236

Received Religions': Calvinist, Lutheran, Roman Catholic, Unitarian. Rumanians' Orthodox Church not recognised.

1599–1600 Moldavia, Wallachia, Transylvania briefly united for first time under Michael the Brave. This was mere territorial expansion; no Rumanian awareness of 'nationhood' in modern sense.

17th century Transylvania prospers under Magyars; life continues hard for peasants but is worse in principalities under native princes, vassals of the Porte. When these princes replaced by Phanariot Greeks, ruling on behalf of Sultan, peasants endure extreme hardship and boyars resent having privileges curtailed.

1718 Ottomans withdraw from Hungary; Habsburgs settle Swabians in the Banat of Timisoara, now a part of Transylvania, to cultivate land regained from Turks.

1773 Joseph II tours Transylvania incognito; unsuccessfully begs his mother Maria Theresa to protect Rumanians in Transylvania from exploitation and discrimination.

1784 Magyars ruthlessly repress Peasant Revolt in Transylvania; many still-remembered atrocities on both sides.

1791 Rumanian religious and political leaders beg Vienna for recognition as 'the Fourth Nation of Transylvania'; plea rejected.

1821 In Moldavia and Wallachia Phanariot rule replaced by native princes appointed by Turks and Russians; peasants benefit only slightly from this change.

1829–34 Both principalities are a Russian protectorate, the Porte retaining suzerainty; valuable reforms initiated by Count Kiselev.

1848–9 Magyars proclaim union of Transylvania with Hungary despite Rumanian and Saxon protests. Vienna seeks Russian assistance to put down Magyars' anti-Habsburg rebellion; Transylvania demoted to Austrian province under martial law. Rumanians now subjected to Germanisation instead of Magyarisation.

1859 Union of Principalities of Moldavia and Wallachia under Prince Ioan Cuza.

1862 These Principalities are renamed 'Rumania' (Transylvania was to be included only in 1920); serfdom abolished; Greek-owned monastic estates appropriated from the Church and sold to peasants thus causing much debt-associated hardship.

1866 Cuza dethroned in bloodless coup and Prince Karl of Hohenzollern-Sigmaringen (later King Carol I) requested to rule Rumania by Bucharest politicians.

1867 Hungary forces Austria to acknowledge her independence and Austro-Hungarian Empire formed. Magyars now free to pursue relentless policy of Magyarisation in Transylvania; they continue until 1918 despite widespread international condemnation.

1907 Carol I deploys 120,000 Rumanian troops to put down Europe's last Peasant Revolt; more than 10,000 Moldavian and Wallachian villagers killed; thousands imprisoned.

1914 Carol I dies on 9 October having failed to persuade his government to abandon their neutrality policy and declare war on Britain and her allies. Ferdinand succeeds.

1916 Entente use Transylvania to bribe Rumania to declare war on Austro-Hungary; army noted for bravery but badly officered and ill-equipped. Germans soon take Bucharest; Government flees to Moldavian capital Iasi.

1918 In May Rumania signs treaty with Germany; on eve of Armistice American Ambassador advises Bucharest to declare war again to strengthen their position at Paris Peace Conference. At Alba Iulia on 1 December tens of thousands of Transylvania's Rumanians gather to declare allegiance to King Ferdinand and proclaim final rejection of Magyar rule.

1920 Treaty of Trianon (4 June) gives Transylvania to Rumania; Hungary has been arguing the injustice of this ever since.

1920–40 Land Reform benefits speculators more than peasants; democracy fails to develop; governments rig all elections; Nazi-type 'Iron Guard' persecutes Jews, killing many especially in northern Moldavia. German influence increases during late '30s when Iron Guard turns on monarchy. Carol II bans all political parties and orders Guard leaders executed.

1940 Carol II abdicates; heir Michael cedes all power to dictator Marshal Antonescu who is forced to return northern Transylvania to Hungary.

1941 Rumania enters war against Soviets in June. Both Hungarian and Rumanian governments collaborate with

238

	Nazis in extermination of Jews and Gypsies.
1944	In August Rumania 'liberated' from Nazis by Soviet Army.
1949	A strongly Stalinist dictatorship established; peasants' resistance to collectivisation causes 80,000 to be arrested, imprisoned and tortured.
1965	Ceausescu takes over; for a decade much more freedom allowed. He develops nationalist economic policy in defiance of Comecon; reliance on Western credits and technical aid gets country deep into debt; insane restrictions on consumption are then imposed in obsessional determination to repay debts.
1989	Nicolae and Elena Ceausescu overthrown in uprising and shot by army firing squad on Christmas Day.